The Problem of the Color[blind]

THEATER: THEORY/TEXT/PERFORMANCE

Series Editors: David Krasner and Rebecca Schneider

Founding Editor: Enoch Brater

Recent Titles:

The Problem of the Color[blind]

Racial Transgression and the Politics of Black Performance

BRANDI WILKINS CATANESE

The University of Michigan Press

Ann Arbor

Copyright © by the University of Michigan 2011
All rights reserved
Published in the United States of America by
The University of Michigan Press
Manufactured in the United States of America
⊛ Printed on acid-free paper

2014   2013   2012   2011   · 4   3   2   1

A CIP catalog record for this book is available from the British Library.

Library of Congress Cataloging-in-Publication Data

Catanese, Brandi Wilkins, 1974–
     The problem of the color(blind) : racial transgression and the
politics of black performance / Brandi Wilkins Catanese.
          p.   cm. — (Theater—theory/text/performance)
     Includes bibliographical references and index.
     ISBN 978-0-472-07126-5 (cloth : acid-free paper) —
     ISBN 978-0-472-05126-7 (pbk. : acid-free paper)
     1. African Americans in the performing arts.   2. African
Americans in motion pictures.   3. African Americans—Race identity.
4. Performing arts—Social aspects—United States.   5. Motion
pictures—Social aspects—United States.   6. United States—Race
relations.   I. Title.
     PN1590.B53C37   2011
     791.089'96073—dc22   2010043128

     ISBN 978-0-472-02792-7 (electronic)

Acknowledgments

I am very honored to have been the beneficiary of all of the support that has led to the publication of this book. Friends and family, mentors, colleagues, and students have all shaped this book, and in the process, have shaped me as well. It is a humbling privilege to begin the act of thanking them with this list of acknowledgments.

I must begin by recognizing mentors who nurtured these ideas in their earliest forms: at UC Berkeley, Saidiya Hartman, Barbara Christian, Margaret Wilkerson, David McCandless, and Dunbar Ogden planted the seeds that prepared me to avail myself of the support and encouragement of Harry Elam, Peggy Phelan, Alice Rayner, and Helen Brooks during my time at Stanford University. Upon my return to Berkeley, institutional support from both the Humanities Research Fellowship and UC Berkeley's Office of Faculty Equity provided time and a room (and laptop) of my own in which to achieve major work on this project. Funds from the Mellon Foundation made its completion possible. My colleagues in the departments of African American Studies and Theater, Dance, and Performance Studies at UC Berkeley have been constant sources of inspiration and support. I offer overarching thanks to all of my faculty and staff colleagues in both departments. I offer special thanks to W. B. Worthen, Charles Henry, and Percy Hintzen for their leadership at the time of my arrival at Berkeley, and to Mark Griffith, Shannon Jackson, Catherine Cole, Ula Taylor, and Stephen Small for their leadership and guidance in subsequent years. I am grateful to each of them for the ways in which they have encouraged my work, and I also appreciate the support of colleagues including Peter Glazer, Leigh Raiford, and Shannon Steen, who responded to my work at various stages throughout this journey. I am exceedingly thankful for the critical and personal generosity they have bestowed upon me. I have tremendous respect and appreciation for the graduate and undergraduate students that I have had the privilege of teaching at UC Berkeley, whose courage, optimism, and dazzling intelligence have influenced my thinking in ways that keep me grounded in my reasons for pursuing a life in this profession.

I am also grateful to a broader web of colleagues who have worked directly and indirectly to support me and this work at various stages: they include Patrick Anderson; Stephanie Batiste; Annemarie Bean; Hershini Bhana; the far-flung members of the Black Performance Theory group; Jennifer Devere Brody; Daphne Brooks; Telory Davies; Tommy DeFrantz; Michele Elam; the other members of the Fab Five cohort: Faedra Carpenter, Shawn Kairschner, Jisha Menon, and Zack; Kathleen Frydl; E. Patrick Johnson; Dwight McBride; Heather Nathans; Elizabeth Nordt; Sandra Richards; Joseph Roach; David Román; Maya Roth; Scott Saul; Arden Thomas; Bryan Wagner; Stacy Wolf; and Harvey Young. The forced periods of isolation that the practice of writing requires were sweetly healed by the fellowship that these scholars and others have offered over the years.

At the University of Michigan Press I have benefited from a level of care, patience, and engagement that begins with the support of the incomparable LeAnn Fields, whose patience and enthusiasm for this project have sustained me on many occasions. Additionally, while I only know to acknowledge Scott Ham and Marcia LaBrenz by name, I offer thanks to the entire staff at the press whose help has gone into making the publication of this book possible. Additionally, while the shortcomings of this book are my own, it has benefited tremendously from feedback during the peer review process, and from the editorial wisdom and encouragement of David Krasner and Rebecca Schneider.

Finally, I offer my deepest thanks to my family, the people who have offered me unconditional love during the immediate process of writing this book, and in so many other ways. My parents, Robert and Vicki Wilkins, have been unerring in their support of my development as a person and as a scholar. I am sure that I will never fully comprehend all that they have done to make the life that I enjoy today possible, but I thank them for their fierce love and the values that they instilled in me. I cherish my brother and sister, Rob and Courtney, for the joy that they have brought into my life and all of the ways that they make me proud to be their big sister. I honor my grandparents, LaVada Wilson and Rose and Leroy Lawson, for the examples of hard work, commitment, and love of family that they have shown to future generations. I thank the entire Catanese family for welcoming me so wholeheartedly into their lives and rituals, and my extended family of aunts, uncles, cousins, and friends-as-family (including my favorite armchair cultural critic Christina Royal, with whom I have thought through more than one of the ideas in this book) for giving me a robust and joyful life that helps me to keep the vagaries of work in perspective.

Without question, the greatest thanks of all go to my husband, Joseph Catanese, and our exquisite daughter, Olivia Rose, and to the long-suffering Miss Trinks, who have patiently endured the days (and days) and nights of work that this project required with extraordinary levels of generosity and sacrifice, and healthy doses of laughter as well. In every way, completing this book would have been impossible without your patient and seemingly limitless love and support. Thank you for being friends of mine.

Contents

CHAPTER 1

Bad Manners: Talking about Race

Let me begin by burnishing what has become, in fairly short critical order, an old chestnut: within the United States, blackness and performance are ineluctably linked. Some of the nodes of this linkage are already quite obvious within black cultural and performance studies: from the ignoble tradition of blackface minstrelsy to contemporary NAACP boycotts of television networks that underutilize black talent on- and offscreen, to Barack Obama's recent history-making presidential campaign, we are by now keenly aware of the politics and burdens of representation within the United States. Critical and political attention to the quantity and quality of black cultural performances is certainly warranted, given the ever-increasing power of cultural representations to shape public attitudes in matters of race, and the global commodity that hip-hop culture—often collapsed into a complicated synonymity with black culture—has become.

What I want to add to this truism, though, is the suggestion that we couple our attention to the power of expressive culture with an understanding that other modes of performance—related to institutional and capitalist imperatives of surveillance, productivity, and efficacy—play equally significant roles in constructing the lived experience and political possibilities of black Americans. As Jon McKenzie illustrated in *Perform or Else,* the isolated valorization of cultural performances as liberatory, transgressive practices risks ignoring the other, more normative registers of power within which notions of performance have always also functioned. He writes: "Our attentiveness to liminal performance has kept us out of the loop with respect to the performativity of power, and in doing so, has limited our liminality," and this is nowhere more true than where black subjects must contemplate which thresholds we may or may not cross during the presentation of self in everyday life and elsewhere.[1] This, too, guides Herman Gray's critique of an outdated mode of black cultural politics that "continues to privilege representation itself as the primary site of hope and critique."[2] Representations in the realm of cultural performance—just like bodies (Butler) and race (West)—continue to matter, of course, but should be analyzed relationally rather than hierarchically in order to understand how the multiple formulations of performance cohere to regulate, to provide pleasure, to enact possibility. For example, if we accept the central role of slavery in the production of the African American subject, we must address not only the performative affect of certain twice-behaved behaviors in stylizing black bodies to occupy a certain social role, but also the economic imperatives that performance opens up in relation to these black bodies at different moments in history. Surveillance of black bodies through the system of slavery, for example, was designed not just to quell any assertions of subjectivity that would threaten white supremacy, but also to ensure that these working black bodies performed their labor tasks as efficiently as possible. Indeed, as Saidiya Hartman's *Scenes of Subjection* demonstrates, the relationship between performance as aesthetic practice and performance as evaluative rubric of labor is not just one of complementarity but of mutual constitution. Observing black bodies engaged in what was acknowledged as physical labor had entertainment value for white spectators, just as "the transubstantiation of abjection into contentment" required a great deal of faith and work, given the abject circumstances into which enslaved blacks were forced.[3]

This supervisory dimension of the national investment in black performance manifests in other areas as well: as a mundane example, library searches for work on "black performance" reveal an extensive bibliography of research not just on expressive cultural forms but also on black academic and athletic performance, and the external factors contributing thereto. This quantitative analysis resonates both in California, where I live and work, and across the country, as efforts to dismantle affirmative action in higher education routinely rely upon disparaging arguments about undeserving, underqualified minority applicants. The argument in favor of California's 1996 Proposition 209, which ended affirmative action programs in the public sector, used inflammatory language to explain why affirmative action was wrong: "set-aside" policies "hijacked the civil rights movement," creating "terrible programs which are . . . tearing us apart," an outcome that "naturally [causes] resentment when the less qualified are preferred."[4] Such rhetoric makes clear that one of the most urgent current discussions of blackness and performance in their many meanings revolves around national anxieties over the racial crossroads at which we have arrived (or stalled): are we a consciously pluralistic nation, or a color-blind one?

This book is an attempt to understand the function of these complementary, even overlapping, modes of performance—aesthetic and efficacious—in settling this question. *The Problem of the Color[blind]* argues that an examination of black performance practices from the last decade of the twentieth century, after the abatement of the 1980s culture wars, exposes color blindness and a strictly quantitative multiculturalism as far more ideologically linked than they are oppositional responses to the politics of racialized representation, and clarifies the need for a new vocabulary and evaluative framework through which to understand how performance in particular might intervene against the limitations that stereotypes impose upon black expression. On both institutional and cultural levels, performance has become the medium through which American anxieties about race (and in particular, blackness) are pondered, articulated, managed, and challenged. Whether we talk about artists who subvert our habits of looking at black bodies or we discuss conservative politicians' attempts to measure and yet detach performed productivity from the racialized bodies that execute various types of work, looking at what black bodies do through the conceptual parameters of performance and its attention to embodiment, temporality, and repetition's concretization of discursive formations allows us to understand the simultaneous, even mutually constitutive, opening up and shutting down of representational possibilities that shifts in our national discourses about race have produced for black performers and black performance.

THE PROBLEM OF THE COLOR[BLIND]

In 1903, W. E. B. DuBois published his landmark text, *The Souls of Black Folk*. A collection of essays that fused culture with politics, *Souls* offered a meditation on the possibilities of black progress within American society, criticizing entrenched racism while carefully enunciating black responsibilities for racial uplift within a society that saw blackness and Americanness as quintessentially opposite formulations. Key among the many foundational concepts that DuBois explicated within his text was the notion of double consciousness, understood in relationship to the system of segregation that the Supreme Court had affirmed in *Plessy v. Ferguson* a mere seven years earlier. DuBois recognized that by declaring the possibility—even desirability—of a nation with "separate but equal" social, economic, and political infrastructures, the Supreme Court had ensured that "the problem of the Twentieth Century [would be] the problem of the color line," a dividing principle that was problematic in part because of the misapprehension of blackness that it fostered and foisted upon whites and blacks alike.[5]

On October 7, 2003, a century after the publication of DuBois's text, California voters participated in an unprecedented recall election that ousted Democratic governor Gray Davis from office, replacing him with Hollywood action hero and Republican party candidate Arnold Schwarzenegger. The spectacle of this election garnered national attention, with movie stars, child stars, porn stars, and career politicians all vying for the top elected position in the state. While Schwarzenegger's eventual victory was a foregone conclusion to many, the fate of another measure on this special ballot was far more suspenseful: Proposition 54, dubbed the Racial Privacy Initiative (RPI), would amend the state constitution to prohibit the "classif[ication of] any individual by race, ethnicity, color, or national origin in the operation of public education, public contracting, or public employment . . . [and] in the operation of any other state operations."[6] Spearheaded by Ward Connerly, who in his previous capacity as a regent of the University of California successfully led the effort to eliminate affirmative action in college admissions (the aforementioned Proposition 209), the campaign for Proposition 54 branded racial consciousness an inherently divisive discourse that only perpetuated, rather than ameliorated, racism.

Voters defeated the Racial Privacy Initiative by a margin of nearly 2 to 1, protecting a place for race in public discourse. However, while the campaign for Proposition 54 was centered on achieving a color-blind society in which racism had no discursive or procedural defense, opponents of Proposition 54 chose not to rely upon the typical, politically inflected critiques of color blindness. Instead, they cannily focused on medical research and treatment as proof of the continuing relevance of race in public life, predicting the disastrous consequences of ignoring health disparities between racial groups, such as unequal rates of diabetes, sickle cell anemia, and osteoporosis. After the election, Ward Connerly conceded, "I think the voters generally embrace the ideas of Proposition 54, but the opposition very, very effectively raised doubts about the health issue."[7] Indeed, Eva Paterson, then-director of the Equal Justice Society, foregrounded health in her celebration of the proposition's defeat: "'The people of California rejected being blinded to race. They realized there were health implications.' . . . It is a great day for civil rights.'"[8] Paterson's conflation of health implications and civil rights strategically reframed the consequential dimensions of race, making it indistinguishable from civic personhood in contemporary political life: the possibility of privacy that the initiative aspired to offer was, in practice, impossible. Or, as one senior scholar quipped when we were discussing the RPI, some of us don't have the option of racial privacy, do we? She and I laughed, imagining the seclusion that would be required to keep our brown skin to ourselves, even as we recognized the political quagmire tactics such as the RPI initiated: privacy is an important and contested privilege in American society today, granted to some and denied to others, but for people who have been denied voluntary, protected access to both private and public spheres of their own choosing, privacy can end up feeling a lot like exile.[9]

While Proposition 54 dealt directly with the proper role of race in American life, it was in fact part of a much larger cultural struggle relating to the tensions between the public and private sectors. Electoral and legislative activity in the earliest years of the twenty-first century have established deeply important yet seemingly inconsistent boundaries between personal and public (group) rights, from the "defense of marriage" statutes that have spread across the country to deny same-sex couples the legal protections that marriage affords to the second Bush administration's efforts to privatize Social Security. In the former instance, the public (and by extension, the government) has a right to structure the most private of relationships between consensual adults, yet in the latter case, the public and government are framed as intrusive presences in what ought to be personal decisions regarding finances, wealth, and quality of life.

In subtitling Proposition 54 the Racial Privacy Initiative, Connerly and his associates exposed and affirmed a racial etiquette that dominates contemporary American culture. As I have attempted to suggest with the title of this chapter, twenty-first-century social graces dictate that references to race always be issued *sotto voce*, so as not to cause any undue discomfort. Proposition 54 extends this logic, in effect criminalizing racial consciousness in the public sphere. Implicitly, the legislation suggests that race is exclusively a matter of private consciousness, only gaining publicly relevant materiality when and if individuals confess their awareness of one another's bodily differences. In this schema, race is the unruly chin hair on the face of an otherwise unblemished America: only bad manners would compel anyone to bring it up, and the politest among us will instead do others the favor of not mentioning a thing that can only cause embarrassment, discomfort, or shame. Anticipating these as the likely and logical outcomes of foregrounding race is a reflection of what John L. Jackson names "racial paranoia," a post–civil rights phenomenon "constituted by extremist thinking, general social distrust, the nonfalsifiable embrace of intuition, and an unflinching commitment to contradictory thinking."[10] Such paranoia overdetermines racial identity rather than racial injustice as the core problem of American society, daring people to speak of race in a perverse game of tag: "whoever mentions race first is the racist in the room."[11]

The irony of such foolish games is their ostensibly benevolent intention. We can read them as facile responses to W. E. B. DuBois's overinvoked claim about the color line. However, DuBois wrote at a moment of unique urgency for black Americans: at the beginning of the twentieth century, decades after emancipation from slavery and the backlash against Reconstruction, blacks continued to exist just beyond the limits of the civic imaginary, to be prefigured, in DuBois's simple yet trenchant words, as "a problem" that could not or would not be solved through incorporation into the dominant society.[12] A century later, we continue to struggle with repairing racial inequality on one hand and, on the other, recognizing the celebratory, emancipatory aspects of both elective and sometimes coerced membership in racialized communities. In fact, DuBois's concerns could now be reframed to assert that the problem of the twenty-first century is the problem of the color-*blind*: those who wish to disavow the continued material manifestations of race in our society. For reasons both well intentioned and sinister, a significant number of Americans believe that a total ignorance of race is the obvious, and only, solution to the problems that an acute attention to race has brought our society.

And yet if I am critical of the rhetoric and enactments of color blindness, the supposed alternative, "multiculturalism," is barely more satisfying. Deeply attached to the culture and canon wars of the 1980s and 1990s, multiculturalism was in part a response to the fact that lopsided representations of American society normalized whiteness by making other racial groups (and by extension, cultures) invisible. It affected school curricula as well as public policy, and according to David Hollinger, manifested primarily through two strains, pluralist and cosmopolitan.[13] In keeping with the second of these strains, Robin D. G. Kelley coined the term *polyculturalism* as an alternative to multiculturalism, "since the latter often implies that cultures are fixed, discrete entities that exist side by side—a kind of zoological approach to culture."[14] According to James Lee, multiculturalism is primarily a discourse of representation that has to date remained detached from materialist concerns over the inequitable distribution of resources.[15] Likewise, after famously arguing "against race" altogether, Paul Gilroy went on to introduce the notion of "conviviality" as an alternative to multiculturalism and its attendant connotations of an impossible "absence of racism or ... triumph of tolerance."[16] Ironically, color blindness, through its efforts to dematerialize racial difference, offers itself as the structural vehicle through which material racialized differences and discrimination will be overcome. Racialized minorities have been forced to navigate an ethical dilemma: visibility where and at what cost?

The competition between color blindness and multiculturalism as the modes through which we could come to know ourselves and others as American was not restricted to curricula or even to court cases about discrimination. Indeed, the "culture wars" moved outside of the university system to include the realm of aesthetic practice, as evidenced most famously by the NEA Four, Tim Miller, Holly Hughes, John Fleck, and Karen Finley, artists who received modest funding from the National Endowment for the Arts in 1990 only to have it revoked because of objections to the content of their work. Although the artists eventually had their funding restored after years of litigation whose costs far exceeded the value of the original grants, the NEA subsequently enacted a "decency clause" that enabled them to censor future funding recipients in order to preserve particular understandings of both "National" and "Arts," and also did away with grants to individual artists, who could be harder to pressure into compliance than organizations relying upon NEA funding for institutional stability and longevity. Notably, most of the artists we hear referenced in relation to government funding conflicts and affiliated concerns over the decency of images produced in the name of publicly funded American art were white. In some instances, these white artists were also engaged in representing blackness, such as Robert Mapplethorpe's controversial nudes, or the Wooster Group's use of blackface in *Route 1 and 9*.[17] For the most part, though, black artists themselves were not as visibly implicated in this understanding of the battle lines drawn in the war over American culture. According to Michele Wallace, "the culture wars represent[ed] a pitched battle among hegemonic white insiders only," because "black artists rarely (actually never) occupied the hallowed berths reserved for art world stars."[18] Nevertheless, black artists and audiences were present in other spheres, especially hip-hop, whose various elements all challenged the spirit of what gets valorized as art that reflects positively upon the nation. From the freestyle lyrics of MCs to the appropriated sounds and lyrics of DJs who sampled existing audio tracks to the writers and b-boys who commandeered public space to make graffiti art or to dance, hip-hop, as Abigail DeKosnik argues, is not only raced but also pulled into questions about ownership, appropriation, and appropriate distinctions between the public and private spheres.[19] The culture wars also provide a useful lens through which to evaluate other sites of black performance, from actors in mainstream Hollywood cinema to playwrights working on and off Broadway. The rhetoric of the culture wars seemed to be about the elite registers of high art and higher education and their trickle-down potential, but as I hope to demonstrate through my analysis of an eclectic, variously situated array of cultural representations, the politics of representation had and have urgent, often material consequences at each rung of our cultural hierarchy in its own right.

My emphasis on theatrical performance and its close relatives in film and television exists in productive continuity with this analysis of how American society grapples with its polyglot status. The term *melting pot*, a metaphor that has long idealized the peculiarly American convergence of multiple races and cultures, comes from the theater. In 1908, Israel Zangwill's play *The Melting Pot* premiered, fittingly, in the nation's capital and offered a romantic narrative of America as the site where cultural difference was transformed into strength that would change the world. The young protagonist, David Quixano, an immigrant of Russian Jewish heritage, spoke of the symphony he was composing in homage to what he saw as America's epic task:

> America is God's Crucible, the great Melting-Pot where all the races of Europe are melting and reforming! Here you stand, good folks, think I, when I see them at Ellis Island, here you stand in your fifty groups, with your fifty languages and histories, and your fifty blood hatreds and rivalries. But you won't be long like that, brothers, for these are the fires of God you've come to—these are the fires of God. A fig for your feuds and vendettas! Germans and Frenchmen, Irishmen and Englishmen, Jews and Russians—into the Crucible with you all! God is making the American. . . . the real American has not yet arrived. He is only in the Crucible, I tell you—he will be the fusion of all races, the coming superman.[20]

A return to Zangwill's words allows us to understand more clearly the raced and gendered assumptions built into this model of assimilation as the key to America's strength. The prototypical American is masculine, and is derived from European stock. Although the character David later expands his vision of the melting pot to include not just the various races of Europe, but also "black and yellow . . . East and West, and North and South, the palm and the pine, the pole and the equator, the crescent and the cross,"[21] the methods by which this amalgamation occurs are incendiary, and violently obliterate any distinct traces of what came before. Excavating Zangwill's actual language helps to clarify precisely why this metaphor has fallen out of favor with those who resist the idea of the complete death of the individual subject (and, implicitly, her past) as the price of inclusion in America, who do not believe that totality must always eradicate the particular. Equally important to note about this patriotic text is the fact that both Zangwill the author and David his protagonist have turned to art to express these nationalist sentiments, to grapple with the question of what it means to be an American. Premiering at a time of massive immigration from Europe, *The Melting Pot* offered powerful instruction to its audiences on how to embrace American ideology performatively. This influence is characteristic of performance's affective potential. Whether through realism, which masks its recursive force with claims to passively reflecting an exterior truth, or through experimental work that actively challenges the prejudices that realism instills, performance gives order to our perceptive abilities, and affects nationalist and racialist discourses alike.

THIS IS NOT A BOOK ABOUT NONTRADITIONAL CASTING

But once upon a time, I thought it would be. This conviction was most likely forged in a woodsy glade on the Berkeley campus in the spring of 1994, where I worked one afternoon with my partner from acting class. We were rehearsing the scene from *Twelfth Night* where Rosalind, dressed as a boy, is plotting with Orlando. It was spring, it was gorgeous outside, and we were both really happy: the scene took place in the woods, and we were actually rehearsing *in the woods!* How Method! Our deep-tissued understanding of the spatial dynamics informing the characters' encounter would certainly yield one of the best scene showings of the semester. Everything was going swimmingly, but I kept getting stuck on this one line, uttered by my partner:

"And I swear, by the white hand of Rosalind . . ."

My hand is not white.

My hand is brown.

My hand, silent yet ever so present, posed an obstacle to my total disappearance into the role. I *got* Rosalind on so many levels, but because I didn't *get* at birth the same skin color that Shakespeare imagined for her, I was forever estranged from the character in ways that some of my classmates could never have understood, estranged through their very eyes as spectators who would respond to the dissonance between words and body in different ways.

How did I resolve this problem, this tension between comprehension and apprehension? When we performed the scene for the class, I made a "bit" out of it: I stood speaking to Gabe with my hands clasped behind my back, and when he uttered the fateful line, I snuck a peek at my brown hand in momentary confusion, then continued to nod encouragingly. The audience laughed, and our scene was a success. I couldn't not acknowledge the material specificity of my body in that moment of performance, but I didn't quite know what to do, so I took it as my responsibility to demonstrate my awareness of my nonnormative performing body, and to diminish its significance by laughing it off. I was, as David Wiles put it, "trying to live in the 'world of the play' while performing in the world of race."[22] While this is one of the most conspicuous examples of my embodied relationship to the questions explored in this book, it is by no means the only one. As an actor and director, I have had to confront the conflicting impulses of recognition and disavowal that race in performance introduces, and as an educator, I have come to understand how deeply it continues to vex even the most recent generation of actors. A few years ago, one of my students explained her understanding of her curriculum in a nationally respected MFA program to me: "They spend the first two years making me believe that I can play anything, and then they spend the last year telling me that I can't, so I should get really good at my 'thing,' which will probably be 'the black best friend.'" Such pragmatism would prepare her to work in regional theater as well as in film and television by making her skilled at and legible within the still-racialized worlds of "mainstream" performance. This book emerged from an effort to understand my own experiences relative to nontraditional casting in the theater and to imagine alternatives, but it has evolved into a broader meditation on the integration of black performance into our conversations about the future of race in national culture. Nevertheless, an understanding of nontraditional casting—its origins and applications—remains essential to this project.

When most people think of nontraditional casting, they think of nonwhite actors in "white" roles, such as Phylicia Rashad's 2009 performance as Violet, the matriarch in *August: Osage County,* or Wendell Pierce's turn as Didi in the Classical Theatre of Harlem's 2006 and 2007 productions of *Waiting for Godot.* As the rough equivalent of affirmative action for the world of performance, nontraditional casting—crudely put—gets underrepresented minorities on-stage. In its affinity with affirmative action, it is a programmatic response to various aesthetic and institutional barriers that have kept nonwhite actors (along with women and members of other minority groups, including the disabled) from finding employment onstage, especially in mainstream theaters.[23] Harry Newman, then–executive director of the Non-Traditional Casting Project, wrote in 1989 of a "four-year study by Actors' Equity Association completed in January 1986 [that] revealed that over 90 percent of all the professional theatre produced in this country—from stock and dinner theatre to the avant-garde to Broadway—was staged with all-Caucasian casts."[24] This discovery motivated Equity's Ethnic Minorities Committee to codify a definition of nontraditional casting that was then "successfully negotiated . . . into several contracts and [began] to get acceptance for the notion, at least from those on the business side of the theatre" (24).[25] Newman's history of the institutionalization of nontraditional casting affirms that its efficacy is defined almost entirely in economic terms: Equity representatives curried business (rather than artistic) favor in the hopes of yielding quantitatively measurable gains for its members, as would be expected of a labor union. Quantity rather than quality of nonwhite representation took the forefront in lobbying efforts, with the tacit assumption that improving the former would improve the latter.

A month after the publication of this 1986 report, Actor's Equity Association helped to support the founding of the Non-Traditional Casting Project (NTCP).[26] Still in existence in the twenty-first century, the organization "works to promote inclusive hiring practices and standards, diversity in leadership and balanced portrayals of persons of color and persons with disabilities."[27] The NTCP moves beyond the quantitative imperatives of AEA and explicitly works for qualitative change in the representation of minorities, "consider[ing] diversity a comprehensive issue which extends to the participation of those who make up the artistic team—actors, directors, designers, writers, stunt performers, choreographers—as well as the production team and administrative staff, board of directors and the audience."[28] In this way, the NTCP recognizes American theater as a microculture reflective of larger social practices that produce and sustain racial hierarchies. The organization's polyvalent mission reflects its awareness that true cultural diversity cannot be localized: artistic choices must be complemented by business practices, the distribution of authority, and other types of institutional reform. Their work emanates from an assumption that the politics of representation are both aesthetic and structural.

Envisioning itself as both an advocacy organization and a practical resource, the NTCP convened the First National Symposium on Non-Traditional Casting in November 1986 in New York City. In addition to panel discussions, practical sessions featured nontraditionally cast actors in scenes from plays that could be successfully realized with actors of any race or physical ability.[29] Selected transcripts of the proceedings were published under the title *Beyond Tradition,* and the speeches and panel discussions documented in this volume make consistent appeals to practitioners and producers with rhetorical strategies rooted in both universalist/transcendent and nationalist discourses. From

Paul Robeson, Jr.'s assertion that "non-traditional casting in its best sense draws upon the enormously rich universality of the best in minority cultures"[30] to Margaret Wilkerson's claim that "the vitality that is a part of our total American culture needs to be a part of our imaginations,"[31] the discourse of the symposium was fervent and optimistic. After a year in operation, the NTCP received a special citation in 1987 from the *Village Voice*–sponsored Obie Awards, a significant recognition of the contributions the organization was making to American theater.

None of this addresses the question: what philosophy of race (in and as performance) implicitly forms the foundation of the NTCP's advocacy platform? In *Beyond Tradition*, Clinton Turner Davis and Harry Newman define nontraditional casting as "the casting of ethnic, female, or disabled actors in roles where race, ethnicity, gender, or physical capability are not necessary to the characters' or play's development."[32] They further divide the practice into four subcategories:

Societal Casting: ethnic, female or disabled actors are cast in roles they perform in society as a whole.

Cross-cultural casting: the entire world of a play is translated to a different cultural setting.

Conceptual casting: an ethnic, female or disabled actor is cast in a role to give a play greater resonance.

Blind casting: all actors are cast without regard to their race, ethnicity, gender or physical capability.[33]

This delineation produces an ideologically fluid spectrum that alternately uses race to Say Something, to Reflect Truth, and at the extreme, to Say Something By Saying Nothing. Although nontraditional and color-blind casting are routinely understood as synonymous, color blindness informs only one of the four practices that NTCP codifies, while the principles of multiculturalism seem in some form to undergird the other three. Mixing what Hollinger would define as cosmopolitanism and pluralism, these other three modes invest, to varying degrees, in the salience of race even to "neutral" narratives. Societal casting seems most cosmopolitan, suggesting that racially homogeneous casts don't reflect the more eclectic patterns of interracial social mobility that we experience today. In truth, it is the one category that justifies all of the other variations on nontraditional casting because it serves a redressive function against the artificially imposed sameness of our theatrical, televisual, and filmic landscapes. It suggests that realism—which is the genre where most conversations about nontraditional casting reside—contains ideological biases that must be laid bare in order to be resolved. Societal casting takes a pragmatic approach to the hypervisibility of whiteness by suggesting that if we only cast our stages as we live our lives, diversity will automatically increase. Conceptual and cross-cultural casting, however, both tend toward the pluralistic, investing in the specificity of racially discrete groups, while also believing that these differences do not preclude an understanding of the racially nonspecific themes a text might address. Conceptual casting (itself a bit of a red herring, as all casting choices belie a production's conceptual orientation) is the most oxymoronic for its simultaneous reliance upon and denial of the significance of race: privileging or harmful definitions of race should not preclude certain actors' access to productions, but the overdetermined (as privileged or harmful) definitions of actors' racial categories provide the "greater resonance" of which a racially nonspecific play is capable.

Blind casting is in some ways the most ambitious of these approaches, particularly if audiences are expected to be blind to more than one social category at the same time (e.g., race and physical ability). Rather than the typical ranking of identity politics through strategic (or not) essentialism, it asks, potentially, for their wholesale erasure. Director and theorist Richard Schechner suggests that blind casting, although utopic, would be possible if we managed to cultivate

a . . . theatre where several different kinds of responses are possible: times when perceiving the race, gender, etc. of performers matters; times when spectators perceive the categories but it doesn't matter; and times when it should not even be perceived—not because of disguise (like in *Le Cage aux Folles*) but because spectators have been trained to be race, gender, age, and body-type "blind."[34]

Schechner's admonition emphasizes the performative dimensions of both theater and race through his recognition that identity categories can be transformed, in real time, by spectators with the cultural literacy to produce alternate readings of how raced, gendered, and variously abled bodies signify onstage.

The production community has taken up the issue of nontraditional casting with a very clear sense of its nationalistic implications. Advocates and critics alike recognize the power dynamics embedded in racialized discourse. Proponents such as Alan Eisenberg, former president of AEA, celebrate nontraditional casting as "a belief in the potential of the American theater."[35] This language offers a backhanded compliment to performance practices that could make greater interventions into the cultural landscape. Rather than allowing complacency to rob the American theater of a potential source of vitality, the thoughtful use of nontraditional casting and its attendant redistribution of artistic authority destabilize the institutional and aesthetic forces that normalize a decidedly un-American monoraciality. Offering a similar defense of nontraditional casting, British director Nicholas Hytner defended his conspicuously multiracial 1994 Broadway production of the musical *Carousel* with the claim, "'This is so quintessentially an American show that it would have been odd to have excluded a large part of America from it. . . . What I would have had to justify is racially exclusive casting.'"[36] As I will discuss in greater detail in the sections and chapters that follow, this perspective—notable because it comes from someone who views America from the outside—recognizes the historical dimensions of racialized representation. Monoracial casting in "neutral" plays, or, as playwright Charles Mee describes it, "the bizarre, artificial world of all intact white people, a world that no longer exists where I live,"[37] often imposes an anachronistic tableau upon American theater. More specifically, it reifies the fiction of American theater as monoracial, when in fact it has always been deeply invested in presenting (and sometimes misrepresenting) racial difference in order to ponder and contain it, whether through explicit representations of racial others (e.g., mixed-race figures who embody the crises of racial categorization and citizenship) or through sublimated meditations on difference (such as Eugene O'Neill's *The Hairy Ape,* which reflected both anxieties over the fraught racial categorization of the Irish and antipathies toward people of African descent). What Mee and Hytner are actually gesturing toward, implicitly, is the power dynamic that expects people who are seen as nonnormative to accept a continued ancillary self-representational status within the institutions that self-identity as leading sites for the production and preservation of America's theatrical culture.

From the opposite perspective, theater critic John Simon is an especially notorious opponent of nontraditional casting. In addition to disparaging Hytner's *Carousel* for racial casting that "'militates against the meaning of the work,'"[38] one of Simon's most antagonistic relationships was with Joseph Papp, producer of the New York Shakespeare Festival. In the 1960s, when Papp began staging Shakespeare's plays with multiracial casts, Simon took great umbrage at Papp's sullying of the Bard's verse:

Out of laudable integrationist zeal, Mr. Papp has seen fit to populate his Shakespeare with a high percentage of Negro performers. But the sad fact is that, through no fault of their own, Negro actors often lack even the rudiments of Standard American speech.... It is not only aurally that Negro actors present a problem; they do not look right in parts that historically demand white performers.[39]

Simon's aversion to the bodies and voices of black actors laying claim to one of the icons of Western high culture is juxtaposed against Papp's determination to create an experience of Shakespeare that made his language accessible and relevant within a specifically American context. Like Hytner's production would some thirty years later, Papp's work privileged the resolute temporality of performance, emphasizing the political realities and frames of reference of the spectators who would see the show in the 1960s (or 1990s, in Hytner's case), rather than asking those audiences to employ habits of mind that were decades, centuries, or continents away.

Recent academic discourse has taken the issue of nontraditional casting and opened it to even greater scrutiny, hoping to explain the mechanisms through which it produces (and denies) racial meaning. Josephine Lee offers a critique of the paradoxical politics of liberalism that often motivate the implementation of nontraditional casting. In "Racial Actors, Liberal Myths," she suggests that nontraditional casting is an extension of the politics of liberal integrationism, which seek at once to acknowledge and efface difference, reifying the desirability of the ideological institution into which the raced body is meant to be assimilated.

Rather than effectively ending the stereotyping of "colored" bodies, the liberal impulse of cross-racial casting, particularly in its color-blind incarnation, wound up complicating the issue of racial visibility. It did so first by de-politicizing the racialized body, imagining race as a superficial quality that had to be transcended in order to ascertain the true merits of the actor. Bodies of color that could or would be so easily de-racinated would in fact be at a loss. This paradox of seeing and not seeing race ... in a sense allows this liberal thought to co-exist with the very racism that it had tried to eradicate.[40]

Lee historicizes the practice of nontraditional casting in order to shed light especially upon the often tacit traditions that it tries to subvert. As a theatrical manifestation of post–civil rights activism, cross-racial casting relies upon the assumption that structural inequality is a thing of the past: enduring cultural and racial differences are reduced to surface distractions that a discourse of color blindness (often connected with notions of transcendence) can remedy. For Lee, the politics of visibility embedded especially in notions of color-blind casting sustain the undesirable meanings of race, and offer hope that actors can leave behind its facade in order to express their true, interior selves. Demonstrating the intersection of theatrical and social discourses of race in performance, Lee connects this notion of color-blind casting to everyday social practices in which nonwhite individuals are turned into "racial actors," the limits of whose agency to act as individuals are experienced when they fail to conform to others' racialized expectations of them.

In a similar vein, Angela Pao discusses the extent to which "national identity is at the very heart of the debates over non-traditional casting."[41] Focusing on the politics surrounding Asian American theater companies' productions of classic (white) dramatic texts, Pao demonstrates that the anxieties about American national identity relate to the physical vulnerability of the nationalist paradigm through the embodiment of culture. All–Asian American casts that perform classics of the American canon performatively produce their equal access to narratives valorized as emblematic of American (theatrical) culture. When they do so in a color-blind way, rather than according to conceptual or cross-cultural conceits, they fail to respect the silent conflation of whiteness with Americanness.

Pao cites productions of plays by Eugene O'Neill and Arthur Miller as proof of this claim: when Asian American actors assumed that their performing bodies were as neutrally available to the texts as white actors', they disappointed critics wedded to the racialized logic of American society (or at least, of the American theatrical canon). However, when Arthur Miller himself directed *Death of a Salesman* in Beijing with an all-Chinese cast, the production served as a successful instance of cultural exchange (if not imperialism) because the Chinese actors' performance in Miller's play at once instantiated the Chinese artists' recognition of an American cultural icon and an acceptance of their literal and figurative distance from it. According to Pao, the transfer of *Salesman* to Beijing served as "a sign of the significance and quality of [the] play, a confirmation of [the] work's high standing in the canon of American theatre . . . a critical step in elevating [the] work from the standing of being just an American classic to a classic of world drama as well."[42] In an American context, quite the opposite occurs: color-blind or cross-cultural productions "ultimately upset the logic and ideology of coherent and homogeneous national identities and cultures."[43]

However, while challenging the purportedly monoracial foundations of American cultural identity, such casting choices rarely effect a total disruption of these foundations. Pao pays attention not only to casting choices but also to their mediation through general audience reception and more specifically, theater critics' responses, whose documentation can not only influence audiences but, as part of the archive, attempt to fix performances within a racial consciousness against which the performers may be working. In citing one reviewer's disappointment at a cross-racially cast production of *Long Day's Journey Into Night* that failed to include any overtly "Asian" cultural references, Pao notes that nontraditional casting can produce contests of interpretation that reproduce, rather than reject, the stereotypical demands placed upon nonwhite performing bodies.[44]

Nontraditional casting practices not only provide opportunities to challenge how we understand the nation as implicitly raced, they also risk acquiescing to a hierarchy of valuation, suggesting that their only function is to improve people of color. White theaters and white texts are affirmed as the pinnacle of artistic opportunity in practices that assume that escaping nonwhiteness is the true task of color-blind social progress. William H. Sun's essay "Power and Problems of Performance across Ethnic Lines" describes the simultaneously political, aesthetic, and educational dimensions of nontraditional casting. In addition to insisting upon an awareness of the various social and cultural spaces within which the consequences of nontraditional casting can be felt, Sun criticizes the disconnect between the universalist discourse that legitimizes nontraditional casting and the decidedly nonuniversal ways in which it is implemented. He asks, "Why do I hear so little about performance across ethnic lines *in both directions*?" but answers his own question by noting that white performers crossing the color line "might bring back the painful memories of blackface minstrelsy" and other racist representational practices.[45] White performers telling nonwhite stories is anything but nontraditional, and in fact constitutes a significant part of the tradition against which actors of color are working. Nevertheless, Sun proposes that there may be contexts in which the educational imperatives of cross-racial casting warrant the risky proximity to an ignoble, performed past. Not only can audiences benefit from seeing that the social constructionist turn cuts both ways, performers themselves might learn from the temporary occupation of different patterns of language, movement, and relationships to history.

BLACK PERFORMANCE: TRANSGRESSION OR TRANSCENDENCE?

Nontraditional casting as such is the most obvious frame of reference for fully appreciating this argument for the relationship between racial representation and racial reality. Attendant to this is the performativity of race, which demonstrates the shortcomings of color blindness's emphasis on transcending racial discourse, while creating a space for thinking through the possibilities of racial transgression as a productive alternative. I align myself with the discourse of race that argues for its antiessential nature without discounting what Harry Elam refers to as its "situational significance."[46] Similarly, cultural theorist Stuart Hall has said that race is "like a language," a sign system whose significance exists within, but not before, the act of social exchange.[47] Race may have no absolute position within biological discourse, but the influence of this "profound ordering of difference instantiated at the sight of the body"[48] structures social situations to the benefit and detriment of various types of bodies according to their valuation within the hierarchy of racial classification. Race, therefore, gains its currency from discourses that enact the reality they describe, meeting the most elemental standards of performativity. Shannon Jackson goes even further in the theorization of racial performativity to argue that racism, rather than race, "is the ultimate performative,"[49] because of its inherently structural and institutional dimensions, which allow us to distinguish between conscious, voluntary notions of race as performed identity and racism as a broader social system that recruits individuals wittingly and unwittingly to fortify the institutions that create distinctions in privilege.

Michael Omi and Howard Winant articulate the idea of racial formation as "a process of historically situated *projects* in which human bodies and social structures are represented and organized."[50] Rather than postulating race as either entirely real (biological) or entirely illusory (social construct), they propose a definition of race as "a concept which signifies and symbolizes social conflicts and interests by referring to different types of bodies,"[51] one that recognizes bodies as the cultural sites upon which ideas are routinely mapped. This intersectional framework is especially valuable when trying to understand nonconforming (perhaps a better word than *nontraditional*) racial casting and performances: sometimes the body doesn't do what it says it's doing, and sometimes this failed correspondence is produced not solely by the performer but partially by the spectator whose interpretive competencies challenge the performing body's efforts to speak for itself—the history of social conflicts and interests of which the spectator is aware, and therefore uses to comprehend an actor's performance, might grate against the narrative circumstances the actor tries to inhabit.

These understandings of race are of course very closely related to Judith Butler's theorization of gender as a "repeated stylization of the body, a set of repeated acts, within a highly rigid regulatory frame that congeal over time to produce the appearance of substance, of a natural sort of being."[52] Performance offers the opportunity for both gendered and racial subversion by allowing social and theatrical actors the opportunity to "restyle" the body and attempt to gain momentum that will cause repetitions of this restylization to spread from their local bodies to broader cultural sites. To borrow from Ann Pellegrini, "'We' (the collective and collaborative 'we' of writer and reader, performer and audience) can only catch ourselves in the act of becoming [racial] subject[s] when we see ourselves as if through the other's 'I.'"[53] I would argue by extension that we can only catch ourselves in the act of imposing racial objecthood upon others when we feel deeply invested in our own racial "I." Understanding race in this way privileges its external dimensions, rather than its private ones, by emphasizing racial categorization of the self and other as the enunciation of a social contract of sorts, an invitation to or provocation of a host of behaviors and expectations that grant one access to society as a member of a privileged or problematized group. Race is best understood as a complex synthesis of involuntary and voluntary attributes and affiliations whose significance is performative, produced through our fidelity to them rather than as anterior, interior fact. Furthermore, this fidelity is structured around the allocation of privilege. In the theater and in everyday life, knowing how and agreeing to perform your racial role correctly is often a guarantor of personal safety, financial reward, interpersonal respect, and even affection, reflecting E. Patrick Johnson's claim that "the pursuit of authenticity is inevitably an emotional and moral one."[54]

It is for this reason that racial categories are so energetically kept "within a highly rigid regulatory frame" in some quarters of society: concepts of race absolutely do not take care of themselves. Andrew Parker and Eve Kosofsky Sedgwick discuss "the torsion, the mutual perversion, as one might say, of reference and performativity"[55] in order to cast doubt upon the functionality of racial meaning as a referential endeavor. The oscillating practices through which the referent grants felicity to the performative and vice versa deny the ontological stability of referential priority. That to which performatives refer is altered in the very act of referencing: "originals" accrue significance in the act of invoking them as worthy reference points, and this accrued significance shapes the ways in which the performance gains sanction as achieving its intended function. Within the discourse of racialized performance, Parker and Sedgwick's exposition of the fragility of ontology reminds us that the discourse of racialized realism is constantly corrupted and corruptible.

So, for example, in the latter half of the mid-nineteenth century, one way of performing blackness may have involved blackface burlesque that articulated a nostalgia for antebellum southern life, but in the twenty-first century, new protocols have emerged. The historical instability of the referent "blackness" to which performative practices must conform demands that new cultural spaces be recruited in the dissemination of racial categories, and blackness as a referent has been dissected and distributed in new ways. Both blackness and performative efficacy have adapted to the cultural circumstances of the new millennium. Harry Elam argues for the dynamic nature of this process when he suggests that "the [black] performer repeats, reinscribes, *or even reconfigures* established gestures, behaviors, linguistic patterns, cultural attitudes, and social expectations associated with blackness."[56] Performance becomes a site of change, and blackness becomes a category open for (re)negotiation. These characteristic components of performance and performativity are ones that nonconforming casting and performance practices seek to harness for a concerted transformation of racial signification processes in American culture.

I conclude this section with a terminological clarification of the terms *transcendence* and *transgression*. In including the phrase *Racial Transgression* in the subtitle of this project it was not my intention to take on a larger debate regarding the term *transgression*'s analytical utility. From the vantage point of art criticism, for example, Hal Foster has suggested that stable boundaries no longer exist, and, therefore, neither can transgression: there are no representational limits left to cross. Both in terms of space, specifically the shifting relationship between interior and exterior social environments (or public and private spheres), and in the figurative sense of stability's supplantation by relationality, postmodernity makes it difficult to locate transgression as a cultural practice.[57] However, where race is concerned, these lines remain clear: as Michael Brown and his coauthors suggest in *Whitewashing Race,* material lines continue to racially demarcate desirable neighborhoods, circumscribe underperforming and underfunded school districts, and regulate entire categories of labor, making transgression not only possible, but urgently necessary.[58] Cultural and aesthetic practices that push at these very finite demarcations of the acceptable and the unacceptable, the just and the unjust, enable us to imagine and then create alternatives for people whose concerns would otherwise be dismissed through the silencing tyranny of color blindness.

Michel Foucault, building upon the work of Georges Bataille, defines transgression as "profanation in a world which no longer realizes any positive meaning in the sacred . . . prescrib[ing] not only the sole manner of discovering the sacred in its unmediated substance, but also a way of recomposing its empty form, its absence."[59] While Foucault was making interventions into different critical terrain, my investment in racial transgression bears some relation to this model. If we think of race as the sacred truth that simultaneously structures social relations in the United States and that we also try to banish from our consciousness (so as not to contend with the ways that it still informs the allocation of privilege), then racial transgression "recompos[es the] empty form, [the] absence," that allows racial privilege to go unmarked. It exposes the limits placed upon racial discourse in order to violate them and force the possibility of progressive action.[60]

Ultimately, though, I find transgression a useful concept primarily because I place it in etymological as well as political opposition to transcendence, a term that is overinvoked in postethnic, postracial, color-blind, and multicultural discourse. Very often, transcendence of racial issues is framed as both the tactic and the goal of contemporary racial politics. This is an objectionable strategy because, fundamentally, asking (usually nonwhite) people to transcend racial consciousness is usually just a more polite way of demanding that they "get over it." The Oxford English Dictionary notes that while the term *transcend* was once invoked relative to "a physical obstacle or limit," that usage is obsolete, in favor of "a non-physical limit . . . something immaterial."[61] Etymologically, it also implies an improvement over some prior state of being, with "to rise above, surpass, excel, [and] exceed" becoming synonyms within one definition. In spatial, physical, and evaluative terms, racial transcendence exacts disavowal of our racially mediated reality as the price of progress toward resolving American society's racial conflicts. It comes as no surprise that color blindness is the tool through which these admonitions are consistently offered.

On the other hand, transgression remains, for me, more rooted in the material. While it shares the sense of violating boundaries that may or may not be material (the OED includes "To go or pass beyond (any limit or bounds)" as one of its definitions), the moral judgment attached to transgression is more resolutely negative and more resolutely social: to transgress is to "violate," to "offend," to "disobey," even to "sin."[62] The "object" of injury always haunts the designation of transgressive action, suggesting that transgressive action contains the potential to injure entrenched patterns of racial discourse. In other words, the judgments demanded of a particular discursive system (in this case, race) are read through that system, not over and beyond it. Furthermore, racial transgression and racial transcendence invoke competing valuations of race: if moving beyond the immaterial boundaries of race is to excel, racial boundaries must be flimsy and inconsequential, while racial transgressions are deemed offensive precisely because of the deep investment we have in these boundaries. Therefore, an emphasis on representations that engage in what I consider racial transgression enables us to interrogate what counts as "offensive," requiring an engagement with the norms that are habitually upheld by producers, actors, and audiences alike. Whether trying to understand how black actors performing the works of Shakespeare could violate social norms about race, space, and art or how performance rewrites the African American past to undo gaps in the narrative of black subjectivity, engaging with race as a dynamic sociohistorical formation rather than simply as an irrelevant framework waiting to be overcome can be the difference between finding hope or despair in the social and political potential of cultural practice.

Finally, a deeper turn toward the vernacular might explain the urgency of a move away from transcendence as the framework for racial healing. I have already suggested that to transcend is merely a euphemistic injunction that labels the one needing to transcend as overly sensitive or irrational, but there is another reading of "getting over" that perhaps explains even more precisely the problems of transcendent approaches to race: in colloquial speech, to *get over on* is to perpetuate a hustle, to scheme for unearned rewards. If racial transcendence not only asks people of color to get over the injuries they already have and continue to experience but also provides an opportunity for those privileged within the racial status quo to get over on, to illegitimately triumph over, efforts to restructure racial interaction, then it is even more sinister a platform than we have previously realized. Transgression exposes the moral limitations of transcendence as a viable strategy for social change by acknowledging the histories of social location that people wear on their bodies and that inform all of our interpretive frameworks.

In practice, I advocate for racial transgression as an alternative to transcendent, color-blind politics and performance practices largely through a principle of subtraction. As attentive to the failures of color blindness-as-transcendence in theatrical and cultural performance as to successful instances of racial transgression, this project approaches color blindness and transgression as strategies that operate on a variety of levels. My examination of race, color blindness, pluralism, performativity, and performance relies upon an eclectic assortment of objects, all of which conspire to demonstrate that absolute color blindness does not exist in American society, and that performance practices prove the divide between the rhetoric and the realities of race in our culture today. Each chapter takes the case study approach, attempting to understand the possibilities for and necessity of a transgressive approach to black performance by attending variously to institutional politics and their influence over the types of performances that get normalized as "mainstream American theater;" race-conscious strategies of mass-market appeal and their indebtedness to heteronormative paradigms; the ways that our gendered and raced historical inheritance attempts to dictate performance possibilities in the present; and the dangers of a too-hasty embrace of the postracial. I turn in chapter 2 to the Theatre Communications Group–sponsored fracas between August Wilson and Robert Brustein (et al.) to think about the institutional pressures influencing black performance in America. I question the material consequences of color-blind casting in American theater, asking if the end of race that color blindness claims to offer is really just the threatened end of nonwhiteness, achieved through an erosion of financial support and expressive autonomy for black theater. Rejecting Robert Brustein's strategically innocent devotion to color blindness as the only alternative to a balkanized America as well as August Wilson's uncompromising overdetermination of the differences between black and white culture that color blindness destroys, I attend to the emotional and political nodes of their immediate dispute as well as to the larger dynamics at play in the country when the dispute took place, arguing that cultural institutions are key sites through which, inadvertently or not, race continues to receive material support belying the simple discursive tricks that color-blind politics attempt to enforce.

Leaving behind the realm of institutional politics and their effect upon (and intimate relationship to) aesthetics, chapters 3 and 4 then function as complementary, gendered examinations of, on one hand, the limits of racial transcendence, and on the other, practical strategies for engaging in transgressive representational work. Chapter 3 moves firmly into the arena of popular culture, using a pair of films starring black actor Denzel Washington to identify (interracial) heterosexuality as the social practice that most limits our ability to employ notions of color blindness in performance. While only one of the two films casts Washington "nontraditionally" in a role intended as a white man, Washington's status as a black actor who has allegedly transcended the limitations of race in Hollywood lends him a cultural color-blindness that makes a reading of the ends to which his sexual subjectivity is put to use—particularly opposite a white woman—instructive. If, as Steven Shaviro suggests, in addition to pleasure, film viewing offers "a rising scale of seduction, delirium, fascination, and utter absorption in the image" that is distinctly powerful compared to other forms of representation, what can we learn from the seductions of seeing Denzel Washington in a sometimes sublimated romantic encounter with a white woman?[63] What do these moments of transcendent celebrity teach us, in spite of themselves, about black masculinity?

Chapter 4 engages with a positive example of racially transgressive performance's unabashed engagement with the past. Originally inspired by my desire to conceive of nontraditional casting as both an embodied and a textual practice, I focus on the playwright Suzan-Lori Parks, particularly her play *Venus,* and examine the relationship between Parks's constructed Saartjie Baartman / Venus Hottentot and the "actual" historical figure, to interrogate the various discursive constructions of Baartman through time: as criminal, as freak show oddity, as scientific specimen, as fodder for art, as subject of plays and poetry. Additionally, this chapter looks at the competing and complementary processes of visual and textual apprehension of subjects. Asserting that a reconceptualization of blackness in performance can occur not only through the integration of black performing bodies into "white" texts to expand their capacity to reflect a "universal" experience, I advocate Parks's deployment of an "oppositional gaze" that allows for critical interpretation of cultural representations and different mechanisms for employing the black female body in performance.

Chapter 5 moves from the 1990s to a moment at the beginning of the twenty-first century, working to locate the ubiquity of the term *postblack* in relation to other theories of postraciality, the latest critical term to attempt to complete the work of social reconciliation that color blindness and multiculturalism each failed to achieve. Beginning with an analysis of some of the artwork included in the Studio Museum in Harlem's 2001 exhibition "Freestyle," whose catalog ushered the term *postblack* into the lexicon, I work to distinguish postblackness from postraciality, in order to link it more productively and accurately with strategies of transgression that represent blackness in a complex negotiation with the past rather than in disavowal of it. I then move on to look at rapper, actor, and producer Ice Cube, whose transformations in the public sphere have much to teach us about how blackness functions in a postmodern, heavily mediated era in which blackness is being constantly redefined to keep pace with the demands of the marketplace. Beginning with his journey from gangsta rapper to family movie star, I look at the ways he is able to insist upon yet not seem commercially constrained by his blackness, before moving on to discuss the controversial reality series *Black. White.*, of which he served as an executive producer. *Black. White.*, I argue, exposes the limits of what nonconforming racial performances in mass culture can teach us about blackness and the extent to which they can participate productively in its redefinition on a wide scale. Ultimately, by directing my attention to high culture and low, to print, to stage and screen, to art galleries, to everyday life without a conspicuously aestheticized frame, I aspire to understand how the black performing body can exist in a space that is critically engaged with history and also willing to be disloyal to its inaccuracies.

A NOTE ON BLACK PERFORMANCE IN THE AGE OF OBAMA

January 20, 2009, was the first day of instruction in the spring semester at UC Berkeley. It was also the day that Barack Obama was sworn in as president of the United States of America. The campus hosted a broadcast of the inauguration on a Jumbotron on Sproul Plaza, and while I did not make it to campus in time to watch the ceremony with the masses who gathered there, I was able to walk to my first class in the wake of the collective energy and enthusiasm that hung in the air after its conclusion. I was off to teach a course that both satisfies a requirement within my department's major in theater, dance, and performance studies and also fulfills a university-level American Cultures requirement. As described on the website for the American Cultures Center,

> The American Cultures (AC) curriculum has been recognized as a national model for its integrative and comparative analyses of race, culture and ethnicity in the United States. AC courses represent an unprecedented departure from existing approaches to teaching about diversity in the United States. Instead of focusing on one or two ethnic groups, AC courses explore the complexity of ethnicity, culture, and pluralism, and their influences on the ways that Americans think about themselves and approach the issues and problems that confront our society.[64]

After quickly moving through "first day of class" business, I began a conversation with the students about theater's origins in ritual, ritual's role in producing and solidifying collective identity, and an acknowledgment of the events of the day. "Today's inauguration was a ritual, right? A private citizen became an official world leader after taking an oath in front of an audience. We had the chance to view this ritual on Sproul Plaza. Why was this special?" Students ventured a variety of answers:

"Because it only happens once every four years."

"Yes," I responded, "but, having been on campus for longer than four years, I can say that I don't recall any other inauguration being broadcast here for public viewing."

"Well, this was the first election that really capitalized on youthful energy to create a grassroots movement that got a candidate elected."

OK.

"There's a lot of international excitement that a new administration will help to repair America's standing in the world community by taking us in a new direction."

Mmhmm.

Things began to peter out.

"Might it have anything to do with the fact that Barack Obama is the first black president of the United States?" I asked, after a pause.

"Well, yes."

It was clear that in several students' eyes, I had indeed violated racial etiquette, I had tainted their good feelings about the day by foregrounding the importance of race to this instantiation of national ritual. One student put this plainly, saying, "It makes me really mad when people say that this is about race, because that's not why I voted for him. I voted for him because I believe in what he stands for." For my students, even the context of having this conversation in a class that was expressly dedicated to "explor[ing] the complexity of ethnicity, culture, and pluralism, and their influences on the ways that Americans think about themselves and approach the issues and problems that confront our society" was not enough to overcome the discursive common sense that says that race is always and only to be discussed as a problem to get over. That Obama's race (or, more precisely, the fact that his race did not preclude his being elected) was one of the things being celebrated at the inauguration was a narrative that some of my students weren't prepared to discuss or to allow to structure their feelings about the day.

Such an attitude is supposed to be the birthright of this generation as citizens of a postracial order, one in which a black person's ability to appeal to and gain the trust and respect of Americans of all races can be taken for granted. Actor Dennis Haysbert believes that he helped to bring about this transformed social landscape by playing a black president on the television series *24*, offering a character in whose fate audiences were positively invested. According to public reports, he declared, "As far as the public is concerned, it did open up their minds and their hearts a little bit to the notion that if the right man came along ... that a black man could be president of the United States."[65] However, David Palmer was but the latest in a line of fictional black presidents: Douglas Dilman. Tom Beck. Mays Gilliam. Dwayne Elizondo Mountain Dew Herbert Camacho. There was even a slave ship called The Black President.[66] (And let's not forget the fact that Haysbert's character Palmer got assassinated on the series, paving the way for his brother Wayne to become the second black president.) In the realm of the representational, black presidents have functioned much as Barack Obama already has, as a diagnostic symbol of America's ultimate triumph over racial prejudice. Consumption of images of black presidents offers American audiences the opportunity to rehearse acceptance of a black person in perhaps the most improbable role available in America (or to confirm such a turn of events as a dystopic national condition). When Obama received enough electoral votes to secure victory on November 4, 2008, the superlative declarations began in full force, announcing the death of a major barrier faced by African Americans. Tom Brokaw, deeply moved as he presided over NBC's live coverage of election night, called the moment of victory "a profoundly important passage out of the deep shadows of our racist past that began with that first slave ship."[67]

Several important rhetorical and political moves are embedded in Brokaw's poetic language. First, Brokaw locates American racism as our shared historical memory, not merely that of blacks, and as a past practice that has merely a spectral rather than material bearing upon the present. Second, he assigns an originary, metonymic function to "that first slave ship" that invites an easy condensation of all forms of racism into slavery, a strategy that supports the preceding claims of a racist past (vs. post-slavery present). Furthermore, the travel imagery of slave ships and profound passages offers historical breadth to the teleology of racial progress that Brokaw wishes to honor. Transcendent to the core, it goes over and moves beyond the painful intermediate historical markers of Reconstruction, Redemption, and a twentieth century full of activism and contention that separate the inauguration of America's slave-dependent economy from the inauguration of America's first black president. Some of this complicated logic may be attributed to the demands that economy of language places upon improvised eloquence in live broadcast journalism, but Brokaw was by no means alone in marking the outcome of this election as a signal shift in race relations and in America's national character. According to the Pew Research

Center, "immediately after the November 2008 election . . . nearly half of whites (48%) and three-quarters of black voters (74%) said they expected to see race relations improve during Obama's presidency."[68]

Nevertheless, personal and political reactions to Barack Obama during his time as president have certainly laid waste to the idea that his election helped to eradicate race-consciousness in our society. From the allegations of racially licensed disrespect levied against southern Senator Joe Wilson after his outburst during Obama's 2009 health care speech to Congress to the embarrassing destruction of Shirley Sherrod's government career in the wake of disingenuous allegations of governmentally empowered anti-white racism in 2010, people on both sides of the political aisle continued to interpret their adversaries' behavior through a racialized understanding of American culture, its mores and morals.[69] However, it would be a mistake to see this racialized political discourse as a fall from some temporary postracial grace that was achieved during Obama's presidential campaign. Even the efforts to dissociate Barack Obama from predominant definitions of blackness—whether on the grounds of his mixed racial heritage or his access to elite educational and professional spheres—remained invested in the truth and pervasiveness of those other modes of black behavior (why else would he be such an exciting candidate?).[70] Race remained an issue, even in the celebrations of its absence.

The real significance of Obama's campaign, I would argue, lies in the ways that he attempted not to ignore race but to transform our understandings of it. This began with his debut as a national political figure at the 2004 Democratic National Convention, where he delivered a keynote address. In the days leading up to and immediately following this speech, Obama's press coverage eagerly anticipated his import as a harbinger of new (black) politics, black but not distractingly so. While still serving as political consultant for Obama's 2004 U.S. senatorial campaign, David Axelrod deemed Obama the American story incarnate, praising his "ability to walk into any room and connect with anybody . . . [because of] the many different cultural strands that are part of him."[71] His convention speech, "Out of Many, One," offered the same promise, through its primary emphasis on a class-based appeal to the American dream of upward mobility. Though it included subtle references to violations of civil rights in a post-9/11 culture and disagreements over international policy (especially the Iraq War), Obama largely attempted to focus on transcendent, quality-of-life goals that united Americans by going over and moving past regional, racial, religious, and ideological divides.[72]

Obama's emphasis on shared aspirations—already displayed in his own campaign efforts in Illinois—earned him the prized national speaking engagement, and was so successful that it became necessary for him to formally declare his racial self-identification in the face of enthusiasms for his postracial possibilities. While in his convention speech he chose to focus on what Americans held (or wanted to hold) in common, he did not implicitly mean to suggest the irrelevance of the particularities of race or place. This much was clear when an interview published the day before his convention speech reported,

> Asked how he defined his own racial identity, Mr. Obama said he considered himself African-American.
>
> "The reason that I've always been comfortable with that description is not a denial of my mother's side of the family," Mr. Obama said. "Rather, it's just a belief that the term African-American is by definition a hybrid term. African-Americans are a hybrid people. We're mingled with African culture and native American culture and European culture."
>
> He added later: "If I was arrested for armed robbery and my mug shot was on the television screen, people wouldn't be debating if I was African-American or not. I'd be a black man going to jail. Now if that's true when bad things are happening, there's no reason why I shouldn't be proud of being a black man when good things are happening, too."[73]

But given our long-standing national investments in phenotype as destiny and hypodescent as law, how did Obama's racial identity, much less authenticity, ever come into question at all? One could argue that this is a reflection of the ways in which Obama confounded racialized expectations about black masculinity and its place in the public sphere. Just as Marvin McAllister has described "whiteface" as encompassing not only a stage affectation but also social practices in which black individuals assume behaviors and roles that are presumed to be the privilege of people living in white bodies, Obama's celebrated ability to relate to individuals across the race and class lines that structure most people's everyday lives represented, for some, a usurpation of white social ease that was fundamentally incompatible with current understandings of how blackness is experienced by individuals and engaged by our society at large.[74]

These concerns about his racial identity returned with vigor during U.S. Senator Obama's campaign for the presidency. Then-rival Joe Biden demonstrated this in early 2007 when he inelegantly described Obama's popularity as the result of his being "the first mainstream African-American who is articulate and bright and clean and a nice-looking guy," implicitly denigrating all of

Obama's black political predecessors on one if not all of these criteria.[75] Such a characterization reinforced a transcendent reading of Obama's performance as a candidate for national office by devaluing black political history in order to recontextualize Obama as a figure who could get past the precedents of how black political figures once engaged with the American electorate. Yet Obama borrowed heavily from those earlier politicians, blending the oratorical style of black America's most prominent leaders (many of whom presided over pulpits at some point in their careers) with the Midwestern affability that paid homage to his matrilineal heritage as well. Beyond Obama's general campaign affect, he engaged the issue of blackness and its place in his own political and personal identity through his "More Perfect Union" speech, commonly referred to as his speech about race, which was treated as a major news event. The address was prompted by the controversy that erupted over Obama's former pastor Rev. Jeremiah Wright, whose brand of liberation theology offered sharp criticisms of certain aspects of American culture. Taken out of the context of the sermons within which they were contained, clips of Wright's especially incendiary rhetoric threatened to undermine Obama's campaign by proving, in spite of his apparent transcendence of race, his actual, deep-seated loyalties to a mode of blackness that was perceived as being hostile to white interests.

Standing at a podium with multiple American flags behind him, Obama used this speech to try to supply the missing context for Rev. Wright's pulpit critiques, and also to distance himself from them. His remarks were intended as a challenge to both black and white Americans to recognize the effort that would be required to work through our complex racial history, rather than simply to overlook it or to dwell in a static understanding of racial dynamics as insurmountably contenious. To that end, he not only borrowed the well-known language of the founding fathers as the organizing motif in his speech, he also supplied some of the history lesson that would be necessary for Americans to embark on a shared project of transformation. By asserting, "race is an issue that . . . this country cannot afford to ignore right now," Obama resisted the transcendent interpretation of his performance as a candidate and potential president.[76] Instead, he could more productively be understood as a transgressive figure, one who, to borrow Daphne Brooks's concept of afro-alienation, "rehearsed ways to render racial and [to a lesser degree] gender categories 'strange' and thus to 'disturb' cultural perceptions of identity formation."[77] Through his exhortations to engage race in unprecedented ways that were accountable to a material history (and the enduring practices) of a race consciousness that emanates from very specific patterns of social stratification,

Obama's individual behavior and the set of social relations into which he invited his audience worked to disturb the racialized practices that have long limited black personal and social possibilities. Preferring the transgressive to the transcendent interpretation of Barack Obama's success means refusing to participate in the devaluation of blackness and instead foregrounding the possibility of black performance as a transformative practice within American culture, a disposition that I hope permeates the analysis that follows.

CHAPTER 2

The End of Race or the End of Blackness?
August Wilson, Robert Brustein, and
Color-Blind Casting

One hundred years from today, Americans are likely to look back on the ethnic difficulties of our time as quizzically as we look at earlier periods of human history, when misapprehension defined the reality.

—Stanley Crouch, "Race Is Over," 1996

While . . . I embrace colorblindness as a legitimate hope for the future, I worry that we tend to enshrine the notion with a kind of utopianism whose naïveté will ensure its elusiveness. . . . Perhaps one of the reasons that conversations about race are so often doomed to frustration is that the notion of whiteness as 'race' is almost never implicated.

—Patricia J. Williams, *Seeing a Color-Blind Future*, 1997

When August Wilson passed away in October 2005, a major voice in American culture and dramatic literature was silenced. Lionized for his project of creating a play for each decade of the twentieth century—an ambitious feat unequaled by peers of any race—Wilson had two public personae, one developed through his dramatic writings and the other through his public speeches. His plays celebrated the black Everyman and foregrounded the musicality and rhythm in African American experience in a way that resonated with audiences of many races and cultures, while his public speeches exposed a different side of his politics, one that left many of his nonblack audiences feeling alienated. Rather than transcending to the universal with his emphasis on the particular (as supporters credited his plays with doing), Wilson's speeches seemed to violate many of the tenets of multicultural America's philosophy of race, which often takes a cautiously celebratory—instead of overtly redressive—stance toward the incorporation of black culture and black people into American social structures. This became clear during the protracted 1996–97 debate between August Wilson and Robert Brustein over the racial politics of American theater. Taking this debate as my central text, in this chapter I will examine the ways in which discourses of color blindness affect the artistic and institutional viability of blackness as a cultural formation. Both August Wilson and Robert Brustein rested their condemnation and celebration of theatrical color blindness on understandings of blackness that were both limited and limiting. For Wilson, color-blind casting in particular placed a specifically politicized notion of blackness under assault, and for Brustein, this very same politicized blackness (antagonistic, if not antithetical, to white culture) formed an interest category that had no proper place within the aesthetics of American theater, and to which color-blind casting offered a welcome alternative. Each man's position overlooked the possibility that what we know as color-blind casting might have transgressive, rather than just transcendent, effects. Ultimately, Wilson's criticisms of color-blind casting exposed the gap between casting decisions and the performance practices they make possible, as well as the affinities between representation and discursive and institutional power.

As an introductory salvo, August Wilson's "The Ground on Which I Stand" speech criticized both the aesthetic and structural biases that persist in American theater and continue to relegate non-Eurocentric works (and cultural workers) to marginal status. Significantly, he situated his critique within a renunciation of the politics of integration and assimilation of blacks into white culture, which he considered an "attempt to blot us out, to reinvent history and ignore our presence or to maim our spiritual product."[1] Wilson suggested that color-blind casting practices were little more than band-aids—cheap healing tools that covered the wound of exclusion with a neutral though not at all color-blind veneer—that formed "an assault on [blacks'] presence, . . . an insult to our intelligence, our playwrights, and our many varied contributions to society and the world at large."[2] Rather than equitably redistributing economic and artistic resources, assimilationist and color-blind policies preserved a racialized theatrical infrastructure that relied upon fictions of black inferiority to justify its practices of resource allocation.

Although he was not present at Wilson's keynote address, Robert Brustein was the one representative of mainstream American theater whom August Wilson criticized directly, and Brustein very quickly responded to Wilson's speech and its charges in an essay of his own, "Subsidized Separatism."[3] Chronicled primarily in the magazine *American Theatre,* a debate went back and forth in print between Wilson and Brustein, drawing in other practitioners and critics, and culminated in a face-to-face showdown, the January 1997 Town Hall conversation "On Cultural Power" between Wilson and Brustein, moderated by actress-playwright Anna Deavere Smith. Their debate remains provocative over a decade later because the concerns to which Wilson was reacting have not significantly changed, and the questions of where and how black theater gets valued and supported remain controversial. An uncritical deployment of color-blind casting invites the question of whether race is truly irrelevant in American performance practices, or if the rhetoric of color blindness only diminishes the value of nonwhite cultures, while leaving whiteness intact. Is Michael Eric Dyson correct when he argues that "the cost of colorlessness is always an investment in whiteness"?[4]

The quotes with which I introduced this chapter advance both complementary and competing concerns over the possible obsolescence of race in American society. Stanley Crouch, the notoriously irascible black cultural critic, predicts the end of race as the inevitable by-product of the "cultural miscegenation" that has always been part of American culture. He sees this, aided by the increased biological disruption of so-called pure bloodlines (as "the current paranoia over mixed marriages [becomes] largely a superstition of the past"),[5] as the primary reason why race will lose its organizational salience within American social and cultural politics. Crouch reinforces this claim in visual terms, conceding that "what such [postracial] people will look like is beyond [his] imagination";[6] nevertheless, his article in the New York Times magazine is illustrated with a gallery of photographs of mixed-race children, from the Pakistani–African American Saria to Keith, who is Filipino-Italian-Russian.

Crouch's optimistic essay manages to invoke many of the discourses that help to construct race: gene pools, visually apprehensible difference, social class, economics, commodification, representation, and institutional networks. Nevertheless, the inexorable slide toward an amalgam American culture that privileges no group according to racial status (because of the dissolution of these groups) may not transpire as the effortless reconstitution of the social sphere that he predicts: what are the terms according to which this integration will take place? Critical race theorist Patricia J. Williams's cautious optimism about America's potential for bringing about an egalitarian revolution is instructive. She advocates an interrogation of the methods that would produce such a signal shift in American racial culture. Williams's primary concern is that whiteness is consistently exempted from consideration when the dismantling of race is discussed. Borrowing John Fiske's concept of "exnomination" specifically to criticize the unnamedness of whiteness as a racial category,

Williams suggests that "exnomination permits whites to entertain the notion that race lives 'over there' on the other side of the tracks, in black bodies and inner-city neighborhoods, in a dark world where whites are not involved," and hence, they are neither capable of nor responsible for helping to solve problems that are articulated in racial terms that do not include them.[7] In the color-blind future, therefore, blacks and other minority groups will experience drastically different lives, having been liberated from racial concerns, but whites, presumably, will step unaltered into a postracial America. For Williams, assuming the vacuity of whiteness as a racial category is a problem: whiteness and white privilege are at least as worthy of interrogation as the more frequently marked and problematized terms of racial discourse (nonwhite Others), and any project for moving Americans into a colorless (or color-blind) future must think critically about how the transformation of American racial culture unavoidably includes disrupting the salience and power of whiteness.

Fellow critical race theorists join Williams in her skepticism toward color blindness. They take greatest exception to the claim that the U.S. Constitution, as a foundational nationalist text, "imposed a rule of color blindness on the government."[8] The Constitution is perhaps one of the more interstitially performative governmental texts we have: it simultaneously makes true those things that it declares, and does what it does through the performative authority of the Supreme Court to interpret it and determine its appropriate application. Justice John Marshall Harlan may have asserted in 1896 that "our Constitution is color-blind, and neither knows nor tolerates classes among citizens," but he made this declaration as the lone dissenter in *Plessy v. Ferguson*: the deciding opinion in that case believed that the Constitution did indeed understand and accept distinctions of class and color, that separate and supposedly equal accommodations were consistent with the Framers' intention to provide and protect the rights of America's free white citizenry.[9] In truth, all efforts to claim the color blindness of the U.S. Constitution are retroactive: OED dates the earliest use of *color blindness* as a figurative (rather than diagnostic) term to 1856, in language describing the Commonwealth of Massachusetts as having "a government color-blind; no distinction of race in the camp or the senate."[10] Nearly a century prior to this, blacks were the "other Persons" who deserved reduced proportional consideration in calculating the composition of Congress, and the possibility of whose escape from conditions of forced labor was considered a matter of federal importance.[11] Calling the Constitution—and therefore, our national ideology—color-blind is at best defensible only in the strictest linguistic sense, but at worst, it "fosters the systematic denial of racial subordination and the psychological repression of an individual's recognition of that subordination, thereby allowing it to continue."[12] Semantic solutions alone cannot solve structural problems: shifting the rhetoric of American discourse to suggest that race is no longer a central feature of public life does little to repair demonstrable race-based inequities. Instead, this strategy simply attempts to eliminate an important vocabulary of analysis, critique, and reform.

In the world of theater, an adamant rhetorical posture of color blindness threatens to bar August Wilson from being able to discuss black aesthetics or the conditions under which black theater is produced. Following Gotanda's critique, color blindness becomes a fiction that divorces itself from the processes of history: since many institutions in our culture were created through concerted inattention to nonwhite culture in order to normalize whiteness, the attempted sleight of hand that is color blindness (as nonrecognition) "ultimately supports the supremacy of white interests" (36) by placing uncritical faith in the color-blind integrity of institutions created through the extreme race-consciousness of America's past. American theater, then, is exempted from having to contemplate its own history and the extent to which past practices of race-based discrimination produced the supposedly color-blind institutions of the present, and more importantly, how some enduring practices perpetuate racialized inequities.

Whether it is framed in social or legal terms, color blindness centers on notions of race as performance. More precisely, traditional color-blind politics suggest that performance (as efficacy rather than as entertainment) is the pathway to racelessness. By placing a priority on individualism, color-blind theories suggest that one may try to escape an ontology of race through performance. Therefore, oppositions to color blindness are in fact objections to a value system that assigns the realness of racial categories (other than whiteness) a continually degraded status as problematic, unruly performatives. In social and legal policy, color blindness gets reduced to a troubling "Don't ask, don't tell" stance, in which the acknowledgment of race is predicated upon its inferiority, and color blindness becomes the condescending favor of ignoring racial identities that nonwhites would do well to disavow. This process does not also problematize whiteness but instead exempts it, and teaches other groups that identity politics only produce the problems they claim to want to overcome.

Nevertheless, color blindness and integration (as new or increased access to space and virtually all forms of capital) are bedfellows. Color blindness is constantly ghosted by the identity politics it professes to disdain. Constant, careful attention to just how many people of color receive access to material resources and opportunities is essential to preserving the distinctions between color blindness, racism, and racial opportunism. It is no wonder then, that many non-white theater artists have deep concerns about becoming signifiers of diversity (evidence of blindness to color as an automatic criterion of inclusion or exclusion) who are always figured as occasional incursions rather than as central and consistent contributors to the representation and production of American culture within the relatively privileged sites of regional theater in particular.

AUGUST WILSON: CULTURAL AUTHENTICITY, "RACIAL STIGMA," AND COMMUNITY

Delivered as the keynote address of the Theatre Communications Group's biennial conference on June 26, 1996, August Wilson's speech, "The Ground on Which I Stand," decried the egregious, systematic exclusion of people of color from American theatrical institutions in both economic and aesthetic contexts. His speech was a plea for institutionalized support for black theater as an antidote to the color-blind casting practices used as recompense for racialized inequities in American theater. Wilson stood before his audience in Princeton, New Jersey's McCarter Theater as a self-proclaimed "race man," steeped in the politics of the Black Power Movement, and rejected "the idea of colorblind casting [as] the same idea of assimilation that black Americans have been rejecting for the past 380 years."[13] Defining race as the single "most important part of our personality," he argued that American theater had a responsibility to recognize this cultural category, which "is also an important part of the American landscape," by including blacks within its institutional framework.[14] Rather than assimilation, which assumed that "black Americans do not have a culture"[15] and could therefore be uncritically absorbed into the existing (white) performance institutions of American theater, Wilson passionately advocated the necessity of black theaters, in which artists possessed "the right to amend, to explore, to add our African consciousness and our African aesthetic to the art we produce."[16] While there is no question that black artists do deserve access to well-funded spaces that allow them to create work that is actively rooted in an African aesthetic, the main problem of Wilson's address is that he makes this appeal through a very restrictive understanding of, to appropriate Stuart Hall, what this black in black performance actually is.

In this section, I will focus on three issues that help Wilson construct his limited definition of blackness, producing its problematic status in order to defend it from continued usurpation by a white culture that cloaks itself in color-blind rhetoric. The first appears at the very beginning of his speech, when he points out, "I wish to make it clear . . . that I do not have a mandate to speak for anyone. There are many intelligent blacks working in American theatre who speak in loud and articulate voices. . . . I speak only for myself and those who may think as I do."[17] Here Wilson immediately embroils himself in dilemmas of cultural authenticity and membership: what are the definitions of blackness that make his statements possible, and how are these definitions of blackness linked to notions of race in and as performance?

Second, the depth of disregard for black cultural products with which he charges mainstream American theater implies the persistence of what Glenn C. Loury has termed the "racial stigma"[18] that attaches to black identity and which, in this case, undermines the prospects for black art's success within American culture, as well as the prospects for color-blind casting's racially transcendent aims. Here, race is formulated as something other than a solely voluntary cultural category—the compulsory performance of race reveals the limits of a notion like color blindness in addressing the realities of how racial concepts function in material terms.

Finally, as Robert Brustein later pointed out,[19] on the rhetorical level, Wilson relies heavily upon the term *we* to create both the urgency and the ethical force of his argument, invoking an invisible community in a gesture that would ordinarily invite audiences to feel a sense of oneness with the speaker. In this instance, though, since Wilson's audience was neither exclusively nor predominantly black, they became both "us" and "them" as needed by his argument, thereby creating simultaneous calls for transracial collaboration and racial/experiential exclusivity, which combined to disrupt the politics of responsibility included within the admonitions of his speech. The most condensed of these instances is a two-sentence paragraph that both unites and divides: "The ground together: We must develop the ground together. We reject the idea of equality among equals, but we say rather the equality of all men."[20] The first "we" includes "them," the white decision-makers in the audience, whereas the second "we" serves as Wilson speaking for "[himself] and those who think as [he] do[es]" and rejecting an ideological system advanced by the heretofore included "them." His rhetorical strategy invites the question, in whose hands do the power and potential to (re)construct racial meaning through color blindness or other means lie?

In grappling with the notion of cultural authenticity, Wilson positions himself as the observant legatee of a two-tiered system of cultural production. Invoking the classic African American communal dichotomy of house versus field slaves, he suggests that within the realm of art and performance, "There are and always have been two distinct and parallel traditions in black art: that is, art that is conceived to entertain white society, and art that feeds the spirit and celebrates the life of black America by designing its strategies for survival and prosperity."[21] If all theater both produces and reflects the culture within which it is situated, Wilson's division between activist and accommodationist art reflects the existence and production of two types of blackness: authentic blackness, which is rooted in a self-determined specificity, and inauthentic blackness, which sacrifices those aspects of black subjectivity that cannot be absorbed into a white mainstream. According to this logic, color-blind casting produces inauthentic blackness by avoiding the historical specificity of black bodies, and to some extent, creates a cadre of artists who reject their "true" racial community in order "to be in league with a thousand nay-sayers who wish to corrupt the vigor and spirit of [their] heart[s]."[22] In commonly used terms, activist art is produced by black artists, whereas accommodationist art (whether in terms of textual products or the service to which actors' bodies are put) comes from artists who happen to be black (or who acquiesce to definitions of blackness that do not threaten the interests of the dominant culture).

This racial happenstance—often aligned with the rhetoric of color blindness, suggesting the literal immateriality and political irrelevance of an individual's racial identity—threatens the purity of Wilson's desired community. If race is paramount in the lives of black people, then those artists who aren't "designing [black people's] strategies for survival" weaken the vitality of the community within which they are nevertheless situated, because regardless of their intentions, their racial specificity provides the lens though which their work will be evaluated by mainstream culture. When assimilationist artists gain access to powerful representational venues, their depictions of blackness achieve a dominant status with which activist black art cannot compete. "Authentic blackness" risks obsolescence without equal access to the production opportunities and audiences that accommodationist art receives. However, Wilson's own career highlights the contradictions within his black art binary: as perhaps the most produced black playwright in America, he has achieved the mainstream legitimacy that makes him more than palatable to white audiences, even while he sees himself as working on behalf of his own racial and spiritual community. His path to success has come not through the independent black theater network, but through mainstream venues not usually credited with featuring works that challenge conventional wisdom about race, demonstrating that, as Harry Elam argues, Wilson "must inevitably conform to a hegemonic system that he concurrently decries for its diminution of black art."[23]

Within Wilson's schema, the difference between authentic and inauthentic blackness becomes both political and ontological. Authentic black artists offer their work as an intervention into a dominant representational regime that is aligned with Eurocentric values that privilege whiteness as "beyond reproach in its perfection."[24] Conversely, those inauthentic black artists who try to modify their racial selves in order to fit within an aesthetic paradigm that has little use for them are taking an ideological stance that affords them an ontological delusion: they may believe that they can control the signification of their blackness by colluding with the dominant culture, but in fact, their escape into inauthentic blackness is temporary, at best, and at worst, preserves the hierarchy that allows white institutions to have control over black expression.

Wilson's entire argument relies upon multivalent notions of race as performance rather than as simple material fact: race figures in his speech as functionality, as embodiment and enactment, and as theatrical tautology. In the first, racial performance is evaluated in terms of the efficacy of conveying a sense of one's racial identity to others in social situations: Wilson argues for race's singular importance because "it is the [category] that most influences your perception of yourself, and it is the one to which others in the world of men most respond."[25] Therefore, social competencies developed in this world of men rely upon certain correct ways of enacting blackness that color-blind casting, which "casts [blacks] in the role of mimics,"[26] undermines. These performative competencies provide the backdrop for the second sense of racial performance, which is situated within the discourses of liveness and materiality: blackness derives meaning from the contexts within which is it enacted, rather than simply from abstract, immanent precepts. The blackness for which August Wilson wants to create an institutional home is an experiential category that has come under assault within American culture. In a rebuttal to Robert Brustein that continues the argument of his original speech, Wilson alleges that "the influence and contributions of black Americans are not recognized by any gain in material culture that would allow us to further develop our arts and establish control over their dissemination."[27] Here Wilson makes clear that any discussion of race is always a discussion of material culture, and therefore of power. As I have already suggested, Wilson is keenly aware of the power of current iterations of blackness within prominent American theatrical institutions (color-blind casting practices, accommodationist art) to reify a racial politics that denies blacks cultural autonomy. This produces an irony for Wilson: at the same time that he stresses the existence of a real (even essential) blackness, rooted in a synthesis of African cultural retentions and present-day American contexts, he recognizes that without this material, external support real blackness might not survive.

The last sense of race as performance contributes most strongly to the dilemma embedded within Wilson's speech. His critique of color-blind casting as ineffectual (or dangerously effectual) relies upon a tautology: one performs blackness onstage because one is black onstage because audiences are aware of (and therefore force one to perform) one's blackness onstage. This cycle relies upon the notions of embodiment and efficacy that I have just discussed. Audiences' social competencies produce the racial meanings that they ascribe to performing bodies, meanings that then circumscribe the signifying potential of these performing bodies. The question of racial signification (as a component of racial performance) partially shifts the locus of agency from the body of the performer to the spectator's act of reception, and to "the shared expectations of [blacks] as a people."[28] Within Wilson's argument, rather than allowing for new meanings of blackness to be produced in performance, the tautology traps both performers and audiences in the reification of race. Actors are seen as conforming to essential notions of race because these are the only notions of race with which audiences are able to evaluate them.

Out of his need to navigate the competing strains of race as interiority and exteriority, Wilson also exercises caution when articulating the difference between race and (racialized) culture: after defining race as "the product of a shared gene pool that allows for group identification," he goes on to claim culture as "the behavior patterns, arts, beliefs, institutions and all other products of human work and thought as expressed in a particular community of people,"[29] which are therefore transmitted and regulated socially. The two halves of Wilson's definition of blackness as genetic inheritance and as lived culture situate self-identified blacks as both performers and spectators, in that they engage in racial performances and also witness and ratify the performances of others (i.e., those actions that express an individual's affinity/identification with black culture).[30] At the same time, though, the fact that Wilson acknowledges culture as socially mediated raises the question of how this mediation affects the agency of the black performer and the extent to which this performer is responsible for using the medium of performance to preserve specific iterations of black identity.

Wilson is strategic in articulating the basis for these cultural responsibilities that attend to black performance: while the notion of a shared gene pool and shared behaviors validates his authority to "speak for [him]self and those who may think as [he] do[es],"[31] it also helps to create both the crisis of authenticity and the tautological core of his speech (i.e., we act black because we are black). For the purposes of his institutional critique of color-blind casting, blackness is something into which one is born, cannot be escaped, and therefore should be exalted as such rather than mitigated through color blindness; however, the reference to shared behaviors also functions as an authenticating tool, making blackness something that one chooses to embrace (or not). The black community is at once fluid and discretely bounded, a formulation evident as well in Wilson's claim that his matrilineal cultural inheritance "could [be] trace[d] back to the first African who set foot on the continent."[32] This description of African-derived black American culture relies upon a notion of cultural production that both diminishes and overemphasizes the import of volitional agency: a seamless transmission of African practices at once empowers individuals to participate in the preservation of black culture and also seems to proscribe the ways in which this transmission takes place, suggesting that individuals choose to participate in cultural processes that they are powerless to affect. In this formulation, color blindness is not an option; it is impossible to transcend race perceptually because it is passed on, intact, through both bloodlines and inauguration as a social subject. Interestingly, though, this conception of race succumbs to the same criticisms of ahistorical naïveté that plague the discourse of color blindness: in the race-conscious paradigm that Wilson offers, the African components of black American culture (already indebted to an essentialized "Africa") are impervious to history in much the same way that certain notions of color blindness resist the histories of subjection that make racial activism necessary.

Nevertheless, within the framework Wilson articulates, his concerns for the institutional longevity of black theater are important. If racial identity is transmitted in absolute terms, successful in every instance and overriding any individual desires for disidentification or other tactics of estrangement, then the performance of race is the *sine qua non* of black art: black cultural forms are ineluctably involved in (re)producing and (re)presenting their constituency. For Wilson, black art cannot occur in color-blind spaces, and a desire for a color-blind theater therefore means a desire for American theater without blackness or black art. His arguments for the institutional validity of black theater as such rely upon the idea that racial categories are at once immanent and yet under assault and in need of defense. In explaining the difference between color-blind integration and a radical restructuring of American theater, he argues,

Doing a black play or allowing blacks to have roles not written for them does not change the nature of the institution or its mission. Blacks come and go and the institution remains dedicated to its ideas of "preserving culture and promoting thought." Our visitor pass expires and we never have a place to hang our hat, to develop our ideas, and to provide our community with a sense of cultural worth and self-sufficiency. The damage this does to our present institutions and our already debilitated communities is evident and significant.[33]

Wilson's visitor pass metaphor indicates that mainstream American theater practices a form of color blindness that does in fact exploit race-consciousness (through strategic, production-specific invitations to black artists) while cleverly diminishing the importance of race (specifically, whiteness as the dominant aesthetic and determinant of power) in order to protect its institutions from criticism. Therefore, color blindness becomes simultaneously a real threat and a social impossibility. The rhetoric of color blindness threatens the realness of racial culture in ways that have material consequences (e.g., disproportionately low resources directed toward specifically black theater), even at the same time that ameliorative measures reveal our heightened awareness rather than ignorance of race.

Aware of this paradox, Wilson structures his argument in order to concretize blackness as a salient racial category and as a culture, in order to expose whiteness as its opposite, and to demonstrate the ways in which whiteness receives institutional support that guarantees its longevity within American theater and culture while blackness does not. In Wilson's view, current color-blind practices deny the specificity of nonwhite cultures as irrelevant and thereby reinforce the value of white culture, perpetuating "the nature of the institution [and] its mission" by suggesting that black actors are best served as artists by having opportunities to escape the confines of works and institutions situated within (or limited to) their own culture.[34] He argues that a more complex approach to racial inclusivity is required, and yet Wilson's own formulations of blackness as a racial category and its "strategies for survival" are so rigid that he does not include those artists who choose to exercise their skills within the dominant value system of American theater because their participation in color-blind productions legitimates a form of condescension that promotes invisibility. Instead, he argues, "We want you to see us. We are black and beautiful," implying that whenever black actors are cast against racial type their blackness disappears, and that the resulting performances cannot have any sort of transgressive potential to expand what we know as black (and beautiful) performance.[35] Wilson rejects the notion that the choice to ignore color is a welcome favor or a compliment, or even an opportunity for complexity that puts pressure on racial discourse, and instead considers it yet another act of institutional violence that denies black culture the right to define itself artistically.

The prospects for creating not just a statistically but an experientially and politically diverse American theater are linked, of course, to economic practices. While Wilson speaks out of a concern for the preservation and propagation of black artistic culture, his political mandate boils down to a critique of the economic structure of American theater, one that requires him to proclaim boldly, "We do not need color-blind casting; we need some theaters to develop our playwrights. We need those misguided financial resources to be put to better use."[36] As I argued previously, Wilson's critique of color-blind casting suggests that the practice renders black subjectivity impossible, and that color blindness operates from an ignorance (real or feigned) of the processes through which (nonwhite) racial cultures are produced and sustained. For Wilson, funds directed toward color-blind casting place very specific conditions upon black participation in American theater: rather than welcoming their racial and cultural specificity into their work as theater artists, color-blind imperatives suggest instead that blacks' participation in American theater is almost entirely predicated upon their disavowal of their culture. This "misguided" approach seeks at once to incorporate black bodies and obliterate black culture, and therefore should be exposed for its racial bias and resisted. Wilson's critique is closely aligned with what Glenn C. Loury refers to as the racial stigma that attaches to persons (and products) of African descent in American culture, limiting their opportunities for advancement within American institutions and social networks.

In his 2002 book *The Anatomy of Racial Inequality*, Loury discusses the competing forms of agency (individual and institutional) that perpetuate blacks' unequal standing within American society: much like Wilson's awareness of both the seeming immanence and vulnerability of black culture, Loury examines the extent to which black people experience their race as both a galvanizing force within a community of like individuals and a category imposed upon them and used to justify inequitable social and economic practices. After defining race as "a socially constructed mode of human categorization . . . for which no deeper justification in biological taxonomy is to be had," he goes on to build upon social theorist Erving Goffman's notions of virtual identity and social stigma.[37] Arguing that the difference between one's virtual (external, ascribed, and relational) and actual (internal, biographically true) identities plays a crucial role in racialized interactions, Loury himself invokes the language of performance to describe the ways in which individuality may be subsumed by the discursive power of race.[38] "As we encounter one another in social spaces," he writes, "we perceive the physical markings on one another's bodies and go on to play our respective parts, enacting scripts written long before we were born."[39] To some extent, this version of race as social phenomenon echoes Wilson's claims about the overdetermined transmission of racial culture from generation to generation.[40] However, while Wilson is saluting the ways that black culture preserves itself, Loury is eyeing with concern the ways in which interracial (as well as intraracial) contact conforms to patterns rooted in a history of racial dishonor, a compulsive performativity that he considers "inseparable from the social meaning of race" in an American context.[41]

Racial stigma, then, consists of "dishonorable meanings socially inscribed on arbitrary bodily marks, of 'spoiled collective identities,'" and keeps individuals from seeing others as "possessing a common humanity with the observer."[42] Therefore, "The idea of racial stigma can be used to gain insight into the problems of perception, representation, and standing in contemporary American public life that adversely affect (some) blacks."[43] Loury's claim for the utility of racial stigma as an analytical construct again focuses our attention on the dialectical roles of representation and perception in matters of race. Certain color-blind practices in American theater reify rather than rectify the racial stigma commonly associated with blackness in aesthetic and institutional domains. In aesthetic terms, black bodies are represented on mainstream stages, but they are not meant to be perceived as such, and therefore their presence undermines the practices of self-determination for which Wilson advocates. Institutionally, the presence of these black artists appears to demonstrate mainstream theater's recognition of the value of black expressive culture, but it may also be perceived as a judgment that black institutions are not viable custodians of black art.

It is ironic that Wilson must rely upon the "spoiled collective identit[y]" assigned to blackness in order to make his argument for blackness's value. In his view, this spoiled definition conforms to the logic of racial transcendence against which he struggles. If blackness is "bad," then rising above it, leaving it behind, is a positive tactic. However, he notes that this transcendence cuts only against nonwhiteness, while allowing the institutional logic of whiteness to remain intact. Wilson exposes this strategic imbalance when he asks, "Why is it impossible to imagine 9 black theatres but not 66 white ones?"[44] That the former should seem impossible while the latter was a matter of course in the self-consciously pluralistic final decade of the twentieth century demonstrates the ways in which an attitude of racial happenstance—dismissing the racialized workings of power that produce disparate opportunities and outcomes—happens to benefit whiteness, which is allowed to remain unnamed until someone like Wilson calls attention to it. This materialist indictment of American theater demonstrates one dimension of racial stigma as defined by Loury: the "disparity occasions no societal reflection upon the extent to which that circumstance signals something gone awry in OUR structures rather than something having gone awry in THEIRS."[45] In this case, the crisis afflicting black theater is accorded no relationship to the relative vitality of (white) mainstream theater—the successes and failures of each institution are seen as discrete rather than interconnected. Robert Brustein seems to succumb to this process of rationalization when, in response to Wilson's critique of these apparently racialized funding practices, he argues that Wilson "sees no contradiction in demanding that white foundations take the responsibility for founding as well as funding black theatres, as if theatre companies were the creation of philanthropic agencies rather than the indigenous outgrowths of dedicated artists and supporting communities."[46] Brustein accepts the centering of white foundations as the "us" to black theater's "them," and even seems to take offense at the attempted irruption of "their" economic concerns within "our" economic framework. The lack of institutional stability in black theater, then, is attributable to the lack of "dedicated [black] artists and [a] supportive [black] communit[y]," rather than a reflection of racial bias that informs an ostensibly color-blind but actually white philanthropic foundation structure.[47]

Although Wilson's institutional and economic critique has very broad contours, his question about the quantity of black versus white theaters was not an abstraction: in 1995, of the sixty-six theaters that comprised the League of Resident Theaters (LORT), a body that politically unites far-flung theaters across the United States into a cohesive negotiating body, only one, Crossroads Theater, was specifically dedicated to presenting theater that reflected African American cultural traditions. The remaining sixty-five theaters were implicitly white, inviting artists of color in on a rotating basis during their producing seasons in an effort to embody the diversity that philanthropic organizations and other internal decision-makers desired. That a significant organization of American theaters would have such culturally skewed membership was, to Wilson, no accident: this statistical reality emerged from the social reality that most of those with the power to allocate resources (from institutional funding to individual production opportunities) failed to see or concern themselves with the merits of institutional longevity for black theater as a site where the cultural and political histories and meanings of blackness should be produced, reproduced, and negotiated. Institutional permanence, therefore, was a reward meted out disproportionately "as a privilege to the overwhelming abundance of institutions that preserve, promote and perpetuate white culture."[48] In Wilson's view, the conditional absorption of black cultural resources into these institutions diluted rather than reinforced the strength of black culture, not because of the undesirability of cross-racial collaboration, but because of the intermittent rather than sustained nature of these mainstream theaters' engagement with black culture, and through the disproportionate number of opportunities extended to black actors in which they could "transcend" rather than engage with their racial and cultural specificity.

As an antidote to these terms of participation in the mainstream, Wilson proposes a meeting of black cultural workers. He argues, "We need to develop guidelines for the protection of our cultural property, our contributions and the influence they accrue. It is time we took responsibility for our talents in our hands. We cannot depend on others."[49] Such guidelines are a form of what Glenn Loury refers to as discrimination in contact, the systems of preference deployed informally in the private sector (rather than formally in the public sector). Loury suggests that black Americans face an ironic choice in their goal to achieve equality of effect—rather than just a supposed equality of opportunity—in American culture: they must "systematic[ally] practice . . . pro-black discrimination in contact," making concerted efforts to aid one another to achieve a more equitable distribution of both resources and opportunities in society.[50] Wilson suggests this as a redressive measure against the somewhat easy access nonblack theater practitioners have traditionally had to black culture: rather than making themselves available to white theatrical institutions that are not committed to their long-term presence, black artists should instead choose only to participate in those productions where blacks retain artistic and administrative control over their cultural property.

In his view, anything less than this racially specific focus on the institutional dimensions of black theater is a betrayal of the black artistic community's needs. In criticizing a black actor for taking on the Shakespearean role of Henry V, Wilson argues, "We will not put our bodies to the celebration of a culture which has oppressed us. Andre Braugher, in playing the role of an heroic English king, is celebrating a culture which has brutalized black people."[51] This interpretation of the cultural and political consequences of Braugher's performance is a way of indicting the naïveté of color-blind casting: it asks black actors and all audiences to ignore the legacies of subordination that black Americans wear on their bodies. For Wilson, this sort of acting risks giving credence to what Loury deems a "brittle, two-step liberalism that enshrines some mythical 'unencumbered self— a 'self' located outside the flow of history and the web of culture."[52] Wilson believes that color-blindly cast black bodies are ahistorical bodies, treasonous to their racial history and community rather than mindful of them. While this critique is valid, in that the social competencies with which audiences view performances are certainly indebted to racialized histories, Wilson's objection seems to assume a single correct set of references and histories against which both the dramatic script and the black performing body are always juxtaposed. This assumption conflates color-blind casting and color-blind performance without interrogating their union, rendering racial transgression through casting against racial expectations impossible.[53]

Wilson's keynote address is not the only place where he offered such essentialist notions of culture as the justification for his protectionist stance toward black cultural products. His infamous op-ed piece, "I Want a Black Director," expressed similar concerns about "whether we as blacks are going to have control over our own culture and its products."[54] Inverting the concept of racial stigma applied toward blacks, Wilson's editorial suggested that in certain important respects, whites did not "possess a common humanity" with blacks, and were therefore incapable of directing his work with the level of care he thought necessary. In describing the qualities he sought in a director, Wilson argued,

> White American society is made up of various European *ethnic* groups which share a common history and sensibility. Black Americans are a *racial* group which do not share the same sensibilities. The specifics of our cultural history are very different. . . . Someone who does not share the specifics of a culture remains an outsider, no matter how astute a student they are or how well meaning their intentions. I declined a white director not on the basis of race but on the basis of culture. White directors are not qualified for the job. The job requires someone who shares the specifics of the culture of black Americans.[55]

Thus the discourse of qualifications, so prevalent in race-baiting critiques of affirmative action and other ameliorative practices designed to provide opportunities to blacks, is adjusted to suggest that racial rhetoric places limits upon the qualifications and abilities of whites, not only of blacks. The inversion is worth noting, but also (and perhaps more) of note is the lack of material consequences attached to Wilson's proclamation of white directors' situational inferiority. Even in the inversion of racial stigma, the power attendant to whiteness silences black art and culture: while he maintains his conviction that no white person could handle the task of directing the film version of one of his plays, at the time of his death, Wilson "[was] still waiting for Paramount to hire a director for *Fences*."[56] The material reality of who controls cultural resources trumps any rhetorical efforts by blacks to reframe in/competence in terms that privilege black artists.

I do not mean to suggest that Wilson is not complicit in this silencing: the failure to produce *Fences* as a movie is a failure produced by both black and white adherence to racial realism: white producers' desire to "hire a 'human being'" who will likely be white is, according to Wilson, a thinly veiled capitulation to the notion that "the only qualification any black has is the color of his skin," while Wilson's unyielding stance on the race of his director presumes that blacks operate within a homogeneous, bounded cultural community to which whites have no access.[57] Both practices of selection and exclusion acquiesce to differences between racial groups that are produced through social practices rather than being inherent in either community. Ultimately, Wilson is attempting to practice problack discrimination in contact, while exploiting notions of cultural authenticity to bolster his claim.

Each time that he offers it, Wilson's critique exposes the invisibility of white cultural forms masquerading as simply human, and forces us to question the inevitability of this potent discursive exnomination. His line of interrogation forces the question, must "American theater" be forever synonymous with the "perpetuat[ion]" of white culture?" Here the rhetoric of Wilson's argument becomes essential. Shifting between a sense of us and them, Wilson at first situates himself within the world of Eurocentric theater, claiming it as the artistic ground upon which he stands, but then locates his personal and political ground as "the self-defining ground of the slave quarters."[58] Deeming himself a hybrid attempting to reconcile disparate elements of his life, Wilson adheres to the familiar adage that marks the personal as political, revealing through his own testimony the extent to which the blackness he attempts to protect and celebrate is produced in multiple social spaces. Citing the difficulty of "dissasociat[ing his] concerns with theater from the concerns of [his] life as a black man,"[59] Wilson locates the ethical urgency of his pleas in racialized personal as well as institutional terms.

In its own way, Wilson's speech also offers an example of the challenges of nontraditional or color-blind casting as an affective, not merely aesthetic, experience: if these casting practices are meant to allow nonwhite performers to identify across cultural lines with characters they are talented enough to portray, they also require the cultivation of a spectatorial sensibility that encourages people to make intellectual and emotional investments that go against habitual deployments of racial consciousness. As fervently as Wilson's speech conveys the necessity of mainstream theater workers strengthening and redirecting their support of black theater toward autonomous black institutions, his rhetorical creation of community also speaks to the ghosted presence of a critical mass of black theater workers, not in attendance at the conference because not enough has been done to support their presence in American theater.[60]

For the majority of those present at Wilson's speech, his syntax unwittingly offers an ethical challenge to participate in a risky exercise of counterintuitive identification. Choosing to affiliate oneself within the shifting racial community Wilson creates in his speech demonstrates the extent to which, as Elin Diamond argues, "To identify is not only to incorporate but to be incorporated. To be radically destabilized."[61] This destabilization comes from the recognition of mutuality that identification forces: the boundaries that separate the self from the other (one of the premises, on a cultural level, of racial discourses) are revealed as permeable, shifting the grounds upon which the self may be defined. Thus, those members of the TCG audience who were not black could opt for a radical destabilization that afforded them inclusion in Wilson's community of people "need[ing] to alter our relationship to the society and to alter the shared expectations of ourselves as a racial group."[62] An allegiance to this strategy vitiates the process of exnomination through which the specific production of white culture goes unnoticed. This opportunity to identify as "we" allows for both unity and specificity, a process recognized elsewhere by Audre Lorde:

> You do not have to be me in order for us to fight alongside each other. I do not have to be you to recognize that our wars are the same. What we must do is commit ourselves to some future that can include each other and to work toward that future with the particular strengths of our individual identities. And in order to do this, we must allow each other our differences at the same time as we recognize our sameness.[63]

As Lorde suggests, rather than failing to acknowledge differences of culture and/or cultural privilege, transracial identification enables political progress by granting different groups equal critical access to "some future that can include each other," and makes productive use of racial difference, rather than simply figuring it as an insurmountable problem. It is this productive possibility that Wilson cultivates in the very act of offering this speech to an audience of mostly non-black theater workers, but at the same time, his insistence upon the fundamental differences of aesthetics, history, and values separating blacks from whites risks closing down that opportunity for progress.

My reading of Wilson's use of "we" intentionally modifies the racial dynamics that he espouses in an effort to expose the imperfection of even the most passionate attempts to define (racial and) communal categories. Wilson's own fluctuating allegiance to an us/them binary reveals both his inability to renounce the simultaneity of his placement within two powerful communities and the way in which his line of argument both demonstrates and undermines his stated desire to bring the two together. In other words, Wilson's structure of responsibility (as both culpability and hortatory potentiality) risks establishing an antagonistic rather than collaborative approach to rectifying real segregation in American theater. If mainstream theater workers are invited into Wilson's ethical community only long enough to be reprimanded ("We cannot share a single value system if [it] consists of the values of white Americans based on their European ancestors"), but not long enough to cultivate a sense of loyalty to and investment in black theater ("we may forever be on the opposite side of aesthetics"), then Wilson's argument simply reproduces the racial stagnation of American theater as a whole.[64] What Wilson seems to argue for, even in the way that he calls for cross-cultural collaboration ("We have to do it together"),[65] is a single institutional logic that makes use of simultaneous difference, hosting many different, discrete cultures while making sure that they do not distort one another. While American history justifies his caution about the possibilities for both economic exploitation and social misrepresentation that attend to the meeting of black and white cultures, Wilson's argument trades one limited notion of cultural pluralism for another. His speech may have been hyperbolic in an effort to incite action rather than just polite applause, but his allegiance to slippery notions of authenticity that separate racial and cultural groups from one another only emphasizes the urgency of moving toward a transgressive framework of cultural practice. Recognizing that black theater acts through and upon American theater (and vice versa) shifts the conversation away from how precious resources might be used to police cultural borders and instead toward how a vibrant American theater might mine its rich historical ground in ways that make constant rather than occasional use of a wide variety of (black) artists and audiences.

ROBERT BRUSTEIN: METAPHOR VERSUS MATERIALITY

As an influential writer for *The New Republic* and then-director of Harvard University's American Repertory Theater (ART), Robert Brustein was an easy target with which to personalize several of Wilson's critiques. Firmly situated within the mainstream establishment of theater, Brustein embodied for Wilson many of the forces that stymied the progress of black art in American culture. Brustein's essays in *The New Republic* during the 1980s and 1990s, for example, consistently expressed his privileging of "common values" over notions of cultural difference in evaluating theater. (Not coincidentally, his *New Republic* column inches also gave voice to his low estimation of Wilson's much-vaunted plays.)[66] In his creative capacity with ART, Brustein produced works from the Eurocentric canon that dominates the stages of many subscriber-based American regional theaters, and one might reasonably assume that the same aesthetic governed the curriculum at ART's Institute for Advanced Theatre Training.[67] While Brustein would probably classify his aesthetic as an unqualified commitment to formal and creative excellence expressed in works that "[embrace] a common humanity,"[68] Wilson charged Brustein with using universalism as a euphemism for Eurocentrism, silently but powerfully marginalizing works by and about people of color.

The culture wars of the 1980s and 1990s provide a context for Brustein's alarm over the perceived shift from universal to relative standards of excellence. During these decades, conservatives mounted an aggressive backlash against what they perceived as the erosion of national culture in favor of race-based particularism that stressed people's differences rather than what they held in common as Americans. In 1992, William Bennett, who formerly served as both secretary of education and head of the National Endowment for the Humanities, described the "culture wars" as

> the struggle over the principles, sentiments, ideas, and political attitudes that define the permissible and the impermissible, the acceptable and the unacceptable, the preferred and the disdained, in speech, expression, attitude, conduct, and politics. This battle is about music, art, poetry, literature, televison programming, and movies; the modes of expression and conversation, official and unofficial, that express who and what we are, what we believe, and how we act.[69]

Bennett's antagonistic stance toward the processes through which culture is produced was warranted, he believed, by the surplus of intellectuals who "have overstepped the bounds of common sense and . . . given up on the disinterested pursuit of truth . . . hitch[ing] their intellect to the service of ideology" instead.[70] He typifies what David Theo Goldberg refers to as "monoculturalist" ideology, expressing his belief that "what ties us together as a people—the *unum* in *e pluribus unum*—is in constant need of support."[71] In this line of argument, the color line is replaced by the culture line, the boundary between good and bad, between the representations and quotidian practices that fortify an endangered American culture and those that threaten to destroy it. The important question becomes, what forms of "support"—or, more bluntly, force—are marshaled to resist our polycultural reality? As Wilson suggests, these are often political, aesthetic, and economic, in ways that cannot be disentangled from one another. To suggest a sequential relationship, whereby aesthetics (common culture) predates the economic and political structures that shape the world that these cultural representations reflect and inhabit, is disingenuous.

In a vein similar to Bennett's, Robert Brustein's writings as a critic of American theater consistently disparaged those efforts that injected politics into "that universal culture called dramatic art."[72] In the 1980s and 1990s, the overt racialization of American theater recurred as a sore spot for Brustein. Despairing over the state of new works in American theater, he wrote, "The new American play, once the proud staple of the commercial theater in the thirties, forties, and fifties, has virtually disappeared from producers' agendas, unless it can be marketed as a variant of affirmative action, alleviating liberal guilt toward minorities or the handicapped."[73] This critique of the cultural politics of American theater stemmed from Brustein's "admittedly unfashionable view that no major work of art ever changed society, however it succeeded in changing consciousness."[74] For Brustein, then, multiculturalism in theater—enacted by privileging racial culture above all other considerations—often (but, he is careful to state, not always) occurred at the expense of artistic quality and was a misguided effort to use art to solve social ills that had economic roots. "New American plays" were no longer valuable as reflections of a galvanizing national culture but as demonstrations of the particularity of micro-constituencies within American society, diminishing rather than enhancing American theater.

Wilson introduced Brustein into his keynote address when he took exception to claims initiated by the latter in the 1993 essay "Diversity and Unity" and later expanded upon in 1994's "Coercive Philanthropy." Here, Brustein critiqued the fact that many funding agencies were attempting to kill two birds with one philanthropic stone by supporting the arts and supporting minorities in one financial gesture. This meant that mediocre productions with strategically appealing demographics would win out over good ones whose demographics were "traditional." The trend was "having a demoralizing effect on artists and artistic institutions"[75] who feared that their work would be judged according to standards it was impossible to anticipate, or that ran counter to creative freedom. Grimly forecasting the long-term consequences of these philanthropic practices, Brustein writes,

> This insinuation of politics into culture comes at a time when tribalism has begun to shatter our national identity, when the melting pot has turned into a seething cauldron. It is only natural, under such conditions, that philanthropy should rush to the aid of racial, ethnic, and sexual groups clamoring for recognition through the agency of creative expression. But the thing about a group with special interests is that in order to achieve power, influence, strength, and unity, it must display a common front. And this often means suppressing the singularity of its individual members and denying what is shared with others— neither good conditions for creating the idiosyncrasy and universality associated with great art.[76]

While acknowledging the fact that discrimination in American culture in general and American theater in particular do exist, Brustein suggests here that the racial categories produced and endorsed through coercive philanthropy rely upon an essentialism that does not serve individual, racialized artists, and more pointedly, that art catering to essentialized communal and philanthropic imperatives is destined to be of poor quality. Wilson takes Brustein's objections to mean that black art—art that engages the politicized history of people of African descent in the United States—does not measure up to the same artistic standards as idiosyncratic and universal art, labels that, not coincidentally, tend to get bestowed most frequently upon works created by white authors. Furthermore, Brustein's remarks suggest that this racially particular art is never even held to the standards of "great" art, a tacit admission of its inadequacy on those terms. Implicitly connected to attacks on affirmative action, this criticism of separate and unequal evaluative criteria has come to be known in the twenty-first century as "the soft bigotry of low expectations," a term that compassionate conservative George W. Bush used on the 2000 presidential campaign trail when arguing against policies that cling too tightly to past wrongs in advocating separate or redressive measures for the disenfranchised.[77] Applied indiscriminately, this criticism fails to account for the harsh bigotry of "high" expectations in the deeply classed high/low cultural divide, which naturalize the superiority of white cultural forms and the disproportionate access they have to material resources that are distributed according to allegedly universal criteria of excellence.

When Robert Brustein responded to August Wilson's attack on his principles, he did so with brio, consistently appealing for a race-blind aesthetic meritocracy without giving meaningful consideration to the structural practices that produced racially identifiable disparities. In a provocative essay titled "Subsidized Separatism," he attempted a point-by-point refutation of Wilson's "rambling jeremiad."[78] While Wilson assessed the state of American theater in order to critique larger institutional issues of injustice consistent with the racist history of the United States, Brustein's response claimed to champion "transcendence . . . recognizing that the greatest art embraces a common humanity."[79] His language of transcendence implied that race was somehow an elective and problematic category of social engagement that we could simply get over without working through it. In fact, in a brief follow-up essay Brustein wrote for *American Theatre* in November of 1996, he asked in hope and frustration, "Can we not at least hope for a day when we are no longer African-Americans, Latino-Americans, or Jewish-Americans, but simply Americans?"[80] Simplifying American identity in this way could only occur by suppressing memories of ethnoracial traditions that lived experience continues to preserve. Additionally, this wish suggests a rupture as essential to the constitution of the American citizen-subject: the political value for many minorities in names like "Jewish-American," "Latino-American," and "African-American" is the ability to conjoin a long memory or diasporic consciousness of traditions that predate immersion in America to an insider status that centuries of American labor laws, immigration and citizenship policies, and civil statutes often aim to deny. Brustein's desire for an age of "simply Americans" exposes simple Americanness as the divisive category, separating people from memories and cultural practices that actually enrich rather than impoverish American culture.

This desire to liberate art from the stranglehold of race, revealed explicitly in Brustein's essay and other previous writings, betrays a tension within his musings on art between race as materiality and race as metaphor. His advocacy of color blindness as the transcendence of inherently divisive racial discourse seizes upon the metaphorical dimensions of race, reducing them to patterns of speech that we might abandon in order to unite by naming ourselves differently. This presupposes a discourse that is detached from the material circumstances that have both enforced and necessitated vocabularies of racial belonging (and exclusion). Brustein's argument conforms to the simultaneously oversimple and overcomplicated notion espoused by William Bennett: "The way to achieve a color-blind society is to actually *be* a color-blind society, in law and in spirit. The way to get beyond treating people as if race makes a difference is actually to treat them as if race does not make a difference."[81] This line of argument, when espoused by both Brustein and Bennett, relies upon the unspoken premise that only nonwhite "races" make a difference, and that this difference is always bad. For Brustein in American theater and for Bennett in American society at large, to contend with blackness as anything other than happenstance is to contend with it as a problem, one that detracts from the quest for a common culture.

When Wilson asserts in his speech that the titular ground on which he stands includes both the artistic ground of the Eurocentric dramatic canon and "the self-defining ground of the slave quarters,"[82] Brustein responds by asking, "Isn't it time to acknowledge that, for all the grim, uncompleted racial business in this country, those quarters have long been razed to the ground?"[83] Brustein's efforts to ignore the metaphorical dimensions of Wilson's claim in favor of a materialist dismissal of Wilson's language imagine a present that can be disconnected from the racialized power dynamics of the past. Beyond an effort to undo the overdetermined nature of how slavery figures in the racial imaginary, Brustein's question attempts to impose a "statute of limitations on white guilt and reparations."[84] He does this in spite of the fact that, quite literally, many slave quarters have not been razed to the ground, as the heritage plantation tours throughout the Southern United States demonstrate. Even this fact offers evidence of the continued visibility of the ignominious history of slavery in the United States, the continued practice of viewing African Americans in relation to this history, and the continued profitability (with money flowing out of black communities) of these sociopolitical relationships that presentist attitudes about how to fix the race problem wish to overlook. Within this context, Brustein's rebuttal to Wilson's self-defining claim offers a selective misunderstanding of Wilson's own fusion of metaphor and materiality. By focusing on the slave quarters as materially emblematic of a long-outlawed economic system rather than focusing on Wilson's sense that the *ground* of the slave quarters provides a foundational social location for African American consciousness, Brustein refuses to engage in a conversation about how the material practices, institutional structures, and aesthetic imperatives of slavery might still structure not only black consciousness and culture but white mainstream culture as well.

Brustein's response to Wilson critiqued Wilson's model of racial discourse, his edicts regarding artistic funding, and his narrow-minded artistic vision for black actors. While these claims cannot be entirely divorced from one another, each area of commentary offers different opportunities for Brustein to expose his rhetorically contingent conception of race and, inadvertently, to offer evidence of the very practices in American theater that Wilson wanted to reform. For example, in expressing his disdain for Wilson's model of funding American theater, he framed race as a problematic, if not outmoded, classificatory term. While Wilson believed that white theaters held privileged status in the competition for funding, Brustein coyly suggested that he was "not at all certain anymore what constitutes a 'black' or 'white' theatre.'"[85] Yet in the preceding paragraph, he utilized the very terms he subsequently disavowed, alleging hypocrisy in Wilson's insistence "that white foundations take the responsibility for founding as well as funding black theatres."[86] Brustein questions the meaning of a white or black (rather than racially heterogeneous/transcendent) theater without questioning the definition or existence of white foundations, implicitly recognizing the consolidation of resources and authority among white people as legible in foundation terms. In the latter (foundations), race as a metric for consolidating resources is irrefutable, but in the former (theaters), where the institutional emphasis is on the far more ephemeral dimensions of race as cultural practice or values, the permeability of boundaries between white and black culture in the United States allows Brustein to question the premise of Wilson's argument. However, while Brustein attempts to suggest that theater as a site of aesthetic practice defies racialization, he fails to interrogate the fact that the racial classification of economic power (which makes these aesthetic practices possible) has retained its logic, or the fact that theaters are both aesthetic and economic institutions.[87]

Of course, when Brustein sidesteps the complex intersections of race, art, and commerce that theater companies manage, he does so only temporarily. As the artistic director of American Repertory Theater at Harvard University, and the former dean of the Yale School of Drama, he is keenly aware of the cultural politics of being considered a white theater during a multicultural era.[88] The difference between Wilson and Brustein therefore becomes one of racial valuation: Wilson values race (especially blackness) as an integral component of American theater, as it is a site for the preservation of specific cultures, whereas Brustein seems to consider racial discourse inherently exclusionary and divisive, to be abandoned. Again, a devout presentism undergirds his sense that the racialization of theater through funding practices is a new phenomenon, linked with coercive philanthropy, but such an attitude obscures the fact that prior to this recent corrective attention to nonwhiteness, these same foundations were almost exclusively helping American theater to function as a site for the articulation of white culture. The subsidized presentation of race in American theater is not new, only the subsidized presentation of nonwhiteness is. Relative to funding standards, color blindness for Brustein becomes little more than white-blindness, or an unwillingness to see the ways in which racial politics did and continue to benefit white culture.

As one ideological intertext of Wilson's and Brustein's 1996 conflict, "Coercive Philanthropy" provides insight into Brustein's passionate resistance to the postmodern problematization of distinctions between high and low culture, opting instead to preserve a set of rigorous standards according to which artistic products may be objectively ranked without attention to racial concerns.[89] The racial biases embedded within Brustein's artistic and economic convictions coalesce when, in this earlier essay, he suggests, "Culture is not designed to do the work of politics. . . . No wonder inner-city children prefer rap or salsa when so few qualified teachers have been employed by the system to expose them to serious theatre, art, or music."[90] In choosing to focus on "inner-city children," a term that already has valences of class and race embedded within it, he condemns the racially marked musical forms of rap and salsa as being mutually exclusive of "serious theatre, art, or music." Furthermore, Brustein admits that these "serious" works of art require institutional force to attain and sustain their supposedly normative superior status, a fact that calls into question the universality of the values that (should) render them supreme.

Brustein's essay contains another instance of reliance upon discursive practices he professes to disavow: in spite of his professions of color blindness, he relies upon racial realism to refute Wilson's claims. While decrying Wilson's submission to the "'ethnographic fallacy' that one [person's] peculiar experiences can represent a whole social category," Brustein nevertheless suggests that Wilson's own success at the hands of the LORT organization that he criticized made it disingenuous and ungracious of him to position himself as a spokesperson for victims of obstructed opportunity within (white) American theater.[91] He contends:

> Wilson is displaying a failure of memory—I hesitate to say a failure of gratitude—when he charges nonprofit resident theatres with using "sociological criteria" in choosing seasons that "traditionally exclude blacks." . . . Is a man who has garnered such extraordinary media attention (not to mention every conceivable playwriting fellowship) really in a position to say that blacks are being

excluded from the American theatre or that these institutions only "preserve, promote and perpetuate white culture"?[92]

This critique of Wilson's politics suggests that Wilson cannot recognize himself to be a privileged member of a still-underrepresented group whose overall status within American theater remains denigrated. Invalidating Wilson's criticisms because of his success simply produces another version of the ethnographic fallacy, whereby Wilson's success is taken synecdochically to prove that blacks are successful within American theater (even when their work does not meet time-honored standards of excellence, as Brustein elsewhere suggests that Wilson's does not).

Ironically, this fallacy unites Brustein and Wilson in their seeming anxiety over the terms according to which cultural membership and legitimacy are meted out within the black community. Wilson strives to make political imperatives and cultural retentions the basis for defining blackness, a combination of voluntary and compulsory forces that produce black subjectivity, whereas Brustein's invalidation of Wilson's critique seems to locate blackness as subjugation, thereby excommunicating Wilson from the community he claims, yet inadvertently reinforcing the terms upon which this community is figured. This inconsistency in Brustein's argument (the simultaneous affirmation of black success in American theater and formulation of black theater workers as a group from whom August Wilson's success distinguishes him) amounts to a conscious disavowal of even his own assessments of the status of American theater. For admittedly different reasons, Brustein comes to virtually the same conclusion as Wilson: very few great artists of color are recognized within the mainstream of American theater. For Brustein, this is less about the invisibility of nonwhite artists than it is about the lionization of nonwhite artists on political rather than artistically merited grounds; while for Wilson, it is about blacks' systematic lack of access to the means of cultural production.

Brustein is not wrong to assert both the material and metaphoric dimensions of race; rather his rhetorical failure emerges from his resistance to accounting for their simultaneity. In his refutation of Wilson's "divisive" remarks, race is either entirely metaphorical—and therefore within our power to ignore or redefine—or entirely material. Furthermore, since the material realities of race have changed, only selected, tangible aspects of the present—such as monies devoted to diversity programming—are worthy of inclusion in a diagnosis of the function of race in contemporary American theater and cultural politics. Compartmentalizing the different frameworks within which racial discourse operates prohibits a sophisticated understanding of the need for practices that produce racial meaning through performance, rather than simply transcending it "to embrace a common humanity."

It is within this material/metaphor divide that Brustein's support for color-blind casting capitulates to problematic definitions of race: whereas Wilson objected to color-blind casting on the grounds that it diverted material resources from the production of authentic blackness, Brustein's counterargument remains wrapped up in the idea, expressed in other writings, that whiteness is an invisible, irrelevant (or worse, wrongly beleaguered) racial category, while blackness represents an overly politicized category from which color blindness provides a necessary escape. Rather than accepting that it is impossible to divorce the production of whiteness and the discrediting of blackness from the structural past and present of American theater, Brustein posits racial ignorance as a cure for the moral and aesthetic relativism plaguing American society, as if the sole alternative to color-blind casting is an alarming return "to the days of segregated theatres."[93]

THE CRITICAL FALLOUT: COLOR BLINDNESS AND PERFORMANCE

How, then, does this contest of wills between two major figures in American theater illuminate our understanding of how race performs institutionally, and of the threat that color-blind casting poses to the seemingly compulsory performance of blackness? Wilson's and Brustein's debate focused national attention upon the roles that whiteness and blackness play in the creation and administration of theater, and provided a level of discursive visibility—however contested—to the practice of color-blind casting. Rather than an innocuous aesthetic choice, color-blind casting became a symbol of the politics of racial performativity, and formed a site within which racially egalitarian aesthetics and politics could be debated as well as created.

After their print war, Wilson and Brustein participated in a live debate sponsored by TCG and savvily marketed as "On Cultural Power: The August Wilson/Robert Brustein Discussion Moderated by Anna Deavere Smith."[94] The event was held on January 27, 1997, at the Town Hall in New York City, a 1,500-seat space that was filled to capacity on the evening of the event. In a live debate, unlike in print, the men could hold one another instantly accountable for their remarks, as could the public that they hoped to influence with their ideas. The live debate offered yet another example of the intersections between institutional and individual acts of racial performance. Both Wilson and Brustein served as representatives of the supposedly adversarial black and mainstream theater communities.[95] As a woman who identifies as black and who performs postmodern works that actively transgress racial boundaries while still earning respect for her craft according to universal standards of artistic excellence, Anna Deavere Smith served as a physical bridge between the absolutes each man was meant to represent. Racially, she functioned as an alternate representative of black theater, and because her gender disrupted "the world of men" upon which Wilson's ideas about race relied, her role suggested the possibility that the evening's dialogue might be forced to move beyond old discursive habits into new territory.

As reported after the fact in *American Theatre,* the event was indeed a site of racialized performance. Situated onstage, in front of a passionate audience, both Wilson and Brustein performed the roles that they had rehearsed against one another and independently for years in their writings and their public personae. Brustein's introductory remarks demonstrated the cultural impasse that their debate would preserve rather than challenge, because "[no] one man can score enough points to prevail over the other . . . nobody can hope to end an argument that has gone unresolved for centuries."[96] Brustein chose to define their debate as less about race than about "the basic function of dramatic art," a universalist move that would relegate Wilson's racially materialist objections to secondary status.[97] In some sense, as a theatrically satisfying spectacle, the task of the debate was to stage the impossibility of bridging the divide between apolitical, universal/white art and political/polemical black art, rather than to challenge such an assumption of insurmountable difference. On these terms, "On Cultural Power" was a success. Just as their print debate had done, the live discussion preserved Brustein's and Wilson's strict notions of blackness and universality, and cultivated in their audience an appetite for these polar opposites.[98] Stephen Nunns's report of the event reveals, "If the participants were generally civil in their critiques, the at-times unruly audience was aching for something a little more rowdy," describing the rote investment in antagonistic definitions of blackness and whiteness that spectators brought to the event and expected to see affirmed.[99] When Brustein and Wilson failed to deliver this strife to the audience's satisfaction, spectators produced it themselves, calling Wilson a "Fascist" and "hissing" at Brustein.[100]

Therefore, the dynamics of the spectacle suggest how central the problematization of race (especially blackness) is in American performance. Brustein acknowledged himself and Wilson as icons of a permanent racial intractability, and Smith, through audiences' awareness of her artistic work, symbolically represented the possibility of ideological reconciliation.[101] However, according to press reports, her "even-keeled arbitration . . . made it clear . . . that she was there only as a medium for the ideas and the discussion between the two men."[102] Without wishing to undermine the gendered critique embedded in this characterization of Smith's role, I would suggest that the representation is probably more accurate than it intends to be. Lamenting Smith's function as "only a medium" in some ways implies a disappointment with her limited influence on the discussion, yet this is precisely what Smith does in her own work as well. Richard Schechner describes Smith's solo performance work as shamanistic, a more ritualized understanding of the term *medium* than the disappointed one that sees Smith in technological terms as one whose presence enabled Wilson's and Brustein's ideas to reach the audience, if not one another. Instead we might see Smith's function as that of witness-participant who, through her presence and incorporation of these conflicting ideas (literally taking them into her body in order to, through her own words, moderate the discussion), reveals here, as she does elsewhere in her own performance work, that the narratives we seek about race and American character are not to be found in one authoritative voice, but instead in the postmodern collage of dissent, misunderstanding, and unintended collusion that is everyday life. The lack of handy resolution between Wilson and Brustein is only a complete failure if we frame an investment in racialized discourse as always and only a problem: in this way, only Brustein's victory would suffice, since a stalemate or Wilson victory would keep the conflict alive. On the other hand, an emphasis on the attention focused—even temporarily—on black theater makes the event provisionally successful on Wilson's terms. Rather than being dismissed from it, black theater becomes central to and the catalyst for this conversation on cultural power.

Both before and after the Town Hall debate, *American Theatre* solicited feedback from various scholars and practitioners on the intersection of race and performance. Some responded specifically to the concerns raised by both Wilson and Brustein; others instead took the opportunity to reflect upon the broader systemic concerns that the debate reflected. From director/scholar Richard Schechner, who agreed with Wilson's calls for greater economic support of black theater but suggested that "to always cast according to type—racial type, especially—is a stupid, short-sighted and inartistic thing to do,"[103] to director Lou Bellamy's concern that "the major institutions' forays into [black art are] colonialist . . . foster[ing] the idea that those they choose to admit are more accomplished or more talented because those artists chose to accept their 'color-blind' invitation,"[104] August Wilson's public critique had at least the short-term effect of making the intersection of race and performance central to the public discourse of American theater. Unfortunately, though, the print debate that unfolded in the aftermath provided quick and uncritical affirmation of the validity of Wilson's institutional critique (yes, black theater is underfunded, and yes, that's a shame) without producing sustained, proactive dialogue on how the conditions that provoked his critique could be rectified. Racial manners dictated a move away from considering the socioeconomic and political valences of back participation in American theater and instead toward asserting American theater's inclusivity.

This lack of resolution instantiated the very substance of Wilson's argument, displacing black concerns with "American" ones rather than fusing the two. While his primary concern was for the economic future of autonomous African American theater, some critics deemed the subsidiary issue of color-blind casting "the most specific aspect of the current disagreement."[105] This in turn prompted others, like performance artist Robbie McCauley, to be "extremely resistant to writing about August Wilson's address [because it] felt too much like being asked to take sides on Wilson's declaration about non-traditional casting."[106] Wilson alleged that "colorblind casting is an aberrant idea that has never had any validity other than as a tool of the Cultural Imperialists who view American culture, rooted in the icons of European culture, as beyond reproach in its perfection."[107] Mingling artistic and cultural objections with economic ones, he identified the money spent promoting color-blind casting as "misguided resources" that would be put to better use if given to black theaters to help them develop new talent and become financially secure. When Brustein defended color-blind casting against Wilson's objections, he chose examples of the practice that reinforced a hierarchy of integration. He wrote,

Are black actors now to perform only black parts written by black playwrights? Will James Earl Jones no longer have a chance to play Judge Brack or Darth Vader? Must we bar Andre Braugher and Denzel Washington from enacting the Shakespearean monarchs? Is Othello not an acceptable opportunity for Morgan Freeman or Lawrence Fishburne? . . . No more *Voodoo Macbeth*s or all-black *Godot*s? No more efforts on behalf of nontraditional casting and integrated theatre companies? Must history be rolled back to the days of segregated theatres?[108]

Each of the American examples that Brustein selected to show the rewards of color-blind casting involved black actors taking on roles in canonical texts written by white authors.[109] Such a framework implicitly endorses a hierarchy in which color-blind casting gives black actors access to great art that would otherwise remain out of reach and leave them with only black art (which, because of its focus on a politicized and historicized articulation of the conditions of black existence in America, must be less artistically accomplished). This way of imagining an inclusive American theater raises troubling questions: are color blindness and the end of race that it seems to promise so attractive because they divert attention away from the material consequences of racial bias against black Americans? Does color blindness in the theater preclude the possibility of seeing race-based structural injustice?

Robert Brustein's remarks suggest that the answer to this last question is yes, at least in part. His easy avoidance—indeed, disavowal—of the institutional differences between black and white theater in "Subsidized Separatism"[110] follows a script designed to refuse proclamations of America as a house divided, from Larry Neal's 1968 assertion that "there are, in fact and in spirit, two Americas—one black, one white," to dismayed reiterations of the same after the riots following the 1992 verdict in the Rodney King beating trial and the mainstream outrage over O. J. Simpson's acquittal on criminal murder charges in 1995.[111] Recognition of the material and psychic divide between different racial communities is often construed as a failing—logical, moral, and otherwise—on the part of the marginalized, whether they be angry militants or ignorant jurors, producing the separation that they claim to want undone. In this instance, Brustein's condemnation of Wilson (and by extension "those who think [like him]") is predicated upon an unwillingness to address the real barriers to participation in American theater that black artists face in the form of unequal access to foundation dollars, aesthetic biases, and social networking systems that build upon the more egregious exclusions of our Jim Crow past. Although Brustein suggests that black artists benefit from the multiculturalist impulse toward "coercive philanthropy," the truth is that these benefits occur only in ways that affirm the power of mainstream institutions: "raceless" theaters receive the funds that enable them to hire specific minority artists in accordance with their grant stipulations, and the institutional power of mainstream theaters remains intact, even increases, since the economic compensation black artists eventually receive for their work is meted out according to the approval of these mainstream institutions. This is antithetical to—and in fact, the source of—Wilson's concern for black theater's institutional longevity, because, as Clinton Turner Davis alleges, "'New audience' initiatives have resulted in substantial grants to large white institutions [but s]maller, culturally specific institutions have again been left out of the loop; application guidelines, particularly those regarding size of operating budgets, exclude most from applying."[112] Trickle-down diversity preserves the jurisdiction of white decision-makers over black art by privileging institutions that achieved a degree of longevity and scale of production that are partly attributable to the earlier distribution of foundation dollars at a time when disinterest in "diversity" initiatives also disadvantaged small black theaters.

However, Brustein was not the only person to privilege discussions of racialized art over racialized economics without closely scrutinizing their intersection. Without mentioning color-blind casting directly, Gitta Honegger commented on the current paucity of true integration in American theater, and noted it as a liability afflicting artists of all races: separatism vitiates conflict, and conflict is the source of all good drama. Therefore, the lack of integrated audiences and production staff robs theater institutionally and aesthetically of the source of its vitality. However, Honegger was also wary of the integrated performance of conflict that the Wilson-Brustein debate seemed to initiate. Noting the "extended and highly successful mise-en-scène of the Brustein-Wilson discussion," she wrote,

> Ironically, in a culture obsessed with free speech, talking becomes an effective tool of censorship. *Talking about* creates the illusion of *doing something about.* Free speech becomes the painless talking cure that gets us over the real problem.[113]

Honneger's critique in some ways mirrors Wilson's condemnation of color-blind casting itself. Color-blind casting, in Wilson's view, allows mainstream theaters to believe that the needs of black artists to exercise their craft have been met fully, and, Honegger argues, talking exhaustively about the state of American theater likewise allows some scholars and practitioners to believe that change is occurring. Rather than material change via economic and institutional reform, the canvas of legitimate topics of discourse simply expands. The speech is free, fully disconnected from material consequences, yet the issues that necessitate the discourse remain untouched, such as the shortage of opportunities for black artists to exercise their craft in "specifically" black roles that makes color-blind casting an expedient and attractive strategy.

Clinton Turner Davis, one of the founders of the Non-Traditional Casting Project, made the same observation about American theater's commitment to fetishizing the problem of racial representation rather than working to resolve it. In a letter to "Members of the American Theater Community," he decried the ineffectuality of conversation as a proxy for social change. Through a combination of inaction and insincerity, the talking cure, he argued from personal experience, had failed black artists repeatedly. Attempting to shift the focus of the conversation from abstract support or condemnation of the principles that fueled Wilson's and Brustein's remarks, Davis instead asked, "Why do artistic and managing directors love to talk about the changes they are making? . . . Why has it taken so long for these so-called artistic leaders to identify and implement the actions they should take?"[114] Within this exposé, Davis also indicted the uninterrogated tokenism that forms the substance of the changes these leaders love to describe: much as Brustein celebrated Wilson's success as something that belied his complaints, Davis noted that "certain theater companies can only identify one or two ethnic directors and designers to work in their theaters . . . [as if] the hiring of one ethnic director . . . preclude[s] the hiring of others."[115] Rather than being infinitely and individually useful (as color blindness claims), ethnic artists become tools of institutional performativity, their carefully quantified presence creating the reality of change, however limited.

Davis's comments highlight the linguistic limitations that the term *color blindness* imposes upon its supposed social aims. Through a heightened and sublimated awareness of race, color-blind casting practices tend to yield an institutional tokenism that is designed to preempt allegations of negative racial bias. In many cases, underrepresented minorities are sought out and given artistic opportunities in order to prove that they no longer face specific barriers to participation in American theater, and once the appearance of equality has been achieved, an ironic form of color blindness emerges, as Davis identifies it, in which decision makers are blind to the talents of people of color who are no longer needed to make a demographic point. Perversely, race becomes useful as an icon of the triumph of racial transcendence. Robert Brustein offered an example of this pattern in his own celebration of Suzan-Lori Parks's play *Venus*, which, he believed, "manage[d] to portray the humiliation of blacks in white society without complaint or indictment."[116] By endorsing the production as "a major advance for an integrated American theatre," Brustein suggested that for American theater to make progress, representations of blackness must relinquish claims to a historicized, politicized context that would indict (for example) the global systems of power that have produced a racial hierarchy with Europe at the top and Africa at the bottom.[117] Brustein believes that Parks's work succeeds because she offers "not so much an indictment of white oppression as

European smugness and insularity," a shift from racial to ethno-continental critique that allows white Americans to distance themselves from the paradigm of subjugation that the play stages.[118]

These strategies of exemption are crucial to color blindness's appeal to cultural conservatives, as Alan Nadel explained in his essay "August Wilson and the (Color-Blind) Whiteness of Public Space." Viewing race as a discourse structured by members of the dominant group to provide a basis for exclusion from their number, Nadel criticizes the language of color blindness for offering only the promised obsolescence of nonwhiteness, rather than a triumph over all racialized thinking. Since the only marked elements in national racial discourse tend to be nonwhite ones, whiteness has always existed as the unmarked, deriving power from its ubiquity and its silence. He argues that Wilson "is attacking the idea that the neutral space is implicitly white and that white culture, all things being equal, does not depend on being perpetuated, only on being protected from defilement, assault, and dilution."[119] He goes on to explain how this affects American theater in particular:

> Colorblind casting is thus a luxury of white theater because black theater always appears within the dominant culture marked by its blackness. Black actors, by definition, have to choose between appearing as blacks or "simply" as actors, with the current state of funding severely limiting their choice. . . . The freedom of a black actor's choice, in the separate but unequal conditions of American culture, must thus be sacrificed to preserve the myth of neutral white space.[120]

In American theater, then, color blindness and multiculturalist agendas are two sides of the same coin: transcendence to a state of racelessness in American theater reproduces the aesthetic, economic, and institutional marginalization of black art, while "multicultural" resources bolster the influence of white art, which remains intact, unsullied by race as a category of exclusion.

One of the objectives of this analysis is to advance a recuperative perspective on color-blind casting that doesn't fall prey to a false innocence or naive ahistoricism that emphasizes its transcendent possibilities. In addition to the fact that the term *color-blind casting* cannot accurately describe a logistical or progressive politics of inclusion, the term also implies a suspended temporality, focusing on actor selection but not on production processes and performance. These last two provide opportunities for color-blind casting to respond to the most cogent criticisms of the practice. For example, Una Chaudhuri has argued that "it is not only black artists but black *culture* that a truly diverse theatre should include, and . . . nontraditional casting, for all its virtues, simply does not contribute to that goal."[121] Chaudhuri actually conflates color-blind casting with all other practices of nontraditional casting, when in fact at least one of the categories of nontraditional casting—cross-cultural casting—by definition aspires to provide an opportunity for the specifics of black culture and the universal claims of canonical dramatic texts to intersect (as might conceptual casting). Even still, I would suggest that color-blind casting does not absolutely preclude the possibility of including black culture in American theater. Rather, as Zelda Fichandler suggests, "Colorblind casting . . . does not say 'I am blind to your color,' but, rather, 'I am blind to the *primary* considerations of color in the playing of this role.'"[122] Therefore, instances of color-blind casting, not just other, more obvious types of conceptual and cross-cultural casting, can lead to transgressive performances that help redefine racial meanings and their relationship to national culture. In defiance of both Wilson's dogma about authentic blackness and Brustein's weariness with "indictment and complaint," color-blind casting may contribute to the multivalence of black subjectivity by insisting upon the relevance of black bodies and the intertext of black culture to a wider variety of narratives than are currently staged.

In practice, color-blind casting actually defies the limits placed upon it by the Non-Traditional Casting Project: rather than preserving the distinctions between different types of nontraditional casting practices, color-blind casting is always, to some extent, conceptual casting. Whether or not the actors' bodies give special resonance to a story, color-blind casting practices always illuminate the racial ideologies that they defy. Richard Schechner asserts that "a production always involves . . . dialogue . . . within the drama and . . . between the drama's culture of origin and its culture of presentation."[123] This dialogue between the culture of the play and the culture of the contemporary world in which audiences are situated underscores color-blind casting's function as one vehicle among many for expanding how we understand blackness and its value.

When color-blind casting allows black actors to take on roles for which they would not otherwise be considered and then gives way to a production process in which the black actor's intersectional identity is integrated into, rather than sacrificed to, the production, the practice does not abandon still-urgent, race-based political inquiry: instead, it acknowledges the multiplicity of the black subject as a political and aesthetic force. Furthermore, understanding race as being produced in and through a variety of performance modes denies absolute power to any single instance of racial production: black performativity must be allowed and required to account for its heterogeneity, which "necessitates incessant reiteration, the conscious and active and repeated renewal of the conditions of its possibility."[124] To discount color-blind casting as one condition of the possibility of black heterogeneity is to reproduce the limitations of universalist discourse.

POSTSCRIPT: THE GROUND ON WHICH [WE NOW] STAND

Even in 2010, August Wilson's concerns about the institutional viability of black theater remained valid: none of seventy-six LORT member theaters then extant was dedicated specifically to the production and preservation of African American (or other nonwhite) culture.[125] This was the case as far back as 2003 when Sandra Shannon and Dana Williams interviewed Wilson. Reflecting upon the aftermath of his speech, Wilson suggested, "I'm willing to bet that if you go back and look that after the speech there was less money given to black theaters than before. And there are reasons for that. And I think it's because in certain ways there's not a value for black theater."[126] To wit: two years after Wilson's speech, Crossroads Theater won a Tony Award for best regional theater; one year later it closed down because of financial and management difficulties. While it has since reopened, it has not yet returned to LORT member status. Philadelphia's Freedom Theatre temporarily held membership in LORT, but has also ceased to do so. This means that there are no African American theaters that meet the eligibility requirements (including season length, duration of rehearsal process, and IRS-approved nonprofit status) and choose to avail themselves of membership in an organization dedicated to "promot[ing] the general welfare of resident theaters in the United States."[127] While LORT statistics are not the only important diagnostic measure of the strength of black theater, the persistent absence of any specifically black theaters in LORT's membership continues to verify Wilson's claim that black theaters lack the institutional stability and national recognition enjoyed by theaters whose audiences, artists, leadership, and production staff are primarily white.

At the same time, the peripheral performance traditions that Henry Louis Gates discussed in his *New Yorker* essay "The Chitlin' Circuit" shortly after the Wilson-Brustein debate continue to flourish. While Wilson disparaged as unacceptably elitist W. E. B. DuBois's belief that a talented tenth of the black community could emerge as leaders to the unfinished masses, his own career lived out the colored contradictions of American theater. Wilson himself was a staple of the regional theater circuit and an individual beneficiary of the white foundation structure that he castigated, while a separate theatrical tradition challenged his assertion that the four characteristics of black theater are that it is "alive . . . it is vibrant . . . it is vital . . . it just isn't funded."[128] Gates's essay explored the lively, vibrant, vital, and well-funded realm of "the chitlin' circuit," a name that recalls the early days of American theater, when touring black performers worked for separate and unequal pay in inferior spaces. In current usage, the designation is less intended to decry the working conditions of these "urban theater" productions than to locate the productions in a specific class register associated with what was once known as the folk. As Gates and subsequent journalists have profiled, urban theater is a very profitable undertaking with tentacles in other representational domains, including publishing, film, and television. This theater relies upon an informal economy housed almost exclusively within the black community, rather than looking toward foundations to ensure its longevity. Urban theater traffics in its own fairly limited definitions of blackness by relying upon stock characters, conflicts, and religiously inflected plot resolutions, and is a far cry from the Aristotelian artistic ground that August Wilson plumbed as one strand of his creative inheritance. Director (and frequent Wilson collaborator) Kenny Leon was blunt about this distinction in 2008, declaring, " 'I look at theater that is produced at some of the regional theaters and theater that is produced on that circuit as two different things. . . . We shouldn't try to make them be the same things.' "[129] Granting these different theatrical forms their separate spheres of influence, audience, and economics is a way of acknowledging the heterogeneous class positions from which black performance can emanate. As much as Wilson understood himself to be advocating on behalf of a broadly based black creative community, some artists questioned the relevance of his subject position on racial grounds: "If the audiences who go to Mr. Wilson's plays are predominantly nonblack, [David Talbert, a leading director on the urban theater circuit] asked, then how significant could he be to black people?"[130] Wilson's privilege, then, made him a questionable spokesperson for the health of black theater not just in Robert Brustein's eyes, but also in the eyes of the directors and producers of a black theater for the masses that already enjoyed the economic self-determination Wilson desired for theaters structured on the regional and resident theater model. These unevenly parallel infrastructures suggest that black artists and theatrical institutions may have either cultural capital or financial capital, but not both at the same time.

As one diagnostic in evaluating the racial dynamics of American theater, the disappointing statistics of LORT membership suggest that color-blind casting practices valuing transgressive rather than racially transcendent politics are more useful than ever. In order for Robert Brustein's claim that what Wilson calls "white theaters" are in fact racially inclusive theaters to be true, color-blind casting must be one of many diversifying tactics employed, so as not to elide the phase of racial representation in which nonwhiteness is valued as such, rather than being tolerated in spite of its still-problematic connotative force. By refusing traditions of segregated stages without refusing racial difference, what we have come to call color-blind casting also has the potential to render whiteness particular rather than universal in its relationship to other racial categories. It would illuminate the ways in which whiteness as endless individuality unencumbered by racialized histories is a fiction that has been maintained by force rather than achieved by happenstance. As David Theo Goldberg argues, the universalist values so often claimed by white art are in fact "no more than the projected imposition of local values—those especially of some ethnoracial and gendered particularity—universalized. The supposed universalism of epistemological politics reduces to the political epistemology of an imposed universality."[131] (White) common sense receives sanction and "create[s] unity by negating [its] difference," and the political, economic, and aesthetic benefits of this dominant status are simultaneously desired and denied.[132] As long as this denial continues unchecked, even the late August Wilson's work will only receive a visitor's pass to what is esteemed as legitimate American theater, with no African American or transgressively coalitional, multiracial theater companies to give it an institutional or cultural home.[133] The end of race will indeed come to mean the end of blackness, and the vivid histories out of which Wilson's work emerges will be denied in favor of a racially transcendent American theater that refuses to acknowledge the full context and significance of black artists' accomplishments.

CHAPTER 3

The Limits of Color Blindness: Interracial Sexuality, Denzel Washington, and Hollywood Film

All concepts of race are always concepts of the body and also of heterosexuality. Race is a means of categorizing different types of human body which reproduce themselves. . . . Heterosexuality is the means of ensuring, but also the site of endangering, the reproduction of these differences.

—Richard Dyer, *White*

As of the second decade of twenty-first century, Denzel Washington is arguably the most successful black actor in Hollywood history. Popular with black and white audiences alike, his movies routinely succeed at the box office as well as with critics, and he has been nominated for five Academy Awards, two of which he has won. Washington is one of the very few actors capable of successfully navigating the space of racial simultaneity: both black and "race-neutral," Washington receives a breadth of opportunities to play roles in which his blackness is meant to signify within the plot as well as those in which it is not. According to Elizabeth Alexander, "He has found a way to assemble a quite remarkable gallery of black male characters for our age that are neither stereotypical nor excessively upright. . . . He alone among mainstream black film actors has given us this range with which to think about, and imagine, black men."[1] However, for most of his career, Washington's racially unprecedented success has been predicated on the careful regulation of his sexuality, primarily by avoiding films that prominently feature heterosexualized romantic narratives. This has proved especially true when Washington plays opposite a white female costar. Standard tropes of romance (or at least sexual attraction) are routinely sublimated when Washington performs in big-budget Hollywood films. This heterosexual manipulation reinforces the bio-logic of race that names color blindness as the emphatic privatization rather than disappearance of the racial dimensions of personhood. Occluding Washington's sexuality grants him entry into the public realm on terms that attempt to make the production—and therefore, reproduction—of his racial identity impossible.

In the mid-1990s, Denzel Washington appeared in two films—both adapted from successful novels—that attempted to exploit a politics of color blindness that would prevent each from being marked (and therefore marketed) as a "black film" with implicitly limited appeal to a wider audience. *The Pelican Brief* features Washington starring opposite Julia Roberts in a role originally envisioned as a white man. In *Devil in a Blue Dress,* Washington stars as a black detective in racially polarized 1940s Los Angeles. Each novel places its protagonist in a romantic or sexual relationship with a white woman, yet each film eliminates this romantic plot line, reflecting the equation, on some deep level, of blackness and masculinity with the problematic pursuit of white women. The foreclosure of Gray Grantham's lust and the erasure of consensual sex between Easy Rawlins and the socially white Daphne Monet affirms the permanence of heterosexualized genealogies of race and the impossibility of color-blind spectatorship. Washington's performing body cannot function or be read outside of the long filmic tradition dictating codes of interracial heterosexual propriety, whether he or his audiences are trying to get over (on) race.

As products of 1990s culture, these films reflect that decade's efforts to publicize black masculinity, most often through representations of infamous black men who functioned metonymically to narrate pressing social problems. The "outing" of black masculinity paradoxically helped to reinforce by negative example the undesirability of allowing race and raced individuals into the public sphere. During her tenure as an associate curator for the Whitney Museum of American Art, Thelma Golden mounted a controversial 1994 exhibition called "Black Male: Representations of Masculinity in Contemporary American Art." As both a part and a critique of this tumultuous decade, the show attracted guarded acclaim for the subject matter as "a rich, timely and complex vein for a museum interested in contemporary art,"[2] as well as vehement scorn for its poststructuralist "nonsense" that "distract[ed]" from the consideration of visual beauty, emblematic of "the repulsive burden that contemporary art places upon" critics.[3] Resentful critics notwithstanding, Golden asserted the necessity of this examination, arguing in her catalog essay, "With the help of print and television media, black men [had] become symbolic icons for this nation's ills. They personif[ied] rampant criminality (Willie Horton), perverse promiscuity (Wilt Chamberlain), sexual harassment (Clarence Thomas), date rape (Mike

Tyson), and spousal abuse (O.J. Simpson)."[4] That Denzel Washington should escape such assignations during this period is remarkable, and certainly the result of his careful social location within his films of that decade.

Washington's performances are most instructive when viewed as keys to the codes of representation that structure our cultural understanding of race through heterosexuality. In particular, *The Pelican Brief* and *Devil in a Blue Dress* demonstrate the persistently ironic role of race in the private/public divide. Through a focus on the possibility of heterosexual activity, race becomes a public (and therefore governable) concern, and yet individuality—the ability to differentiate oneself from a public aggregate and lay claim to a (sexual) private sphere—is also figured as a privilege incompatible with the racial signification that Washington cannot escape, in spite of his seeming crossover to the realm of color-blind success. Put plainly, the heterosexualization of the films' narratives causes Washington to signify as black first and individual second, requiring nimble shifts of representational strategies to prevent this blackness from overwhelming each film's intentions to exceed the limitations of race. Washington's black performing body both involuntarily summons and consciously avoids a fraught genealogy of representations of black masculinity. In the interests of both the narratives and their reception beyond the frame, white women become the sexual barrier that Washington can neither transgress nor transcend. Despite liberal aphorisms to the contrary, love in Hollywood films is not (color)blind.

The fact that Washington's blackness is most conspicuous when juxtaposed against the presence of white women in performance suggests that racial agency becomes indistinguishable from sexual agency for both blacks and whites. The cultural and at times legal rules that structure interracial conduct do so through the maintenance of a strict heterosexual order. And while the focus of this chapter is black masculinity as exemplified by Denzel Washington, I should be clear that a broader gender critique is implicit in this line of analysis. Black women and white men do not escape the raced, gendered, and heterosexed principles of color blindness under investigation here. They are essential players that complete the heterosexual quadrangle at the heart of the black/white binary. And of course, attention to queer sexualities further distorts this quadrangle into something less symmetrical by functioning beyond these heteronormative vocabularies.

As Richard Dyer observes, heterosexual contact functions as a site of racial preservation. Sexual practices and possibilities assign meaning to socialized bodies with the disingenuous assumption that desire works only, effortlessly, and consistently along racial lines, in order to naturalize and perpetuate difference. In practice, however, interracial desire and heterosexual contact disrupt the seeming inevitability of racial boundaries. The libidinal logic of interracial sexuality, therefore, exposes the discursive illogic of racial categorization (loyal as it is to notions of racial purity that actual human behaviors belie), thereby putting it at risk. As Dyer goes on to assert,

> Inter-racial heterosexuality threatens the power of whiteness because it breaks the legitimation of whiteness with reference to the white body. . . . if white bodies are no longer indubitably white bodies, if they can no longer guarantee their own reproduction as white, then the "natural" basis of their dominion is no longer credible.[5]

Panic over the sexual reproduction of whiteness reveals the symbiotic nature of materialist and ideological appeals to race as ontology. The two spheres must act in concert with one another in order to maintain their social power. Thus, the persistent appeal of exteriority, of fecund, visible bodies as the locus of racial identity, poses problems for arguments that presume the possibility of racial transcendence (i.e., color blindness). Although barriers to equal participation in American society may fall down, the very fact of heterosexual reproduction and the racial classification that inevitably follows from it prevent the true obsolescence of racial categories.[6]

Therefore, we can infer from Dyer's statement that heterosexual contact represents the physical limit of any program of color blindness. The reproductive potential of heterosexual relationships foregrounds the partners' racial identities as well as their role in reproducing or undermining their own racial communities. According to this logic, while it may be possible to ignore it in other contexts, it is impossible to ignore race in sexual relationships because they are the means by which (racialized) families are produced—both in the biologically reproductive sense and even in the practice of extending kinship networks to include marital, step-, half-, and in-law relationships. While other institutions that are subjected to integration are often understood in structural rather than reductively material terms,[7] the nuclear family becomes important not just as an ideological formation but also as a set of social and sexual practices that produce, to borrow Judith Butler's phrase, bodies that matter.

BLACK SEXUALITY IN HOLLYWOOD

The terms of Denzel Washington's crossover success cannot be understood outside of Hollywood's historical treatment of black sexual behavior, particularly as emblematized by the master filmic narrative of black men's bestial, dangerous sexuality, which went hand in hand with the film industry's efforts to legislate transgressive sexuality out of the popular imaginary. Also instructive are the unspoken conditions through which Washington's crossover predecessor, Sidney Poitier, was able to achieve success. Taken together, they create a powerful frame of reference for understanding how Washington could become such a bankable Hollywood commodity around the turn of the twenty-first century, during the height of anxieties about the necessity or desirability of acknowledging, accommodating, and embracing racial and cultural difference as such.

Of course, no discussion of blackness, sexuality, and Hollywood film would be complete without addressing Hollywood's first bona fide blockbuster, D. W. Griffith's 1915 technical masterpiece, *The Birth of a Nation*. Griffith has been understandably saluted for his formal innovations that advanced the art of filmmaking, if not narrative, but there is little need to rehearse those accolades here. More important to this project is the fact that Griffith realized these technical triumphs through a romantic narrative of the development of the Ku Klux Klan in the southern United States (itself indicative of the rebirth of a white supremacist nation) as a backlash against Reconstruction, in which blacks were given economic, educational, and political opportunities to participate more fully in the public culture of the United States. By serving "as a midwife for . . . the birth of a new, virile American whiteness, unencumbered by the historical memory of slavery, or being enslaved,"[8] D. W. Griffith's *The Birth of a Nation* effectively provided a set of instructions to future artists on how to demonize blacks as despoilers of supposedly timeless American values, in particular by viewing their sexuality as the primary threat to national aspirations toward unity.

A few scenes from the film stand out in their efforts to make explicit the complicated intersections of race, nation, and desire upon which America's racial mores rely (and now, to which black performers are beholden).

In the first:[9]

Lillian Gish plays Elsie Stoneman, romantic heroine of the film, and the heart's desire of good Confederate soldier Ben Cameron, a.k.a. "The Little Colonel." One of the earliest images in the film is of Ben looking at Elsie's picture, her beauty acting as a salve to his weary, war-torn body and spirit. When they meet later during peaceful times in the South, he hopes to kiss her on the cheek, and instead receives only her hand. Director D.W. Griffith cultivates Elsie throughout the film as an elusive object of desire for both white and black men alike.[10]

Another important scene depicts

A rally taking place in the South, meant to galvanize black support for a Reconstruction government. The Reconstruction platform, as it appears on a poster toted by one of the already converted, is:

EQUALITY
EQUAL RIGHTS
EQUAL POLITICS
EQUAL MARRIAGE[11]

When the Reconstruction government finally takes control of the legislature, black men sit with bare feet propped up on desks, swilling drinks and eating in chambers. An intertitle screen reads:

"Passage of a bill, providing for the intermarriage of blacks and whites."

Griffith cuts back to a shot of blacks in chambers and in the viewing balcony (who are, not incidentally, white actors in blackface), who all erupt into celebration at the news that the fullest manifestation of their freedom is the ability to sully white family lines throughout the South.

Finally, the melodramatic episode that clarifies the stakes of Griffith's work comes when:

Towards the end of the film, the malevolent, power-hungry mulatto Silas Lynch unknowingly initiates a conflict that serves to unite Northern and Southern whites in a racialized concept of both family and nation:

"Lynch, drunk with wine and power, orders his henchmen to hurry preparations for a forced marriage."

Elsie Stoneman is his would-be prize, and he goes to talk with her father, his mentor, about his plans:

"'I want to marry a white woman.'"

In a classic male homosocial gesture of congratulations, father Stoneman claps his protégé on the shoulder and shakes his hand, until he hears:

"'The woman I want to marry is your daughter.'"

At which father Stoneman gets deeply offended, realizes the error of his racial equality-spouting ways, and (through a series of plot machinations) is rehabilitated into the family of American white supremacy.

Forgive me if I am presumptuous in not calling out the most infamous scene of the film, in which the black soldier Gus stalks the pure, chaste, white Flora Cameron, who jumps off a cliff to her death rather than submit to the bestial desires of a black man (a death that serves as the catalyst for the formation for the Klan).[12] I have chosen to emphasize other moments that more explicitly articulate the national stakes of the sexualization of race and racism in America. Silas Lynch's attempted marital abduction is foiled by a white man invested with nationally sanctioned power before it has a chance to come to fruition, while Gus's attempted rape—foiled only by his intended victim rather than by a heroic intercessor—points out the white man's temporary impotence and inability to protect the women closest to him (and motivates the Klan's brand of simultaneously preemptive and retributive violence). Each of these scenes demonstrates the ways in which white women are prized as trophies in America's sociosexual hierarchy, but they also reflect the imbrication of heterosexual politics into the functioning of the nation-state, the state's role in maintaining a sexual status quo that articulates and protects racial difference through sexual contact. According to Cedric Robinson, it was part of a historical "moment during which the mapping of American culture was reinscribed, when the contours of the social practices which came to characterize twentieth-century American society were fixed."[13] *The Birth of a Nation* illustrates the often-unconscious attitudes about race and sexuality that inform even current spectatorial practices, and with which black actors working inside of Hollywood's popular culture system must contend.

The lasting influence of Griffith's epic extends beyond the strict category of "race(d) films": even contemporary Hollywood's romantic genre is predicated on representing white heterosexual womanhood as the *ne plus ultra* in its economy of desire. As the tangled relationship between "realistic" representations and "real" life attests, in American culture, sexual access to white women remains a sign of success and masculinity, and for black men in particular, these relationships are often perceived as an emblem of their escape from (or disloyalty to) their race. Conversely, the failure—not to be confused with refusal—to enter into such a taboo relationship is read as a reinscription of his race onto the black male body, a reminder of the limits of his social freedom. Within film, this means that Hollywood is willing to (color)blindly allow black men into fictive military hierarchies, science labs, congressional halls, corporate boardrooms, and even superhero costumes, but the white woman's bedroom (even in the realm of the representational) continues to be figured as a site of cultural anxiety into which the always already polycultural reality of contemporary American society may not tread.

This heterosexual conservatism is linked not only to the specific representations contained in *The Birth of a Nation,* but also to the explicitly articulated politics of race, sexuality, and representation subsequently enumerated in the Motion Picture Code of 1930.[14] Drafted by William Hays, the code focuses on "the high trust and confidence which have been placed in [the film industry] by the people of the world," and accepts the fact that while "motion pictures [are] primarily entertainment without an explicit purpose of teaching or propaganda ... the motion picture within its own field of entertainment may be directly responsible for spiritual or moral progress, for higher types of social life, and for much correct thinking."[15] Films that respected a segregationist social logic suggested that "correct thinking" should privilege whiteness as paradigmatically American. Disavowing interracial sexuality was central to this effort: according to the Code, "Miscegenation (sex between the black and white races) [was] forbidden."[16] To control black sexuality and its representation was to control and conscript black identity in order to fortify whiteness's cultural hold over the public imaginary.

Sidney Poitier began his iconic career twenty years after the Hays Code's creation. His rise to prominence followed from and extended shifts in American racial politics that created new opportunities for black performers on-screen. Oscar Micheaux and other black filmmakers created race films in the second and third decades of the twentieth century, beginning a tradition of black independent filmmaking that functioned almost exclusively within the black community: black actors, directors, studios, and distributors set the celluloid politics of respectability in motion, but also addressed controversial topics. In particular, Mark A. Reid credits Oscar Micheaux's 1919 film *The Homesteader* as being possibly "the first . . . American film [in which] a sexual relationship between a black man and a white woman was not portrayed as the rape of a white woman."[17] A few decades later, Hollywood also began to expand the range of characters black actors could portray. In the 1950 film *No Way Out,* Poitier embodied the masculine grace and dignity that black America longed to see writ large on national screens, providing "the complete antithesis of all the black buffoons who had appeared before in American movies."[18] After earning a safe place within Hollywood culture as what Donald Bogle calls "the model integrationist hero," Poitier was probably the one actor who could safely star in a film that pushed social integrationist ideology into the domestic sphere: *Guess Who's Coming to Dinner?*, released in 1967.[19] Portraying Dr. John Prentice, the black fiancé of white Joanna Drayton (played by Katherine Houghton), Poitier was the future son-in-law any family of any race would want: educated, accomplished, polite, and handsome. However, Poitier's iconic sexual redemption within the film was achieved, in part, by giving the character Prentice no sexuality at all, supplanting it with intelligence and professional accomplishment. Poitier's asexual presence in this film was nothing new since "scriptwriters [routinely kept] Poitier's sexuality well-hidden," with the effect that "Poitier's sexual neutralization [was] embarrassingly apparent" by the time *Dinner* was released.[20] Hollywood's efforts to reimagine black men's sexuality transpired at a glacial pace, reflecting the continued discomfort felt by (and, arguably, cultivated in) the American public.

Within *Guess Who's Coming to Dinner?* Dr. Prentice's relationship with Drayton is almost entirely factual rather than physical, as they never consummate their love within the embodied narrative. Framing the movie as an exploration of family members' responses to an interracial romance rather than as an exploration of the romance itself granted director Stanley Kramer valuable distance from the codes of Hollywood romantic narrative that *The Birth of a Nation* helped to articulate. Therefore, race is able to figure differently within the film: Poitier gains access to middle-class social and sexual respectability because his contact with Houghton is constantly chaperoned (and this is indeed about Poitier as much as, and more than, it is about the fictional Dr. Prentice). The one kiss shared by John and Joanna in the entire movie is seen through a white cabbie's rearview mirror, doubly mediated for audiences, and literally framed within the purview of the white male gaze. Within the Drayton household, Katherine Hepburn and Spencer Tracy as the white parents provide another legislating gaze that controls the couple's behavior, preventing any physical contact that would foreground either character's sexual agency rather than their presumed social equality and thereby expose the complicated impact the former has upon the latter. Denied access to a private or a public sphere within which to locate this relationship, the triumphant message of love's transcendent power relies upon the no-space that the characters occupy. Ultimately then, Kramer's film offers a capitulatory vision of the politics of interracial sexuality, one that concedes to rather than alters the traditional representation of black men's sexualized physical presence around white women. In effect, the narrative circumstances banish Poitier's sexuality so that white characters in the movie do not have to.

Despite (or perhaps because of) its limited social ambitions, *Guess Who's Coming to Dinner?* was a commercial success, garnering ten Academy Award nominations and two wins, for Katherine Hepburn as Best Actress and for William Rose as author of Best Screenplay.[21] However well received it was by the Hollywood establishment and the viewing public, the film did not inaugurate a new era of films depicting successful interracial relationships. Interracial sexuality remained taboo, and in a sense represented the limit that could not be crossed by actors of color who seemed otherwise to transcend traditional racial boundaries. If Poitier bore any burden of representation in this film, his performance functioned simultaneously as instruction and caution in the rules of success for black men in Hollywood. Both formally (in terms of narrative and visual cinematic strategies) and discursively, Poitier's black performing body exposed the perceptual and social practices necessary to any program of aesthetic color-blindness. What made Poitier successful in this role was his physical detachment from Houghton, rather than audiences warming to enactments of interracial desire.

By the time *Guess Who's Coming to Dinner?* was released, the motion picture industry had abandoned the Hays Code and moved toward a system of rating and self-governance that allowed filmmakers to address issues of race, sex, and nonconformity in ways that had previously been forbidden. However, the cultural anxiety reflected in the Hays Code's prohibitions against interracial sexuality has not disappeared, decades later. While Denzel Washington's success depends upon the partial dissolution of the Code's ideological premises, the underlying notion that American film should offer idealized representations of American culture especially through the valorization of monoracial domesticity (and romance as a vehicle to the attainment of this domesticity) continues to structure much of Hollywood's current output. Nevertheless, by regularly limiting the representation of sexual acts within his films, Washington has achieved a level of mainstream success that is not traditionally afforded to black actors within Hollywood.[22] As a beneficiary of the integration of Hollywood film, he has been seen and promoted as the all-American black man. Both all-American (good, wholesome) and black (cool, sexy, powerful when he needs to be), he built his early reputation and commercial bankability by taking on good-guy roles that place him on the correct side of a moral conflict and repeating Sidney Poitier's accomplishment of making black people look good in the national imaginary.

Such "goodness" occurs through a process of undoing, whereby Washington's performances trouble the referential history of Hollywood's production of blackness. His performing body serves as a host and traitor to the cinematic antecedents of black masculinity. To borrow Hazel Carby's notion of "filmic genealogy," Denzel Washington "carries with him a built-in reference system from his previous roles . . . that resolves any hesitation on the part of the audience about his possible allegiance . . . a genealogy which film directors know exists in the popular imagination."[23] Each new Denzel Washington film helps to reframe our understanding of the possible performance of blackness within popular American culture, as he enters representational spaces that seem alien to the performative production of blackness. Perversely, this is so even when he takes on unsympathetic roles, such as his Academy Award–winning turn as a breathtakingly corrupt cop in *Training Day*. With roles such as this, Washington seems to enter that space of individuality which rejects any burden or politics of representation, famous enough that he can play a villain simply because it offers a meaty acting challenge, unconcerned that such a performance will limit his future career options. Fundamentally, then, Washington's success always depends upon his race, even when it seems not to.

HOLLYWOOD'S NON-NATIVE SON

The Seventy-fourth Academy Awards seemed to celebrate the past, present, and possible future of black Hollywood: Sidney Poitier received an Honorary Award "'for his extraordinary performances and unique presence on the screen, and for representing the motion picture industry with dignity, style, and intelligence throughout the world,'"[24] and Denzel Washington and Halle Berry took the top acting prizes against formidable competition from established colleagues. In the weeks leading up to the awards, much was made of the fact that three of the ten nominees for the leading acting prizes were black (Washington, Berry, and Will Smith, for the title role in the biopic *Ali*), which was taken to suggest both a new level of appreciation for black talent and the disappearance of barriers that kept blacks from enjoying large-scale success in Hollywood. When she received her award, Halle Berry articulated a similar sentiment, dedicating it to the black actresses, past and present, whose work paved the way for her own opportunities, and also to "every faceless, nameless woman of color that now has a chance because tonight this door has been opened."[25]

Denzel Washington's victory was a surprise upset over Russell Crowe, who was widely expected to win for his performance as mentally ill mathematician

John Nash in *A Beautiful Mind* (which won several other awards that night, including Best Picture). Perhaps accordingly, Washington betrayed a slightly more cynical attitude than Berry during his acceptance speech: before launching into the obligatory thank-yous, Washington's first words at the podium were, "Two birds in one night, huh?"[26] Washington recognized with suspicion the tidy narrative of racial triumph that Hollywood could write to account for his and Poitier's awards. On the surface, Denzel Washington's Best Actor win cemented his status as inheritor of Sidney Poitier's legacy. As Washington himself said, "Forty years I've been chasing Sidney [Poitier], they finally give it to me, what'd they do? They give it to him the same night. I'll always be chasing you, Sidney. I'll always be following in your footsteps. There's nothing I would rather do, sir. Nothing I would rather do."[27] However, one might just as easily compare their victories and arrive at a different conclusion. Thirty-eight years earlier, Poitier won a Best Actor award for his role in *Lilies of the Field*, portraying a handyman who helps a group of celibate white women (East German immigrant nuns in search of America's famed religious freedom and opposition to Communism) do God's work. Washington, on the other hand, received recognition for his portrayal of a scheming, violent police officer who is undone in part by his principled young white coworker. Poitier's role helped to make the argument that black men were unthreatening, and could in fact be agents of good, while Washington's role confirmed, for many black critics, all the worst stereotypes of black masculinity save one: no white women were harmed in the making of the movie (his interracial love interest in the film was Latina, played by Eva Mendes). Poitier's "roles measure[d] the limits of black masculinity"[28] during the mid-twentieth century, but Washington's win seemed to proclaim the postracial limitlessness of black masculinity (he's a crooked cop who happens to be black) and also to offer a throwback to abiding anxieties about black men and their proximity to power.

Washington's Academy Award–winning performance makes the title of this chapter section a little bit incongruous. By referring to him as a non-native son, I am invoking two intersecting genealogies: first, I am claiming his outsider status in Hollywood's commercial, aesthetic, and nepotistic systems, and second, I am suggesting that—*Training Day* notwithstanding—Washington has cultivated a reputation as the opposite of Bigger Thomas, the opposite of the black man who poses a physical and implicitly sexual threat to white women. The sense of unbelonging that is central to Washington's success and its constraints emerges at the very beginning of his film career, with his starring role in 1981's *Carbon Copy*, which tells the story of a young black man trying to establish a relationship with his white father in defiance of racial custom. Roger Porter is the young, ambitious son that millionaire Walter Whitney never knew he had, and whom his white associates—including his current wife—encourage him to ignore. The film's narrative demonstrates the impossibility of a racially transcendent reconciliation between the two: race matters, and while father and son might attempt to transgress the raced and classed codes that obstruct their sense of belonging to one another, they never occupy a color-blind social space. At the film's conclusion, Walter has been stripped of most of his class privilege because of his refusal to disown his son, demonstrating that there are material consequences to violating the boundaries that separate races and classes from one another. No longer traveling in the corporate Rolls-Royce, the two men ride off into the sunset in Roger's broken-down car, toward an uncertain future.

Over twenty years and several accolades later, we can read this film as not only the chronological but also the conceptual beginning of Washington's filmic genealogy, questioning the legitimacy of his place within a cultural institution that resolutely normalizes its whiteness and its patriarchal nature. This normalization requires concerted effort, though, and *Carbon Copy* takes note of that: Walter Whitney is a Jewish man who changed his last name at the recommendation of his father-in-law in order to aid his professional and social rise through white society; and even though the seventeen-year-old Roger Porter seems to confirm white expectations when he reveals that he doesn't attend high school, we learn in the last moments of the film that this is because he actually graduated from high school early and is about to return for his second year on the premed track at Northwestern University, his father's alma mater. An unacknowledged legacy in more ways than one, Denzel's first character confronts, toys with, and ultimately disproves stereotypes about black masculinity. All subsequent performances in some way extend from this film's interrogation of the racialized intersections between desired, enforced, and prohibited systems of belonging, marking Washington as a performer who has a perhaps unique charge to challenge the exclusivity of Hollywood's representational apparatus.

Since his debut, Washington has received acclaim for playing roles that rely upon his blackness to address social issues (such as *Glory,* for which he won a Best Supporting Actor Academy Award, *Malcolm X,* and *The Hurricane*), but Hollywood has also appropriated him as a symbol of its ability to be colorblind, to cast the best actor in the role regardless (or in spite) of his race, in films such as *Much Ado About Nothing, The Bone Collector,* and *Man on Fire.* Douglas Brode, in writing about Washington's career, suggests that this is as much by Washington's design as by Hollywood's. Making a claim for Washington's significance as a black celebrity that in some ways mirrors Donald Bogle's allegations about Sidney Poitier, Brode claims that Washington

> seeks out . . . roles originally written as white. Doing so allows him to prove, through his talent, that such parts can be handled as well by black actors, the issue of color dissipating if the viewer is as willing as the performer to relegate it to insignificance. . . . Even in plays and films that have nothing to do with racism, he implicitly [strikes] a blow for civil rights, of the integrationist order, by helping, via drama, to make America color-blind.[29]

By claiming integration and color blindness as equivalent structural terms, Brode conforms to the model of nontraditional casting that marks blackness as problematic and transcendence of a negative racial category as the precondition for inclusion in an ostensibly nonracial mainstream. His characterization denies the transgressive potential of Washington's performances by taking integration (a spatial model that preserves the central power position of the normative) as the ultimate manifestation of freedom.

Although Washington the actor has served for some as an emblem of color blindness, Washington the celebrity receives press attention that clearly marks him as black. Even the accolades he receives for transcending race serve as reminders of his blackness: "Denzel's leading-man status transcends race: he is not a gorgeous black man (Wesley Snipes, Laurence Fishburne), but a gorgeous man who's black."[30] Invoking Washington's race only to deny its importance makes clear that troubling perceptions of black masculinity remain in circulation and help to frame black performers' visibility and legibility in the mainstream press in particular. While in 1996 *People* magazine declared Washington the first—and so far, only—black man to merit the title "Sexiest Man Alive," such recognition reinforces Washington's status as the exception to Hollywood's race politics, rather than the harbinger of some new rule. Locating his success as a feat of transcendence rather than transgression allows the history of Hollywood film and its legislating impulses to remain unmarked as the thing against which Washington's appeal is figured.

"MR. GRANTHAM . . . WOULD YOU MIND SLEEPING ON THE SOFA?"

Alan Pakula's 1993 film *The Pelican Brief* is an adaptation of the 1992 John Grisham novel of the same name. Set in New Orleans and Washington, D.C., it tells the story of a young law student who unearths a conspiracy to kill two

Supreme Court justices. The story has all the necessary pieces of a compelling suspense tale: illicit sex, car bombs, national crisis, unavenged deaths, moral dilemmas, and budding romance. As it is written, the book pays little overt attention to race, only racially marking the occasional nonwhite characters in the book. The few black characters are an older man named Sarge who does housekeeping work near the Oval Office of the White House, and his son, a police officer who also works in the Washington, D.C., area. The romance within the story adheres to the American tradition of making the white woman an elusive object of desire: after the death of Darby Shaw's law professor and lover, Thomas Callahan, she embarks on a quest to locate the mysterious and controversial Pelican Brief that caused his death. Within this search, she comes to work with journalist Gray Grantham, who develops an attraction to her. There is a chemistry between the two that goes unconsummated for some time because of both Grantham's journalistic ethics and Shaw's grief over the recent death of Callahan. However, Grisham does eventually offer narrative satisfaction by concluding the novel with Darby Shaw and Gray Grantham on the cusp of a romantic relationship.

Warner Brothers released its screen version of the novel in 1993. Starring Julia Roberts as Darby Shaw, Denzel Washington as Gray Grantham, and Sam Shepard as the doomed Thomas Callahan, it was a box office hit, earning over $100 million in U.S. ticket sales alone.[31] *The Pelican Brief* met with slightly less success from critics, many of whom found fault with the film for preserving "the rickety flimflammery of Grisham's tale."[32] Reviews paid special attention to Julia Roberts because this was her first film since her two years of tabloid-worthy personal relationship drama, and generally left Washington alone except to say that he did as well as could be expected with limited material. Washington's credibility as a black man playing a role that was assumed to be white within the novel received little comment, as reviews focused instead on the quality of his performance and of the film overall.[33] However, behind the scenes, Washington's race allegedly caused novelist Grisham some concern. According to *Newsweek* magazine,

Reports were flying that the studio was offering Washington his entire salary to leave the project. According to several people who worked on the film, author John Grisham hadn't envisioned the leading man in his novel as black, and was demanding that Washington be removed. "He saw himself in the role, and obviously I'm not like him in looks or otherwise. I wasn't what he wanted, and that was made clear," Washington says. That's not Grisham's recollection. "Alan

Pakula called me about casting and said they were considering Denzel. I said fine," is all the author will say about "Pelican Brief."[34]

This alleged resistance suggests that, counter to Stanley Crouch's assertion that "a sufficiently gifted performer can rather quickly get an audience to see his or her character, not skin tone,"[35] talent rarely receives the opportunity to trump racial signification within an industry primarily governed by unabashedly mercenary goals. Instead, as Linda Williams argues, "The mere appearance of the black male body on the film or television screen . . . creates a heightened expectation for the expression of extreme good or extreme evil."[36]

Grisham's purported objections to Denzel Washington's attempt at racial transcendence foreground a three-way dynamic of racial meaning between the text, the actor, and the audience that resembles the triangulated space of social discourse Amy Robinson defines when she discusses the phenomena of racial and sexual passing.[37] Robinson counters the traditional notion that passing is a strictly binary process, involving the person who passes and the person who is duped by the racial or sexual charade. Instead of relying upon a two-way formulation of racial performativity, Robinson asserts the key role of a third party: the in-group clairvoyant. This person, a member of the group out of which the passer is trying to move, witnesses and is often complicit in the passer's successful performance for the dupe. However, Robinson is careful to explain, the in-group clairvoyant at the scene of racial charade does not reinforce the essential truth of the identity category the passer hopes to trespass, but recognizes "the machinery that enables the [racial] performance."[38] In other words, to the in-group clairvoyant, the "repeated stylization[s] of the body" that generate identity categories become transparent rather than simply natural.

In *The Pelican Brief*, the film's audience is encouraged to assume the role of in-group clairvoyant, affirming the success of Washington's racially transcendent performance at times, while recognizing his blackness at others. What defines the group in this instance is not necessarily a shared racial identity with Washington but a shared racial literacy. American audiences have been trained to see race when we watch Hollywood film, and Washington likewise understands the impact his race could have on the story's development. However, in taking this role, he becomes the actor attempting a racially transcendent charade, and therefore, the racially marked text becomes the dupe. Since audiences don't allow their recognition of Washington's blackness to subvert his "pass" into the mainstream of the plot, it is the text of *The Pelican Brief* that must be duped into accepting Washington's performance. Grisham's novel, with its implicit though deep investment in whiteness (especially heterosexual white masculinity), must be duped into allowing Denzel Washington's black-yet-crossover body and filmic genealogy to reside within its narrative as it moves from literary to cinematic form. A text predicated on the inevitable culmination of sexual desire between a white man and a white woman must be duped into accommodating Washington as an actor whose blackness cannot be detected or pose problems to the narrative as a whole. Washington's deception is not visual, since his brown skin cannot disappear, but connotative, regarding the surplus meanings his presence as a black actor will or will not introduce into the film.

This structure of recognition emphasizes the impossibility of the color-blind space that the film attempts to create. What become clear to us as we watch *The Pelican Brief* are the formal mechanisms of heterosexualized Hollywood romantic performance (the narrative conditions, the composition of shots, the use of music, and even a physical vocabulary) and the importance of the racialized history of Hollywood film to their successful enactment. As Amy Robinson suggests, "Considered as a hostile encounter between two *ways of reading*, the pass offers competing rules of recognition in the place of discrete essences or 'natural' identities."[39] In this instance, the competition between ways of reading emerges from two contexts: the cultural connotations of Washington's particular black masculinity that audiences will bring to their viewing of the film and the racial plausibility of *The Pelican Brief*'s narrative circumstances. An examination of key scenes from the film and their divergence from Grisham's novel suggests that what Pakula's *Pelican Brief* actually stages is the tacit failure of the racial pass onscreen.

Within Grisham's novel, Grantham's attraction to Darby Shaw is a constant refrain for readers, and Grisham allows the reciprocity of attraction to develop slowly over the course of the novel so that their pairing provides a satisfying resolution to the narrative. Within the film, though, this romantic element has all but disappeared.[40] Washington's Grantham is too focused on solving the mystery of the Pelican Brief, and Roberts's Shaw is too frightened and grief-stricken for there to be any discernible attraction between them. The absence of romance offers the site for the competing modes of reading Washington's race: he is black, and this is why a romantic relationship with Roberts's character would not offer a satisfying narrative element to the film, and at the same time, we can de-emphasize his black masculinity because it is not problematically juxtaposed with Roberts's white femininity in a romantic relationship. Eliminating the romantic plotline therefore produces the formal means through which the filmic text invites Washington to attempt his passing performance.

Washington's race is alluded to in only a few scenes, and these allusions are divided between verbal and visual modes of representation. At the beginning of the film, Washington's costume includes a sweatshirt from Howard University, a historically black school, marking him as part of a racialized community. In a later scene, Grantham is dressed in drab jeans and a hooded sweatshirt, and in the heat of an investigation, he tries to hail a cab. A driver slows down, approaching Grantham, only to leave him standing on the side of the road as an icon of frightening urban black masculinity.[41] The last time Washington-as-Grantham is explicitly racialized is when the character meets up with his boss to discuss his progress on the Pelican Brief article and to answer for his defiance of his (white) boss's work orders. Smith Keen, played by John Lithgow, says, "I've thought of dropping you into the ranks of the unemployed, but I know damn well you'd slap me with a discrimination suit."[42] Two of the three references to Washington-as-Grantham's race render it a problem, thereby producing the familiar understanding of blackness that Washington otherwise attempts to transcend throughout the film. Within the structure of racial disavowal I am suggesting, Keen's statement functions not only as a warning to Grantham but also as a form of assurance to the audience that the social problems commonly associated with blacks in white society will not attach themselves to Washington in this narrative, and should not be ascribed to his presence within the film.

Aside from these moments when blackness is problematized explicitly, *The Pelican Brief* invites audiences to sanction the film's color blindness, and at the same time renders that sanction impossible. Color blindness is exposed as largely a visual strategy that cannot work because of the inherent racialization of aesthetics. The triangular structure of passing privileges the visual dimensions of embodiment (rather than notions of racial essence predicated upon interiority), and this is what allows us to recognize the codes of performance that enable racial actors to produce their desired racial identity for the dupe's approval. Within *The Pelican Brief*, the mechanisms of hetero-racial performativity are largely visual rather than verbal. Pakula creates images that cannot help but invite audiences to expect conventional romantic encounters throughout the film, but Grantham, as coolly played by Washington, refuses these traditions in an effort to exist in a deracinated space. His Grantham cannot be white, because then he would be able to take advantage of the mise-en-scènes created to stage the sexual attraction between the characters, but he also cannot be black, because even the imputation of romantic possibility between the black Washington and the white Roberts would undermine the other narrative strains of the film by insisting upon the relevance of race and interracial social contact to the entire narrative.

Robinson's discussion of passing suggests that the recognition of performance mechanisms reflects a "shift from a politics of substance to a politics of optics,"[43] and this is what *The Pelican Brief* offers. Rather than any truth (substance) of Washington's racialized presence, the film instead capitalizes upon the disappearance of any narrative moments that would disrupt the transcendence toward which his performance aspires. In this way, the elimination of the novel's romantic storyline from the film offers "the false promise of the visual as an epistemological guarantee."[44] Because we don't see the consummation of sexual attraction between these two actors, their interracial specificity cannot matter to the narrative. However, the false promise of the visual is doubled in this case: the film exploits the visual codes of romance in order to suggest both the desirability and the illicitness of such an interracial pairing between the two lead characters. In some ways, the dialogue and plot offer the politics of substance (a platonic storyline) with which the politics of optics (conformity to the visual codes of cinematic romance) compete.

From the time that Darby Shaw's storyline physically intersects with that of Gray Grantham, a "politics of optics" subtly reinforces the dialectical relationship between white womanhood and black masculinity, even as the film's dialogue tries to create a color-blind space within which Washington's character may reside. In the initial scene between Darby and Grantham, our first glimpse of Julia Roberts is through a partially ajar door, with the protective chain stretched across Roberts's face, an image that subtly suggests Roberts's fundamental unavailability to Washington. Once Washington enters the hotel room, he maintains a distance from Roberts that supports the platonic, color-blind intentions of the text. However, these color-blind intentions only come through a significant divergence between Grisham's novel and Pakula's film. Grisham characterizes the first meeting between Grantham and Darby as one tinged with mutual desire. The brief chapter of their introduction alternates between references to each character's appraisal of the other. After Grantham notices Shaw's figure in her fitted jeans, Shaw

watched him carefully. He'd published a book six years earlier on HUD scandals, and though it didn't sell she'd found a copy in a public library in New Orleans. He looked six years older than the photo on the dust jacket, but he was aging nicely with a touch of gray over the ears.[45]

While Shaw's admiration is fairly benign, Grisham first paints Grantham as a giddy schoolboy, only to rescind the sexual tension and restore the narrative primacy of the mysterious Pelican Brief:

> He was looking at her. Trying to be cool, not like a gawking sophomore, but he was looking. The hair was dark and very short, and quite stylish, but he liked the long version in yesterday's fax. . . .
>
> Suddenly Grantham realized she was not just a hot little coed, but a widow in mourning. The poor lady was suffering. She had not been checking out his hair or his clothes or his eyes. She was in pain. Dammit![46]

In the filmed version of this scene, there is no suggestion of romantic attraction between the two characters. Instead, Washington is detachedly professional, while Roberts is both fragile and edgy. Camera angles in the scene seem delicately designed to protect the color blindness of this intimate space as it alternates between exploiting the cultural celebrity of the actors and supporting the narrative.[47] Washington is repeatedly shot in close-ups, giving the audience time to savor his good looks, and Roberts is shown in three-quarter body shots, keeping her a bit more distant from viewers. In this way, Washington's sexual appeal as a celebrity is exploited and differentiated from the demands of the character Grantham's placement in the narrative: the distance the camera places between Washington and Roberts enables the invocation of Washington's attractiveness at the same time that it underscores Roberts's elusive status. Her physical distance from viewers signifies her sexual distance from Washington.

The conclusion of this introductory scene elicits competing readings of the heterosexualized dynamics of Shaw's relationship with Grantham. As Grantham prepares to leave, Darby heads into the bedroom of her hotel suite. Before he can make it out of the room, though, Darby stands framed in the doorway of her bedroom and asks, "Mr. Grantham, I know it sounds silly, but would you mind sleeping on the sofa?"[48] The traditional romantic conclusion to a scene between two attractive adults (an invitation to stay the night, offered from the bedroom threshold) is transformed here into a protective gesture that subtly fixes a social distance between the two that will remain intact throughout the film. Washington's sexual signification is neutralized in this film by making him a protective figure to Roberts's vulnerable young white girl.[49] The optics of the scene prey upon audiences' in-group understanding of the visual codes of romance (and the sexualized celebrity of both Washington and Roberts), but the substance of the dialogue runs counter to this logic.

After summoning this sexualization of Grantham and Shaw via Washington and Roberts, the substance of the dialogue may then playfully hint at romance, knowing that previous dialogue will limit the signification of these later lines. After agreeing to stay in Darby's room for her protection, Grantham asks, "Listen . . . at the risk of sounding old-fashioned, don't you think it's time I knew your real name?" and Shaw obliges.[50] Washington is able to indulge in this chivalrous behavior that references the flirtatious dialogue of classic Hollywood romances because the sexual potential of his gestures has been erased. This becomes clear in the final lines of the scene, which restore the white patriarchal order that renders true romantic chemistry between Washington's and Roberts's characters impossible:

GRANTHAM: What made you pick me, Darby Shaw?

DARBY: (whispers) Callahan was a fan.[51]

With these lines the ghost of Callahan, Darby's slain, older (white) lover, himself a father figure of sorts, becomes a part of Darby's relationship with Grantham, a chaperoning figure that determines the nature of their relationship. For the rest of the film, however close Darby and Grantham become, it is always only in ways that do not supplant Thomas Callahan's symbolic sexual and authoritarian status. The invocation of Callahan provides an outlet for Darby Shaw's sexual signification, thereby allowing recognition of Roberts's heterosexual appeal within the narrative without making demands upon Washington's sexual signification. Washington may attempt to pass as raceless because the heterosexual dynamics that Grisham always intended to be a part of the story do not have to involve him.

The rest of the film builds on this play between the platonic substance of the plot and the potentially sexualizing optics of the cinematography. One especially titillating visual occurs after an intense scene in which Grantham and Shaw discover that their key source in the Pelican Brief investigation has been murdered. Whereas Shaw and Grantham have never shared bedroom space within the film (Grantham sleeps in the sitting area of Shaw's suite before resuming his separate accommodations), this scene finds them together in a small hotel room. The scene begins with a close-up of Julia Roberts in bed, in a tangle of covers. Viewing audiences will recognize this image of a woman in bed as a common representation of postcoital repose. However, the substance of the scene allows Washington's Grantham to disavow this interpretation when the camera pans out to reveal Washington, sitting fully dressed on the other side of the bed, with his back toward her, making arrangements with his boss to continue researching the story. His professionalism distances him from the sexual implications of the previous image of Roberts. In this competition of meaning, Washington's actorly substance trumps the camera's optics. After the phone call ends, the dialogue places even greater distance between the two characters as, out of concern for her safety, Washington gently declares, "I want you to leave." The line follows in the tradition of the "breakup scene," and although the visually cultivated intimacy of this encounter supports the imputation of romance, it receives no further support through the dialogue or the actors' performances.

In the film, Roberts refuses Grantham's offer of escape, and their platonic partnership resumes. The hotel scene in the novel is almost exactly the opposite:

> Gray paced along the bed, holding the phone and waiting for Smith Keen. Darby was stretched out on the bed with her eyes closed.
>
> . . . He enjoyed this brief moment of uninterrupted staring without getting caught.
>
> "Are you staring at me?" she asked.
>
> "Yes."
>
> "Sex is the last thing on my mind."
>
> "Then why'd you mention it?"
>
> "Because I can feel you lusting after my red toenails."
>
> "True."[52]

The persistent sexualization of both Grantham and Shaw in this passage is incompatible with the color-blind politics to which the film must subscribe if Denzel Washington's pass out of Hollywood's brand of black masculinity is to succeed. Giving this dialogue to Washington and Roberts would destroy Washington's racial neutrality. The image of a Grantham as a black man lusting after a white woman's red toenails would invite problematic readings of black men's insatiable desire for white female flesh. His gaze would be rendered predatory, and just as D. W. Griffith equated blacks' allegedly color-blind, post-Reconstruction status in *The Birth of a Nation* with opportunities for "Equal Marriage," including this scene in the film would confirm Washington's association with definitions of black masculinity that the film is determined to ignore.

In scene after scene, the film fights its inability to overlook the sexual signification of both Washington and Roberts, its inability to be duped into completely tolerating Washington's deracination. His and Roberts's bodies and language engage in a discordant dance of double meaning, as they both suggest and occlude the romance that the novel initially scripted. Their final scene together provides perhaps the clearest example of this process. Darby Shaw's sentimental escape is filmed like a classically tragic romantic farewell between Washington and Roberts. On the airplane, Roberts wraps herself around Washington's arm as she sleeps; Washington, in turn, looks at her protectively. As in the hotel scene at the beginning of the film, Washington's response to Roberts ensures that protection is not mistaken for attraction, that his agency as a performer will not be overridden by the optical imperative to sexualize Grantham's relationship with Shaw. The contest of meanings continues when Washington and Roberts stand on the tarmac looking at the material consummation of their characters' relationship, the newspaper article about the Pelican Brief conspiracy with both of their names on the byline. Instead of a mixed-race child destined to become a tragic mulatto, the newspaper article allows their platonic relationship to produce something outside of the reproductive economy of heterosexual race relations, and therefore the film maintains its color-blind intentions. This professional focus is necessary to neutralize the romantic connotations of Roberts's departure: as the lush musical score swells, Roberts kisses Washington lightly on the cheek and walks away, head down, before turning and running back to him for a fierce embrace. Those of us who have seen enough Hollywood romances recognize that this should be the moment when the characters enjoy one last kiss before a heartbreaking separation, or when they decide to challenge the odds and pursue love despite difficult circumstances. Instead, Washington offers a restrained performance that helps to rescue the meaning of the scene from the realm of the romantic: deeply affected by their farewell but attempting stoicism, Grantham stands clenching his throat to keep from crying at her departure as Shaw disappears to an unknown locale.

Washington's vulnerability and isolation in this moment undo the heterosexualization of the scene by inverting the gender roles typical of such an encounter. Rather than the man marching bravely into the unknown, leaving an emotional woman behind, this scene allows the white woman to leave. The black man stands alone, his emotional reserve failing him, and the image serves two purposes: it finalizes the distance that makes sexual contact between Washington and Roberts ultimately impossible, and it undoes a hypermasculine signification that is tied to blackness, demonstrating, as Philip Brian Harper suggests, that passing narratives never grant black men full access to masculinity.[53] Strictly within the representational strategies of the film, this conclusion affirms the failure of Washington's attempted racial pass. On the optic and substantive levels, spectators familiar with Hollywood romance as a genre, the intertext of Grisham's novel, and the cultural codes of race and sexuality recognize the limits Washington and the filmic text place upon one another: Washington's Grantham will not be sexualized because to do so would invite a reading of the film within the history of representations of interracial heterosexuality (a proof that his race does in fact affect the narrative), and the film will not succumb entirely to the desexualization of narrative upon which Washington's color-blind status seems to be predicated.

My reading thus far has emphasized how the triangulated structure of passing allows us to investigate the ways in which the film attempts to coerce both a romantic and a platonically color-blind performance from Denzel Washington. This positions spectators to understand Hollywood's romantic tropes well enough to recognize their deployment and also to recognize why they can only be alluded to, rather than realized fully within the color-blind politics to which the film attempts to adhere. However, the filmmakers' desire to use Denzel Washington in a color-blind narrative in spite of John Grisham's alleged objections explains only some of how race structures the relationships between optics and substance, between passer, dupe, and clairvoyant within the film. After he was cast, Washington himself vetoed the romantic storyline between his character and Roberts, for reasons connected to the history of blacks' presence in Hollywood film as well as for reasons very explicit in contemporary racial discourse. *The Pelican Brief* was released between the Willie Horton era and the O. J. Simpson era, both of which featured black men who were accused of using literal and figurative social mobility to place white America (especially white women) in grave physical danger.[54] Washington's refusal to perform the (now interracial) romance called for in Grisham's original story can therefore be read as a refusal to help popular culture further fetishize or demonize black men and interracial sexual contact. Washington himself claims that his editorial decision was a principled one:

> Washington says there were several reasons the interracial love scenes were deleted, and one was indeed the fear of offending some moviegoers—and the viewers he worried about crossing were black women. Washington learned full well the danger of stepping over that line during test screenings of 1989's "The Mighty Quinn," where an onscreen kiss with Mimi Rogers drew loud boos from the audience. Washington had the studio delete the kiss, and decided that he wouldn't be doing many love scenes in films at all, particularly since Hollywood seemed to show no interest in black love stories. "Black women are not often seen as objects of desire on film. They have always been my core audience," he says.[55]

This information makes clear that Washington understands the significance of both his own filmic genealogy and his relationship to broader antecedents like *The Birth of a Nation*. Recruiting his sexuality into the script's narrative—rather than just into its tantalizing optics—would foreground Washington's race and his racialized responsibility to multiple audiences.

By voluntarily perpetuating the prohibitions on representing interracial sexuality, Washington himself complicates readings of the racial power play at work in the making of *The Pelican Brief*. Not only the attempted passer within the narrative and the production of the film, on the cultural level, Washington also becomes an in-group clairvoyant, keenly aware of the mechanisms of racial accountability that will structure reception of his performance. Publicizing the reasons for his refusal to perform the romantic subplot allows Washington to transgress the history of heterosexualized interracial performance. From this perspective, elimination of the romantic subplot is in fact a transgressive engagement with black masculinity in performance, rather than just a transcendent disavowal. Washington's refusal grants him some control over how his body signifies within Hollywood's representational economy. It becomes an attempt to undo the sexual pedestalization of white womanhood and to invite black women into a more prominent position within mass culture—as spectators whose practices of looking are normalized even if their performance presence remains undervalued. However, the racial and gendered dynamics of Hollywood film do not completely succumb to Washington's desires. Pakula's directorial choices counter and threaten to overwhelm Washington's choices as an actor to portray Grantham as staid, professional, and impeccably platonic. Pakula uses formal techniques to coyly reassert the film's romantic valences and thereby restores the legibility of white womanhood upon which Julia Roberts's pedestalized character relies. When taken together, Grisham's alleged objections to Washington in the leading man role, Washington's objections to the romantic plot, and Alan Pakula's unwillingness to forgo this romantic plot—which leads him to stage its failure—all implicitly agree upon the problematic presence of the black man cast against racial type in heterosexualized Hollywood narratives.

Asserting Denzel Washington as a transgressive rather than transcendent force within this film is unquestionably complicated, since efforts to transgress against social rules may not always occur within theatrically or cinematically enframed representations. Instead, they sometimes function extradiegetically, where their force can be harder to recognize. In the mid-1990s, popular entertainment still affirmed a diegetic hierarchy in which films came first and everything extra was indeed extra (if not sequentially, then in order of importance). Reading the broader social implications of this film by synthesizing Washington's performance as Gray Grantham and the performative effects of his practice of everyday life is far easier from the vantage point of the twenty-first century, in which the extradiegetic almost threatens the irrelevance of "pure" entertainment narratives. Nevertheless, discussing *The Pelican Brief* as a failed attempt at color-blind adaptation and filmmaking allows us to understand the concertedly historicized, raced, and gendered mechanisms through which racial transgression modifies the location of blackness in the public sphere.

"'TOO BAD WE WON'T HAVE A CHANCE TO GET TO KNOW EACH OTHER, EASY'"

If *The Pelican Brief* demonstrated the impossibility of locating a color-blind performance within a film beholden to heteronormalized genre conceits, *Devil in a Blue Dress*—another cinematic adaptation of a novel—demonstrates the impossibility of using color-blind strategies to convert a black film into a film that happens to be black. Despite many efforts, director Carl Franklin could not recruit Denzel Washington's crossover success to diminish the racialized import of the world Walter Mosley created in his novel. Published in 1993, *Devil in a Blue Dress* introduced readers to Ezekiel "Easy" Rawlins, an army veteran turned private detective in post–World War II Los Angeles. Mosley situates Rawlins firmly within the black community, using the first in his series of Rawlins mysteries to delineate the racial tensions that characterized life for the city's black residents. In *Devil*, Rawlins receives his first investigative commission by accident: knowing Rawlins is in need of cash after losing his job, his bartender friend connects him with a white man who is trying to find a missing white woman who frequents the black side of town. The hunt for Daphne Monet allows and requires Rawlins to transgress the color and class lines of mid-twentieth-century Los Angeles, employing what film critic Ed Guerrero calls a "double consciousness [that] facilitates double vision. Easy can see deeply into both the black and white worlds and find out not only what powerful whites want to know, but also what they don't want to know, or at least what they want to deny and hide."[56]

Exploring the heterosexualized complications of attempted color blindness is perhaps more intricate in *Devil in a Blue Dress* than in *The Pelican Brief*. In the latter, a white director worked to make the only major character played by an African American a color-blind part of his political thriller, representing the cultivation and negation of a romantic narrative in implicitly racialized though explicitly disavowed ways. By contrast, *Devil* features a black director working with a largely black cast to prevent the film from being overwhelmed by its black sociocultural milieu. All at once, Franklin explicitly depicts the role of race in the sexual infrastructure of 1940s (and 1990s) Los Angeles, the limitations of retroactive color blindness, and the uneasy appeal of narratives of racial melodrama. Additionally, the interracial relationships that disallow color-blind reception of *Devil* are multiply dispersed throughout the narrative, rather than consolidated around Denzel Washington and his crossover success alone. His character participates in only two of the three interracial relationships that Franklin must manage. One places Easy opposite a somewhat anonymous young white woman in a public space; the other pairs him with Daphne Monet in private spaces. The third interracial relationship features Daphne Monet with her white fiancé Todd Carter as they wrestle with whether or not to take public a relationship that would challenge the sociosexual segregation of their time. Because Mosley situates *Devil in a Blue Dress* in the summer before the California Supreme Court's 1948 decision in *Perez v. Sharp* that overturned statutes banning interracial marriage in the state, characters within the novel and film are tempting the law when they act upon attraction across the color line. They are also acting at a time when lynchings of African Americans—particularly men—continued to function as a spectacular corrective tool throughout the United States, often employed to punish fabricated violations of the sexual color line in order to preserve the assumption of difference between the black and white communities.

To the extent that this was the sociopolitical climate within which Walter Mosley situated Easy Rawlins, this story of "a man becoming cynical,"[57] as film director Carl Franklin described it, is also a narrative of the crisis of white American heteronormative domesticity. Romance throughout the world of both Mosley's novel and Franklin's film serves to illuminate the imperfection of the white family as a locus of racial security. Easy's job is to find the elusive Daphne Monet, whose departure has stymied the romantic culmination of her relationship with prominent Angeleno Todd Carter. Monet vanishes because Carter's political rival, mayoral candidate Matthew Terrell, has discovered that she is a mixed-race woman passing for white, and threatens to reveal this information in order to shame Carter into abandoning his campaign. Carter's relationship with Monet is supposed to render him unsuitable for the office of mayor and the authority to protect racial order that comes along with it. However, Matthew Terrell is an ironic instrument of white patriarchal law: as

Daphne Monet learns through a retaliatory investigation, Terrell is a pedophile, having most recently adopted a "son" from Mexico. Terrell's adoption and sexual crimes violate not just general standards of morality and the incest taboo, but also the racially pure dictates of white family embedded in the California Civil Code, revealing that the white American family is often less white (and less American) than idealized representations purport it to be.[58] Such familial inconsistencies reflect what Richard Dyer refers to as the "terror of white reproductive inadequacy."[59]

Although legal scholar Rachel Moran characterizes *Perez v. Sharp* as a symbolic end to the prohibition of marriages that were already tolerated in a de facto sense in Los Angeles,[60] nearly forty years later, the violent deaths of Nicole Brown Simpson and her friend Ron Goldman placed the supposed danger inherent to interracial sexuality back in the forefront of public consciousness in mid-1990s Los Angeles and across America. Football star O. J. Simpson, Nicole Simpson's ex-husband and the prime suspect in the murders, was consistently reinscripted within an understanding of black masculinity that relied upon stereotypes of lawlessness and brute physicality after a lengthy celebrity career as athlete-turned-actor and product pitchman predicated on his transcendence of race. From the notorious June 27, 1994, cover of *Time* magazine that featured a darkened "photo illustration" of his mug shot[61] to the strategic demographics of both the prosecution and the defense teams in the criminal trial, black performativity was everywhere present in the life of a black man who, according to Ralph Wiley, "tried and almost succeeded at being everything *but* a black guy."[62]

Simpson's temporary and partial success at transcending race (and the associated weight placed upon his masculinity) served as an alternative to the racial melodrama that, according to Linda Williams, structures so much of our culture's public discourse about race. Traditionally, she asserts, the melodramatic mode provides moral intelligibility to its audiences, and within the sphere of race, deploys the "paradoxical location of strength in weakness" to produce moral revenge for those who have suffered wrongly at the hands of the powerful.[63] Simpson's rise to crossover success did not conform to the melodramatic narrative mode, as popular attention focused not on his weakness but on his skill, attractiveness, and charm. Instead, Simpson served as an emblem of the material rewards American society had to offer to any and all of its citizens, regardless of race. When charged with murder, though, Simpson became the star of a melodrama that robbed him of his racially transcendent status and placed him quite clearly in the role of villain: the slain white womanhood of Nicole Brown Simpson—and by association, of all (white) women who suffered violence at the hands of (black) men—held the moral authority, and Simpson's race and gender became integral to his status as the evildoer within the narrative of the crime.[64]

Tracing Simpson's transition from color-blind celebrity to national infamy, Williams writes,

> Simpson's athletic and social success, his historic crossing of the color line to sell products to white and black audiences alike, his possession of a Brentwood mansion where African Americans had once been barred, his possession of a white wife where miscegenation had once been a crime, made him seem race-neutral. . . . But because "color blindness" was never an accomplished fact, Simpson's race now emerged as an inchoate but morally significant fact. . . . Race became legible as a mute melodramatic sign.[65]

Simpson's new—or resumed—racial legibility demanded a rereading of various elements of his life. His marriage to Nicole Brown, "once-glamorous, now demonized," was suddenly interpreted through the "black beast" scenario that emphasized her weakness and suffering in the face of his physical, monetary, and social power.[66] The speed with which Simpson's racial signification changed demonstrates the fragility of color blindness, the complicity it demands of one's social environment, and also "the gaps between the color-blind ideology and the dynamics of racial power."[67] In his trial and the media attention surrounding it, Simpson's power was emphasized in order to endow him with something that could be taken away in a proper ending to the melodramatic tale of his downfall and return to a degraded black masculinity, with all of its criminal and disempowered connotations.

While the Simpson trial performed retroactive color consciousness to cast him as the black villain necessary to the exercise of interracial strife (and from another perspective as the black victim of intrinsically racist law enforcement and judicial systems), Carl Franklin's direction of *Devil in a Blue Dress* employs an opposite temporal strategy to limit the racial politics that may be attached to the black characters within the film. In Franklin's hands, color blindness is a strategy of control, preventing potentially troubling definitions of race from structuring the meaning of his actors' performances. Although the film is obviously about racialized relationships, Franklin attempts to contain its representations of blackness within their historical context by refusing to allow contemporary racialized practices of spectatorship to distort the meaning of his work. Manipulation of racialized sexuality is his most potent tool in this effort.

Franklin controls the signification of black sexuality within the film by making significant adjustments to Mosley's original text, choices that seem designed to neutralize the offense contemporary audiences will take at the ways race and heterosexuality intersect.

The first of the film's three interracial relationships, which takes place on a pier in Malibu, stages what Dyer describes as whites' fear of reproductive inadequacy by paying attention to the racialization of space in 1940s Los Angeles. While waiting to meet DeWitt Albright, his boss for this detective assignment, Easy is pulled unwillingly into a conversation with a young white woman at the Malibu pier. Just as Alan Pakula's *The Pelican Brief* employed visual codes to register the unspoken dynamics of Grantham's relationship with Darby, Washington's physical choices in this scene demonstrate the tremendous social divide between black men and white women of the period in public. Washington makes Easy both polite and wary, remaining vigilant throughout the conversation, lest some white male onlooker misconstrue the situation. He uses rigid posture, terse language, and virtually no eye contact to register both physical and social distance from his scene partner. Nevertheless, when the character Barbara's friends race down the pier in a panic to rescue her from Easy's company, they immediately racialize the situation, saying, "This nigger's trying to pick up on Barbara."[68] With this sentence, Easy becomes an inferior "nigger" subject to the young men's power, and Barbara is symbolically elevated as a social cause yet erased as a source of knowledge: her protestations that Easy is not dangerous carry no weight.

As the young white men prepare to attack, DeWitt Albright appears, brandishing a pistol, and corners one youth while the others flee. Suddenly the power struggle shifts from one between a black man and white men over a white woman to one between white men over a black man. Albright forces the young man to his knees and orders him to perform fellatio upon Easy to show his remorse for threatening him. Just before the young man can comply, Albright calls him a "sick fuck," beats him on the head with a gun, and tells him to leave. The homosexual threat Albright employs here challenges the masculine power of each character, including Albright: in the symbolic realm of racial and sexual violence as negotiations of power, Albright loses some aspect of his heterosexist white male prerogative whether he affiliates himself racially with the white man forced into fellating a black man, or heterosexually with the black man, who is forced to expose himself in order for the white man's punishment to take place. As long as the punishment is imagined rather than enacted, Albright retains control over the situation, making both the young man and Easy susceptible to his power, which is all the more meaningful for not having to be fully exercised. Franklin's film, while unavoidably racialized, shifts the site of sexual alterity from black men to white men, while placing the taboo of homosexuality rather than crisis of the white woman's virtue at the center of the conflict. This decision makes it difficult for contemporary audiences to read 1990s valuations of black masculinity onto the narrative circumstances of Easy Rawlins.

While the tension in the pier scene largely pertains to racial and sexual anxiety, Carl Franklin describes it instead as being about "yet another fear for the character whose central premise in a lot of ways is overcoming fear. This particular fear is fear of what he might become, and it comes from his background in the war."[69] Additionally, Franklin (as the writer of the screenplay) chose to deviate from the novel's dialogue in subtle ways that attempt to diffuse the role of race in the conflict. In Mosley's version, the white men punctuate their arrival with the words, " 'Hey, black boy!' . . . 'We don't need ya talking to our women.' "[70] Though Easy is outwardly respectful in order to keep the situation calm, internally he rails against the racist condescension of these teenagers who call him a boy, "thinking to [him]self, Why the hell do I have to answer to you?"[71] Franklin is understandably concerned that such resistance (even when only expressed internally) to the racialized power dynamics of the encounter might overdetermine the scene's meaning for audiences steeped in the social and historical context of 1990s America.

Mosley's Albright is even more aggressive in taunting the boys and playing on their sexual anxieties. Holding the authority in the scene because he has a weapon, he says, " '[Easy's] a friend of mine.' . . . 'And I'd be proud and happy if he was to lower himself to fuck my sister *and* my mother.' "[72] With this assertion, Albright acknowledges and challenges the racial and sexual exclusivity upon which white male privilege is predicated and which black male sexuality allegedly jeopardizes. Claiming friendship with Easy rather than loathing him, and presuming Easy's social superiority to his own white female relatives, Albright's words temporarily disrupt the logic of white supremacy. By avoiding these explicit references to race and sexual terror within his film, Franklin forfeits an opportunity to highlight the role that paternalistic anxieties played in maintaining racial divisions during the time depicted in Mosley's novel.

While Franklin's adaptation drastically reduces the importance of white women to the power struggle on the pier, the social responsibilities and codes of white womanhood are central to the film's other two interracial pairings. Within the film, missing person Daphne Monet personifies one of the most recognizable conceits of the film noir genre: the femme fatale. Beautiful and dangerous, the femme fatale embodied the threat of emasculation in an industrial age, with filmmakers of the period creating villainous female characters as repositories of masculine terror.[73] Both in spite of and even because of her racial ambiguity, Daphne Monet is an icon of this type of lethal femininity that jeopardizes the (white) social order. Jennifer Beals, an actress best known at the time of *Devil*'s debut for having starred in the 1983 film *Flashdance*, took on the role of Daphne Monet. Beals is herself a mixed race woman, an identity that has attracted anxious curiosity over the years about the burdens of representation that could and could not fairly be attached to her performances. In most of her roles, spanning film and television over the past two decades, Beals's characters seem not to be drawing upon the specific histories of African Americans, but are instead racially marked as neutral. Nevertheless, Beals has been marked as a black woman by the press since the beginning of her career, from her nomination and subsequent win of the NAACP Image Award for her role in *Flashdance* to interview materials noting her parentage in order to explain her dark beauty.[74] The conceits of noir and Mosley's novel may both have provided opportunities for Beals to offer an intersectional performance that challenged the coherence of racial and gender categories, but instead Franklin's film turns her into a tragic figure in a racial melodrama that reaffirms the rigidity of racially separatist ideology.

Much like *The Pelican Brief*, *Devil in a Blue Dress* cultivates in its audiences a scopic desire for white womanhood. Just as the first scene between Julia Roberts and Denzel Washington in Alan Pakula's film offers a visual and narrative payoff in placing the two in the same physical environment, the mystery of Franklin's film also objectifies the character Daphne Monet, and the explicitly transgressive nature of Rawlins's first encounter with Monet derives from each character's racial identity. Like Gray Grantham and Darby Shaw, Easy Rawlins and Daphne Monet meet in her hotel room, to which she has summoned him. Daphne Monet (who in the novel invites Easy to her house, a more intimate space, for their introductory conversation) is staying in the white section of a segregated hotel, and therefore Easy has to be smuggled into her room by a colluding white bellhop. The rules governing the physical space of the hotel assign both Easy and Daphne to their racial categories and demand certain behavioral protocols. The matter-of-fact way in which the bellhop ushers Easy into Daphne's room reveals the role white men play as gatekeepers of access to white female sexuality, forbidding public interracial intimacy but also having the ability to broker private, illicit liaisons between white women and black men.[75]

Once Easy enters the hotel room, the conversation between the two bubbles with innuendo that demonstrates the pleasure Daphne takes in her raced and gendered power to make Easy uncomfortable. For example, when the conversation turns to murderers' weapons of choice, Easy asks her, "And what do you prefer to use as your weapon?" to which she replies, "Why don't you search me and find out?" The double entendre of this response includes both an aggressive offer of sexual availability and a threat: Easy has no authority to interrogate her, and she could at any time accuse him of the inappropriate behavior that she has just suggested that he undertake. In the semiprivate space of the hotel, where Daphne has asked him to "come over and explain [himself] to [her]," Easy is both more comfortable with and more vulnerable to white womanhood. The racial codes governing the space of the segregated hotel simultaneously matter and cease to matter when the two characters are beyond the purview of a social panopticon that is figured as white, heterosexual, and male. Daphne's performance of white womanhood consistently invokes and transgresses the de facto laws limiting the ways that black men and white women are supposed to relate to one another. Alan Pakula's *The Pelican Brief* attempted to transcend race by desexualizing the narrative so that attributes other than Washington's blackness and sexual desirability could propel the plot, but Franklin's *Devil in a Blue Dress* cannot help but contend simultaneously with the sexualization and racialization of its characters.

In Mosley's novel, Daphne taunts Easy with sexual commentary and behavior. Their first meeting begins in Daphne's house but leads them to a home where they discover a dead body. In this charged environment, she kisses him aggressively and says, "Too bad we won't have the chance to get to know each other, Easy. Otherwise I'd let you eat this little white girl up."[76] Her comment creates desire and danger as two sides of the same coin, the currency that purchases black-white (sexual) interaction. This dialectic forms the substance of Easy's relationship with Daphne in the novel, but in Carl Franklin's film the specter of desire is raised only when Daphne attempts to manipulate Easy. The hotel scene relies upon Daphne's willingness to flout convention in order to flaunt her sexuality to Easy, but this is not done out of desire: as played by Jennifer Beals, sexual attraction is but one in a range of emotional tactics Daphne pursues, hoping to find the one that will induce Easy to divulge the information she needs.

The rest of Franklin's *Devil in a Blue Dress* refuses to foster any desire in its audience for romantic consummation between Easy and Daphne. However, Washington does perform a sex scene with a black female character, allowing the film to make use of Washington's sexuality and to locate him specifically within the black community without the desire to transgress its boundaries or sexual codes. Unlike *The Pelican Brief,* which used cinematography to belie the platonic nature of the dialogue and narrative circumstances, *Devil in a Blue Dress* uses chiaroscuro to willfully obfuscate that which would otherwise foster libidinal viewing. The sexual banter between Washington and Beals has its place at the beginning of the movie, but quickly disappears, replaced instead with Easy's fear and virtue. This shift away from Easy and Daphne as potential romantic partners in spite of their (supposed) racial difference symbolizes Franklin's move into a form of racial melodrama that employs a logic of moral intelligibility to codify race relations within the film. Easy becomes a representative of the underclass who attempts to triumph over those more powerful than he, and unsanctioned sexual activity would compromise the clarity of his ethical position within the film.

Nevertheless, Daphne attempts to kiss Easy later in the film because sexual access to Easy means physical access to the incriminating photos she wants to retrieve from him. Easy sees through her feigned attraction to him and stops the kiss, retaining ownership of the valuable photos as well as his moral authority. As the only explicit sexual gesture between Easy and Daphne, the manipulative kiss almost casts interracial sexuality as a desperate act, but is neutralized immediately by Daphne's confession that the black liquor dealer whom Easy seeks is her half-brother. Her exposed racial identity rationalizes this reckless act, and the transgression is contained, if not revised. Thus the film ironically stages the suppression of the original narrative of Mosley's novel in order to reify in 1990s America the color line that Mosley allowed Easy and Daphne to subvert in his 1940s setting.

In his director's commentary, Franklin explains why the physical relationship between Easy and Daphne was eliminated from the film:

> Originally there was a romantic connection between Easy and Daphne and it actually even started to play in [the hotel] scene in the book . . . but because we had shifted the focus of the film from an objective perspective to a subjective perspective, telling it through the eyes of our character Easy Rawlins, it was important for us to keep it subjective so that we discover the mystery through his eyes, and also, because in the book she had already made the determination to leave Carter, we decided that it was important that she have a problem that she's working out throughout the film, and . . . what she was trying to do was get some information that would allow her boyfriend Todd Carter to be able to go into the mayor's race . . . and if we had had a romantic connection between the

two then it would have invalidated that relationship and it would have totally destroyed her character.[77]

Offering clear evidence of his wish for moral intelligibility, Franklin chooses to avoid the ambiguity of having Daphne's socially white character consummate an attraction to Easy while still in love with Todd Carter. Franklin relies upon nonracial attributes to describe his strategy for protecting her virtue, emphasizing infidelity rather than interracial sex taboos as the lapse to be avoided.

Even so, the demands of white female performativity structure this moral system. Beals as Daphne can only succeed in her racial pass (Beals must make us suspend our memory of her racialized public biography lest she give away the plot simply by being cast) if she adopts the chaste disposition of white femininity. Perhaps even more so than Denzel Washington, Jennifer Beals's performing body, in all of its phenotypic ambiguity, must avoid certain narrative and visual environments in order for the supposed truth of her racial identity not to impede this film that aspires to avoid 1990s racial politics.[78] Taunting Denzel Washington but ever succumbing to the vulnerability of mutual desire, Beals as Monet must enact the constant disavowal of erotic (rather than strategic sexual) contact with Denzel Washington. Anecdotally, the excision of the romance may help both Beals and Washington to cross over into different performance territory, but it also apparently hoped to help the film's national appeal. According to the *New York Times*, Walter Mosley "was told that a dark-skinned Washington could not kiss the lighter-skinned lead, Jennifer Beals, 'for fear we're going to lose Alabama.'"[79] This concern shifts the stakes of moral responsibility from the narrative of the piece to the way it will circulate, explicitly naming the raced, sexed constraints upon the national imaginary.

If we account for the performative problematic that Beals as a mixed-race actress introduces to this representational effort (even if we discount the Alabama concession as hearsay that should not displace the authority of Franklin's commentary), Franklin's limited and limiting narrative rationale is strategic at best: Easy is the first-person narrator of Mosley's novel, so it, too, unfolded through his eyes and according to his timetable, and his grappling with the codes of racialized romance forms an important part of his relationship with Daphne, structuring his involvement in the plot. If, as Franklin elsewhere suggests, the story is a mystery that allows us to see the transformation of a man, then a relationship between Easy and Daphne would certainly have aided the representation of that trajectory. One of the things that makes Easy cynical by the end of Mosley's novel is the fact that Daphne holds such power over him, making him want to flout the cultural (even legal) codes of the time, and denying him the ability to do so. After their sexual encounter, Mosley's Easy says, "We don't have to listen to them. If we love each other then we can be together. Ain't no one can stop that,"[80] but Daphne refuses. Her refusal denies Easy the opportunity for further racial transgression, proving that racial identity is produced at the complex intersection between self-determination and external, interactive regulation.

Shortly after this appeal in the novel, Mosley reveals that Daphne is a biracial woman passing for white, providing the rationale for her refusal to continue a relationship with Easy: her racial status as white is precarious within the cultural and political climate of the day. The tactics necessary to maintain Daphne's performance of whiteness leave no room for obviously transgressive sexuality.[81] If, to return to Dyer, interracial sex threatens the process of "categorizing different types of human bodies which reproduce themselves," Daphne's biracial body is the incarnation of this ontological crisis, and a relationship with Easy undermines the validity of the racial distinctions that she reifies through her passing performance. Whereas Mosley used Daphne as a pivotal character to expose the construction of race through heterosexuality in her relationships with both Easy and Todd Carter, Franklin's film instead offers a retributive version of interracial sexuality that repeats the narrative of the tragic mulatto, sentenced to death because of the black blood that precludes any desirable romantic (and implicitly socioeconomic) outcomes.

Before the conclusion of Franklin's film, Daphne's relationship with Todd Carter is the only—albeit temporarily—successful interracial relationship, though it is never depicted onscreen, but rather taken as a fact that enables the filmed narrative in which its success is in jeopardy. If Easy's encounter with Barbara at the pier reveals the homoerotic panic underpinning white disapproval of sexual relationships between black men and white women, and if Easy's (lack of) relationship with Daphne stages sexual volition as a cornerstone of racial identity, then the ostensibly endogamous relationship between Todd Carter and Daphne Monet reveals, through its dissolution, the impossibility of domestic and therefore romantic color blindness by framing the heterosexual nuclear family as an inherently raced institution. Choosing to depict Todd and Daphne together only after she has been exposed as a black woman reinforces this perspective on the film. The success of interracial romance cannot be represented, even in a film that attempts to be retroactively color-blind, while the impossibility of such a romance is hypervisible within the moral groundwork Franklin employs throughout the film.

Unlike the sexually color-blind (i.e., platonic) interracial farewell scene between Julia Roberts and Denzel Washington in *The Pelican Brief*, *Devil in a Blue
Dress* stages its most race-conscious scene in the farewell between Todd and
Daphne. If Daphne's charade can be read as an attempt to cultivate color blindness in her future husband and his family—a color blindness that emphasizes
her individual performance above the connotative power of her genealogical
blackness—then the farewell scene at the end of the film offers us the social and
political reality of race as proof of her color-blind agenda's futility. Viewed from
a distance, so that only snatches of the conversation are heard, the scene plays
as the exact opposite of *The Pelican Brief:* where Darby and Grantham are com-
posed yet deeply emotional, Daphne and Todd are passionate and unruly. The
forced insertion of blackness into a white, normative narrative begets behaviors
that stress the antagonisms of interracial sociality, much less sexuality. Easy witnesses the entire scene from afar, including the dissolution of Daphne's naïveté.
Washington's performance in this scene rewrites with difference the secrets that
a triangulated relationship between a white man, black man, and passing-for-
white woman must contain. Instead of the bellhop who literally opens doors
that help to formalize the success of Beals's and Daphne's racial pass, Washington becomes the figure that ushers Beals as Daphne out of whiteness, physically
marking the location to which Daphne must return after being excommuni-
cated from white society. The film posits interracial sexual contact as the act of
transgression that the narrative cannot accommodate. In avoiding the actively
transgressive elements of Walter Mosley's original narrative, Franklin's efforts
at selective color blindness end up displaying a 1990s obedience to the logic of
the color line that mirrors that of his characters set in 1948.

The farewell scene ends with an image of the woman in tears, not half of a
tragic romance, but a lonely, tragic mulatta, whose black blood stymies her opportunities to find love and sends her into despair. Daphne's final act as a white
woman is to return to the back seat of Easy's car, assuming what was previously
a position of raced, classed, and gendered privilege. With the vulnerability of
her racial performance exposed, Daphne cries as she is transported literally and
figuratively out of white Los Angeles and deposited at the home of her brother
Frank in the black part of town. In effect, Daphne Monet ceases to exist, and her
creator, Ruby Hanks, is remanded to her rightful place in a segregated society.
Furthermore, the film concludes with the final discursive punishment of
Ruby/Daphne: when Easy returns to her home a week later to return her
money, she and her brother have disappeared, most likely to reinvent themselves in another town. This departure suggests that there is literally no place

for those who attempt and fail at transgressive performances of race within an environment structured around principles of racial conservatism.

According to Linda Williams, "Melodrama focuses on victim-heroes and on recognizing their virtue. Recognition of their virtue orchestrates the moral legibility that is key to melodrama's function."[82] The conclusion of Franklin's film allows both Easy and Daphne to emerge as victim-heroes in the racial melodrama the director has shaped. The immorality of racism is condemned through Easy's moral rectitude and the pathos of Daphne's heartbreak. After enduring several harrowing experiences, Easy's victory comes in part through the financial security that drove him to accept the detective job at the beginning of the film. While he was repeatedly victimized along the way to solving the mystery, he ends the film secure in his home ownership and contemplating an entrepreneurial move that would keep him in business for himself as a private investigator. Daphne's victim-hero status is more ironic: after attempting to exploit the racism of American society to her advantage, she is victimized when her charade is exposed and brought to an end. Her victory comes through the salvation of her virtue, earned through her refusal to accept anything other than a legitimate relationship with Todd Carter.

Mosley's novel, on the other hand, squarely refuses Daphne the legibility of a victim-heroine: she leaves Los Angeles on her own terms, choosing to give up her relationship with Todd and accept a cash payment to finance a new life elsewhere, but she does so with the veneer of white female privilege intact. At the same time that Mosley concedes the racial divisions that govern life in American society, he also reveals their artifice through a character who understands the fictions well enough to perpetrate some of her own. Immediately after sharing an intimate experience with Easy in private quarters, Daphne resumes her performance of a distant whiteness in public, threatening to scream if Easy touches her and insisting upon the public negation of their private relationship: when the cabbie arrives, "She ask[s the cabbie] to carry her bag. She put[s] her hand on his arm to thank him but she [won't] even shake [Easy's] hand goodbye."[83] This erasure of their private encounter marks Daphne's encounter with Easy as transgressive rather than transcendent, rooted in a willful disobedience to, rather than an ignorance of, racialized codes of sexual behavior. Furthermore, her ability to move so quickly between the two without any apparent ambivalence or guilt is essential to the difference between Mosley's novel and Franklin's film: the latter is a racial melodrama, the former challenges racial melodrama by refusing to assign moral clarity to the constantly shifting logic of this inherently immoral racial system. To moralize the American system of race would be to place credence in it, and Mosley refuses American racial constructs this power, choosing instead to challenge them through a rejection of the narrative mode that irrationally structures national discourse.

The Rawlins books were meant to spawn a series of films of which *Devil in a Blue Dress* would only be the first. However, poor box office performance put an end to talk of any further installments.[84] According to Ed Guerrero,

> When one considers the role of race in the film's demise, what happened offscreen is not much of a mystery at all. *Devil in a Blue Dress*, like *Strange Days* [a sci-fi thriller starring Ralph Fiennes and Angela Bassett], had the great misfortune to be released at the moment of the O.J. verdict, and that was the kiss of death at the box office. The film did not cross over. Racial divisions and tensions throughout the country were running as high as they have ever run, and angry, post-O.J.-trial whites were in no mood for L.A.'s black world, 1948 or otherwise.[85]

After the public dismantling of O. J. Simpson as a color-blind hero, even Denzel Washington's crossover appeal could not draw in his usual diverse audiences. Viewed within the context of the racial illogic that the Simpson verdict represented, the semiotic stability of Washington's filmic genealogy was compromised. The very contemporary racial attitudes that Franklin seems to have tried to suppress within the film by carefully managing racial representation became a part of the spectatorial baggage that audiences would bring (or refuse to bring) to his film anyway. One's perspective determined which players in the O. J. Simpson melodrama were victim-heroes rather than villains, and Franklin's film was not well equipped to compete with the sensibilities of audience members who brought contradictory moral codes to the film. Even though Franklin's film suppressed the sexual relationship between Easy and Daphne that would have (temporarily) brought up the resentment of black male sexuality that contemporaneous events fostered, the centrality of racial ambiguity to the plot may have been too much for audiences at a time when the nation seemed to long for clearer, more unanimous moral distinctions between black and white.

Taken together, *Devil in a Blue Dress* and *The Pelican Brief* reveal the difficulties and the necessity of attempting transgressive performances within the deeply racialized Hollywood film industry. The long history of narrative constraints and financial repercussions attached to movies—and individual performers—that attempt to ignore these precedents proves that color-blind transcendence of the raced, sexed, and classed rules of Hollywood is impossible. The lessons learned by analyzing Denzel Washington's performances in these two films expose heterosexualized protocols that structure his entire body of work. The only film to date in which Washington has ever voluntarily kissed a white woman onscreen (or at least, in which that kiss has made it to the final cut)[86] is Spike Lee's *He Got Game,* in which this liaison is criminalized (Washington's character is a prisoner on furlough and his sexual partner is a prostitute), and which received press coverage for the memorable reactions it elicited from black women viewers who confirmed the concerns Washington expressed in his interview with Allison Samuels. One newspaper reported, "At a New York screening, the audience loudly responded to the interracial love scene [between Jake and Dakota]. Lee draws out the build-up for that first kiss for a long, long time, and the crowd noise grew steadily and then exploded on lip-impact. One woman screamed, 'Denzel! You promised!' "[87]

This alleged cry of betrayal demonstrates the performative dimensions of racially transgressive performance efforts. The individual act of placing one's body in service to a narrative is performatively constrained, both by the precedents determining whether a single performance constitutes a citational repetition or a revision of the stylized behaviors that make certain identity categories—such as black masculinity—legible. Likewise, the effort to assert the citational significance of an individual performance thrusts the representation into negotiation with an audience that, depending upon its social location, has the ability to assert the felicity or the infelicity of the attempted transgression. A black female spectator may not normally be understood as having the authority to dictate the viability of mass media representations, but when her scream of dissent is recorded, reproduced, and distributed in and by the archive, it marks the contestatory dynamics to which black performances are always beholden.

Ultimately, a focus on the relationship between Denzel Washington's sexuality and his celebrity status clarifies the differences between color blindness as an ideological strategy and as an embodied practice. The color blindness that Hollywood claims to grant Washington is ideological and conditional: at times, traditional definitions of blackness will be irrelevant to his function within a narrative. However, this color blindness is never embodied: as black women spectators will attest, Washington's race is never invisible. The essentialist definitions of blackness that attach deep significance to the body as a site of racial reproduction never entirely disappear, and the act of heterosexual contact (rather than simply the idea of heterosexual appeal) underscores this fact. The black body is always located within a cultural genealogy that relies upon sexual interaction to sustain the relevance of racial difference.

CHAPTER 4

Transgressing Tradition: Suzan-Lori Parks and Black Performance (as) Theory

If Denzel Washington's filmography demonstrates the impossibility of transcending race in and through performance by simply ignoring the cultural histories within which performance practices are located, playwright Suzan-Lori Parks moves in the opposite direction. Rather than transcendence, she works toward the active transgression of textual, historical, and theatrical traditions that place strict limits on black performance. The color blindness / multiculturalism binary that reduces redressive strategies to these two options is inadequate in trying to understand Parks's contributions. While many of her plays ask broad questions about the relationship between black people and the past, I am interested in paying special attention to *Venus*, which many scholars have examined for its raced and gendered body politics. I will focus especially on what Suzan-Lori Parks's text has to teach us about the possibilities inherent in black performance practices. By engaging with a specific historical narrative, *Venus* attempts to recuperate the historical subjectivity of the black female performer in particular. In this instance, racial transgression occurs through the interrogation and theorization of performance as an expressive genre.

Parks has published several essays that articulate her philosophies regarding black theater. In "Possession," she claims the theater as precisely the place where the meaning of history may be negotiated, since "the history of History is in question."[1] "H"istory becomes an epistemological frame distinct from "h"istory, the latter of which instead consists of experiences, memories, and individuals waiting to be organized and narrativized into a cohesive Historical continuum. By calling the history of History into question, Parks demands that her audiences attend to the practices through which select narratives of the past gain the power to determine how we understand and behave in the present. In making no effort to occupy the allegedly superior ontological space of History, Parks instead takes advantage of "literature and the special strange relationship between theatre and real-life [to] locate the ancestral burial ground, dig for bones, hear the bones sing, [and] write it down," to use "theatre like an incubator to create 'new' historical events."[2] This is a twofold strategy: Parks situates herself within the genre of dramatic literature, and thereby places her investigations on a par with other textual investigations of the black past. Additionally, through the public embodiment offered in live performance, her plays augment material history: in each production of a Suzan-Lori Parks play, black bodies "actually [happen]" in ways that must now be accounted for in historical (and even Historical) retellings of black subjectivity. In other words, as Freddie Rokem suggests, "Theatre performing history . . . connect[s] the past with the present through the creativity of the theatre, constantly 'quot[es]' from the past, but eras[es] the exact traces in order to gain full meaning in the present."[3] Rather than transcendent ignorance or reiteration without contestation, transgressive black performance has a historical efficacy that transforms our relationship to black presence and the black present.

"An Equation for Black People Onstage" challenges the traditional binary, antagonistic relationship between blackness and whiteness that is enacted in contemporary American performance and cultural politics. For Parks, traditions of black performativity need to be redressed through both embodiment and textuality, and in her body of dramatic work, the latter produces the former. However, this is not the only thing that black performance in print can do: in her estimation, the playwright's challenge is to "get tough and write literature instead of just writing a show. . . . It should be literature, a show, and some sort of historical document—which is what a play is. Why not do all three?"[4] Parks's own plays intervene into and augment aesthetics, practices of spectatorship, historical narratives, and other textually generated forms of subjectivity. Through the coalescence of these practices in a single performance text or performance event, Parks rejects the compression blackness usually receives in literature, history, and performance.

In the discussion that follows, I will take Parks's mandate and use it as the analytical throughline for my claim that her work offers an alternative to racial transcendence as the only technology of healing available to those working to avoid totalizing discourses of blackness: as historical document, as literature, and as show, Parks's plays offer new possibilities for black signification in performance. In particular, *Venus*'s textual and embodied strategies demonstrate how black subjectivity provides the site for what Parks herself describes as "NEW TERRITORY":

BLACK PEOPLE + *x* = NEW DRAMATIC CONFLICT
(NEW TERRITORY)
where x is the realm of situations showing African-Americans in states other than the Oppressed by/Obsessed with "Whitey" state; where the White when present is not the oppressor, and where audiences are encouraged to see and understand and discuss these dramas in terms other than that same old shit.[5]

Here Parks explicitly rejects "that same old shit" that places black bodies in service of timeworn narratives of oppression. This does not mean that there is no awareness or critique of oppressive systems in her plays—issues of class, sexism, and even racial fetishization appear throughout her interrogations of historical processes and their effects upon black subjects—however, Parks does not take Whiteness as the animating force of black life. Instead of an obsessive investment in whiteness (as one of my students once trenchantly though erroneously quoted George Lipsitz), Parks creates and investigates black history as a means to understanding black life on its own terms, in which whiteness is but one of many interstitial forces at work. Parks's preoccupation with performing history foregrounds blackness as a historically contingent category, while also claiming performance—as a temporal form—as a legitimate discursive space within which to transform rather than eradicate racial systems of belonging.

Venus retells and responds to the story of Saartjie Baartman,[6] a South African woman taken from her homeland and displayed throughout nineteenth-century Europe as an oddity because of her distinctive genitalia and buttocks, prompting Sander Gilman's now-famous proclamation that Baartman, as representative of "Hottentots," became "the central nineteenth-century icon for sexual difference between the European and the black."[7] A combination of historical extracts, hypothesized encounters, and metatheatrics, Parks's play takes the complicated, incomplete history of Saartjie Baartman's transformation into the Venus Hottentot as emblematic of the multivalent processes through which blackness and subjectivity are mutually constituted. During the course of the play, "The Girl" (representative of but not identical to Saartjie Baartman) is taken from South Africa on the promise that she can perform there for a few years and earn enough money to return home and live a wealthy life. Instead, however, she is sold to a ruthless Mother Showman and exhibited in a freak show, which begins her life as the Venus Hottentot. While in England, her presence causes social uproar and she is brought to trial on charges of public indecency, after which she is purchased by the French Baron Docteur (modeled on Georges Cuvier, author of her autopsy), who takes her to France as his lover, teaches her European languages, and allows his fellow scientists to conduct preliminary examinations of her while she is alive, knowing that upon her death they will complete their investigation of her body. By the end of the play, Venus dies in the lonely company of the Negro Resurrectionist, who has been paid to sell her body back to the Frenchmen who abandoned her to the streets, thereby ensuring her return, even after death, to a central place within the looking relations that helped to sustain racial hierarchies in nineteenth-century Europe. Parks examines and exploits the spectacular nature of freak shows, the metatheatrical device of a play within the play, the legal system's performance of justice, and the discourse of science in order to ask, how can someone like Saartjie Baartman (or the Venus Hottentot) become a subject in (rather than simply the object of) her own historical narrative? In what ways can this subjectivity be produced through performance?

On the surface, this complex play seems to be a capitulation to the commonplace spectacularization of black bodies within the modern world, living as it does within the frame of the freak show. However, I want to suggest instead that the play contests several things that would otherwise occlude the title character's subject status: the traditional representation of Saartjie Baartman as a passive victim of the whites who exploited her, the iconic reduction of black women to the sexual utility of their bodies, and the conflation of black sexuality and criminality. Parks's incredulity toward the racial presuppositions embedded within traditional historical narratives does more than attempt to spare one South African woman the penury of history; rather, it points out much larger institutional structures that have cohered throughout time to problematize black identity in and through performance.

VENUS AS HISTORICAL DOCUMENT

In his essay "Between Memory and History: *Les Lieux des Mémoire*," Pierre Nora theorizes the relationship between these two related yet distinct epistemic modes.[8] According to Nora, *lieux de mémoire*, or sites of memory, are those places where history (as rational discursive mode) is overtaken by memory (personal, subjective, affective remembrance). He writes,

Lieux de mémoire originate with the sense that there is no spontaneous memory, that we must deliberately create archives, maintain anniversaries, organize celebrations, pronounce eulogies, and notarize bills because such activities no longer occur naturally . . without commemorative vigilance, history would sweep them away. . . . [However,] if history did not besiege memory, deforming and transforming it, penetrating and petrifying it, there would be no *lieux de mémoire*. Indeed, it is this very push and pull that produces *lieux de mémoire—* moments of history torn away from the movement of history, then returned.[9]

According to Nora, *lieux de mémoire* produce action and exist in a space of collectivity that history attempts to deny in its fixity of the past. Yet, at the same time, Nora reveals the symbiotic relationship between the two: it is history's process of stultified remembrance that produces both the need and the desire for alternate patterns of engagement with the past. In *lieux de mémoire*, elements invested with socio-symbolic weight insist upon the presence of the past in the present, and they run counter to the singular, aggressive linearity of traditional history.

Diana Taylor has further illuminated the variability in remembrance strategies by articulating the relationship between the archive and the repertoire. The first comprises ostensibly unchanging materials and artifacts that can be separated from the conditions of their production, while the latter "enacts embodied memory: performances, gestures, orality, movement, dance, singing—in short, all those acts usually thought of as ephemeral, nonreproducible knowledge."[10] The two paradigms may seem compatible, but Taylor emphasizes that her schema does not "[segregate] history and memory as opposite poles of a binary."[11] Our entanglements with the past, she argues, rely upon both the archive and the repertoire, both history and memory. Both Nora's and Taylor's claims prove useful in this effort to understand *Venus*, as binaristic attitudes about our relationship to the past remain deeply influential, even while Taylor's newer formulation offers a reprieve from them.

Because Saartjie Baartman has attained status as an icon of racialized and sexualized alterity, Suzan-Lori Parks's deployment of the trope of performance in *Venus* suggests Saartjie Baartman / Venus Hottentot's status as a *lieu de mémoire* through which audiences are invited to call into question the role of history in enshrining Saartjie Baartman's supposed inferiority, and by extension over time, that of an entire race of people. While making this claim, it is important to keep in mind the arguments of Zine Magubane, who points out that Baartman's iconic status—as emblematic of a generalized blackness and of blacks' difference from whites—has been imposed many years, if not centuries, after the fact. She suggests that ahistorical poststructuralist moves to condemn Baartman's treatment as evidence of the reprehensibly concerted construction of blackness as marginal or subhuman often tend to "valorize the very ground of biological essentialism they purport to deconstruct," refusing to attend to the social relations rooted in specific times and places that would better reveal Baartman's significance both in her own lifetime and to present-day efforts to understand the past.[12] In an effort to honor the spirit of this critique, I want to make clear that these discussions of Baartman are really discussions about how we—critics, historians, artists, audiences—need her to figure in our understanding of the raced, gendered workings of the past. In particular, I do not want to elide without comment the fact that Baartman was from South Africa, not the United States, and therefore the contemporary American politics of race do not describe her social location on another continent in another century, even though they do help to frame the ways that her story circulates today. If my discussion of her participates in the project of claiming Baartman as "transnationally black," I also want to be clear that I do not intend to "overrule [Baartman's racial or ethnic] difference from a North American vantage point . . . [and] reproduce the extant power differential between those of us positioned within the Western academy and the majority of the world's peoples."[13] Instead, I want to understand how an engagement with Baartman's continued narrative visibility, her deeply burdened representation, prompts Suzan-Lori Parks to imagine a way out of overwhelming misrecognition on the grounds of faulty understandings of race.

The ways in which Parks both incorporates and interrogates the received narratives of Baartman's life produce her body (and the body of material that constitutes much of our knowledge of her) as a site through which to understand broader mechanisms of racial production. Parks's play functions as an act of "commemorative vigilance," allowing contemporary audiences to consider Baartman in ways that exceed the traditional history of her life, supporting Nora's claim that "to interrogate a tradition . . . is no longer to pass it on intact."[14] Rather than reducing Baartman to a passive icon of difference constituted entirely by the gaze of her audience, Parks re-members this historical figure in order to foreground the questions that we must constantly ask about the conditions of black performative agency. Without the dynamic valences of a repertoire of enactments of blackness grating against a robust archive documenting problematic performances thereof, the significatory potential of the black performing body would indeed remain shrouded in what Parks terms "that same old shit."

Nora's description of a crisis of memory itself invites a productive consideration of *lieux de mémoire* as instantiations of repertoire. He argues that "true memory" has virtually disappeared from contemporary culture, and has been replaced by "memory transformed by its passage through history," which disrupts the integrity of personal narratives of the past by subjecting them to Historical logic, seeking to explain the past by eliminating ambiguity and mitigating affective forces. Even when we believe ourselves to be engaged in conscious acts of remembrance that summon us into collectivity, we are instead experiencing memory "as a duty."[15] True memory, Nora asserts, is unruly, and "has taken refuge in gestures and habits, in skills passed down by unspoken traditions, in the body's inherent self-knowledge, in unstudied reflexes and ingrained memories,"[16] rather than being "deliberate" like historicized memory. In these terms, true memory can easily be understood as cultural performance. It is embodied, it often exceeds the realm of institutionally validated discourse, and it contains within itself the possibility of subverting the context within which it functions. By contrast, history is commonly understood to fix and reduce meaning and agency, and the historical fetishization of Saartjie Baartman (versus the "true" remembrance of her) is a process that obscures her subjectivity in the narrative of her own experience. Suzan-Lori Parks's theatrical effort to recover—or more accurately, fashion—a "true memory" of Baartman relies upon the embodiment of codes of black performativity and the history of that representational difference. Her work asks, as Harvey Young phrased it, "Can historical documents represent the experience of the black body? Can the experiences of the displayed black body get reclaimed by theatre?" and the answers to those questions are almost less important than the fact of their being asked.[17]

One could argue that Saartjie Baartman's status as *lieu de mémoire* invited postmodern theatrical treatment rather than being produced by it. Baartman's progression from South African colonial subject to European spectacle did not end with her death. Upon her demise in 1815,[18] famed French scientist Georges Cuvier subjected Baartman to an autopsy intended to yield more detailed information about the racial group she represented, and after this procedure, her genitalia and brain were preserved in formaldehyde and displayed (along with her skeleton and a plaster cast of her body) in Paris's Musée de l'Homme well into the twentieth century. In the museum's custody, Baartman's skeleton became the property of France, and remained so until a protracted legal and cultural battle begun in the 1990s culminated with the repatriation of her remains to South Africa in 2002.

Led by the Griqua National Congress, the "Baartman [campaign became] the rallying cry of a new South African movement to reclaim the past."[19] Critical of her continued status as a symbol of racial spectacle within France, the Griqua (descendants of the Khoikhoi people, South Africa's indigenous population) claimed Baartman as a member of their community and demanded that her remains be returned to South Africa for proper burial among her people. Their goal was to disrupt Baartman's literal attachment to the legacy of the Venus Hottentot: burial in South Africa would remove her body from the compulsive signification of alterity that characterized her lived and posthumous captivity in Europe. In this sense, the Griqua's campaign operates at the intersection of history and memory: the Musée de l'Homme historicized Baartman's body in ways that occluded the "true memory" of her—the actual behaviors that embedded her within her own culture became less important than the meanings ascribed to her within multiple European socio-racial hierarchies, and even within the critical body of literature (including this analysis) that tries to understand her story.[20] Baartman's remains become a site in which memory—as a collective process through which Baartman might be constituted, always to serve our interests in the present—resists imposed colonial histories that deny black people control over the representation of their bodies. To some extent, Parks's play *Venus* adds to the remains of Baartman's body and life by subverting the seeming intransigence of historical narratives through which she is misremembered.

The symbolic weight of the Griqua's request does invite methodological questions: given the spottiness of the archive, how can we ever know if Baartman was really an ancestor of their community?[21] Might this ethnic subgroup's request simply be a symbolic attempt to spare an(y) African woman further posthumous exploitation by Europeans? If the answer to the latter question is yes, the tactic demonstrates performance's power to augment history: by claiming Baartman as a Griqua in order to extricate her from her iconic function in France, the Griqua intercept the rigid pastness of Saartjie Baartman, thereby redefining her in the present. In other words, Baartman's exploitation in life and death is only possible when a European history of domination overwhelms systems of memory that recognize Baartman's (and other black women's) subjectivity. At the burial ceremony in August 2002 in which Baartman's skeleton was laid to rest in the town of Hankey, South African president Thabo Mbeki declared, "'The story of Sarah Baartman is the story of the African people. . . . It is the story of the loss of our ancient freedom. . . . It is the story of our reduction to the state of objects who could be owned, used and discarded by others.'"[22] Mbeki's claim for Baartman's significance emphasizes a specific aspect of the burial as ritualized performative act: her physical reassociation with South Africa figuratively helps to sever the colonial relationship of exploitation between Africa and Europe. Through the burial ceremony, Baartman is rescued from France's historicizing acts, which arrested her narrative at her body's ability to represent the primitivism of Africans, and becomes instead a present memory of the resistance and restitution of black subjectivity. Although these repatriation efforts concluded long after Parks's play was first produced, the political and artistic work of each represent challenges to the received history of the black woman's body as sexual object. These efforts to redefine Baartman augur new and multiple modes of signification for blackness within history, within literature, and within performance.

In *Venus*, this challenge emerges through both form and content. Parks describes her use of repetition and revision—"Rep & Rev"—as a means through which she gains access to the past (both historical and theatrical) and at the same time takes the liberty of estranging it from itself. This formal strategy, also seen in other forms of black cultural expression like jazz, produces sites of contestation and dissonance that imbue traditional narratives with new meaning. Parks calls this strategy "a literal incorporation of the past," and claims that its use helps her to "[find] the only way that [a] particular dramatic story can be told."[23] Her work thereby poses an epistemological challenge to notions of history that fail to incorporate a strategy she recognizes as "an integral part of African and African American literary and oral traditions."[24]

Venus relies upon the multiple discourses that have coalesced to produce a tradition of problematizing the public black female body, and yet Parks's temporal distance and artistic license enable her to destabilize these problematic definitions. As one example, Parks re-creates Georges Cuvier as the Baron Docteur, and this figure reads portions of Baartman's autopsy report, to potentially suffocating theatrical effect, during the play's intermission. The intention and force of this document are clearly situated within a racist, sexist discourse of domination when the document in performance is placed after a scene in which Baartman chooses a risky relocation to Paris over the continual degradation of her plight as a freak in the Mother Showman's English spectacle. This repetition of autopsy as historical fact revises its meaning by connecting it to other practices of objectification that Saartjie Baartman experienced. As Parks asserts, "Rep & Rev are key in examining something larger than one moment": in the present, Cuvier's autopsy tells us less about Baartman's body than it does about the racist curiosity legitimated within scientific inquiry, and liberating Baartman (who has become an icon of degraded black womanhood) from the truth claims of this historical document provides discursive space within which Baartman and the category she has been assumed to represent may be redefined.[25]

Parks also uses the character of Venus herself to make a larger claim for the type of historical documentation she effects with this play and its performance. While it is the theatrical frame that calls the autopsy-as-received-history into question and changes its meaning for a contemporary audience, Parks creates a scene in which the Venus simply amends the historical record in the first person: "A Brief History of Chocolate" provides a metaphor for the colonial appetite and its effect upon the Venus's life.[26] She relates this history of domination figuratively, and yet, according to Parks's stage directions, at the moment when this history is related, "the planets align," affirming this different perspective on the past.[27] Coming at the end of the play, without the labeling of the earlier "abstracts" with which Parks has compiled the received history of Baartman's life, this history of chocolate does more than simply codify the difference between the present and the past. Chocolate becomes a parallel for Baartman's own experience in the circuit of colonial traffic: "The *cacao* bean, once used as money / becomes an exotic beverage," just as Venus herself shifts from a form of human currency within her Dutch colonial context in South Africa to an exotic object consumed by European spectators.[28] Likewise, the etymological development of chocolate reflects its different utility in the multiple contexts that it occupies: "The Aztec word *cacao* literally 'food of the gods' / becomes *chocolate and cocoa*" through a process that mirrors Baartman's shift from indigenous subject whose birth name we will never know to Saartjie/Sarah to Venus Hottentot.[29] Finally, the frenzy induced by Venus's presence in European society is likened to the European church's "campaign against chocolate / on the grounds that it was tainted by the character / of its heathen inventors."[30] This nontraditional history lesson casts the project of colonization—and its role in constituting blackness—in a different light, emphasizing the contingency of value systems, nomenclatures, power relations, and even conditions of mobility, all of which cohere in various times and spaces to influence black subjectivity. This history of chocolate both describes and instantiates the dynamic rather than static nature of blackness and the role of performance in this dynamic social relation.

"Brief History" functions outside of the formal register of the rest of the play, in that it isolates the actress playing Venus from the gaze of other figures, and it leads into the scene in which "The Venus Hottentot Tells the Story of Her Life" to the Negro Resurrectionist in more literal terms.[31] Significantly, the history produced in this scene is that of the Venus Hottentot, not Saartjie Baart-man. Baartman was absented so long ago from the trajectory of the narrative that her story is utterly unavailable for our understanding. Nevertheless, the story Venus shares is almost allegorical in its paucity:

> *I was born near the coast, Watchman.*
> *Journeyed some worked some*
> *ended up here.*
> *I would live here I thought but only for a minute!*
> *Made a mint.*
> *Had plans to.*
> *He had a beard.*
> *Big bags of money!*
> *Where wuz I?*
> *Fell in love. Hhh.*
> *Tried my hand at French.*
> *Gave me a haircut*
> *and thuh claps.*
> *You get the picture, huh?*[32]

The brief history of chocolate is intentionally unconventional and figurative, but the history of the Venus Hottentot's life underscores through its brevity and gaps the lack of access we have to both Baartman and even the Venus Hottentot as an agent in her own experience. The Venus Hottentot is depicted as figure rather than fact because the materiality of her life has been sacrificed to other narratives intent upon producing the racial difference that they then chronicle. To some extent, it is this very absence of binding fact that makes both Baartman and the Hottentot so seductive as critical/theatrical/historical subjects: they provide points of departure for the production of racial truths without de-manding fidelity to facts that don't exist because they have not been recorded through traditional means.

Venus's history of chocolate places a higher premium on the social relations produced through chocolate (itself something of a *lieu de mémoire,* in that it of-fers a way of remembering that helps constitute the collective identities of col-onizers and colonized peoples) than on the times, dates, and places where these relations occurred. Likewise, the textual structure of *Venus* engages in a sym-bolic act of interpretation. Dividing the play into thirty-one scenes plus an overture, Parks uses and undermines a retrospective structure to suggest the impossibility of defining the past as the past in order to abandon it there: while the ordinal titles of the scenes count backward from thirty-one to one, the action of the play moves chronologically forward. This formal device reveals the palimpsestic nature of history: the numerical ordering of scenes running in one direction as the plot moves in another creates the sense that in telling Baartman's and Venus's stories, Parks is sifting through accretions of information from the past in an effort to understand the mechanisms of historical narrative. Scene 31 shows Saartjie Baartman at the moment when her Dutch owners plan her future as the star of a spectacle, while scene 1 is the scene in which the cast announces that the Venus Hottentot has died.[33] Scene 1's last/first death announcement for this historical figure suggests that Venus's absence is the point of departure for all subsequent narratives of her life: it is her death that makes these historicizing efforts possible and even necessary. The multidirectional narrative structure destabilizes history, thereby legitimizing the transgressive performance of black female subjectivity that *Venus* provokes.

Not everyone celebrates the liberties that Parks takes with history in her dramatic reconstruction of Saartjie Baartman's life. In her frequently referenced essay "The Re-Objectification and Re-Commodification of Saartjie Baartman in Suzan-Lori Parks's *Venus*," Jean Young condemns Parks's play for suggesting that Baartman could have been complicit in her objectification in Europe.[34] Furthermore, Young contends, "Parks's portrayal of Baartman draws on cultural images and stereotypes commonly used to represent Black women in demeaning and sexually debased roles, the objectified oppositional 'Other' measured against a white male 'norm.'"[35] Of greatest concern to Young is the fact that Parks's play suggests that Saartjie Baartman was complicit in her exploitation, when the historical record (specifically, accounts of her indecency trial) suggests otherwise. By examining the historical documents that chronicle Baartman's treatment by her many European handlers, Young argues that Parks willfully misinterprets historical fact and perpetrates a neoracist, sexist exploitation of Baartman for her own selfish artistic ends.

Young's critique relies upon a fidelity to historical record that Parks obviously does not share, by alleging that in taking such great historical license, Parks cruelly silences her subject, repeating the moral crimes enacted against Saartjie Baartman without revising them. From one perspective, this is an easy argument to make, but what would happen if we instead read the play as a corrective against the damage that traditional history has done to Baartman's experiences? Parks begins from the assumption that there is no way ever to know the real Saartjie Baartman's life: as a *lieu de mémoire* Baartman would "have no referent in reality; or rather, [she would be her] own referent: pure, exclusively, self-referential [sign]."[36] Once Baartman transcends status as a historical object and becomes a *lieu de mémoire*, the documentation of Baartman's life takes on a different meaning: these artifacts become chronicles of the subjectivity of their authors, each of whom constructs Baartman anew for their own purposes.

If Baartman is one of the figures occupying—to borrow a conceit from *The America Play*—the great whole of history, then perhaps the best use of her current historicity is to extrapolate narratives that help us to understand how this unknowable past figures in the present. Parks's goal is not to offer a literal representation of the particulars of Baartman's life, but rather to investigate the social processes that encourage us to construct her as totemic, unassimilable Other. We can never verify the degree of complicity Baartman bore in her life experience, but encouraging audiences to ponder it in her play allows Parks to alienate audiences from what we think we know of Baartman's history. Even as it takes her legend as a point of departure, this strategy relieves Baartman from the pressure of serving as what Diana Taylor calls a "limit case," something placed "at the outer edges of intelligibility, at the very boundaries of representation," that demands "the language of exceptionalism."[37] Undermining our relationship to standard histories of black female sexuality invites important questions: why is the display of the Venus Hottentot still so provocative in the present day? What continuities between early nineteenth-century Europe and America today make the sight of a black woman's buttocks so provocative nearly 200 years after the historical Venus's death?[38] Is Baartman's story only worth remembering when she is cast as an uncomplicated victim of white exploitation, or does such a depiction of her repeat, from another vantage point, the erasure of her subjectivity?

Given the rigorous skepticism toward even her own creation that Parks demands, in what way does *Venus* function as a historical document? If our time demands that the historian as "erudite transparency . . . an absence obsessed with objectivity" disappear, to be replaced instead with one who "is ready to confess the intimate relation he maintains to his subject," then *Venus* documents, as much as anything, Parks's ability to challenge contemporary audiences to revisit historical archives through the perspective of a black woman— whether that woman be Baartman or Parks herself.[39] Parks's membership in the cultural category Saartjie Baartman was taken to represent forms "the means of [her] understanding" Baartman two centuries later. In depicting Baartman as potential coconspirator, Parks offers a nuanced, historicized interrogation of the very notion of black agency, both theatrically and more broadly. What does "choice" mean if Baartman's options were public exhibition as part of a European freak show or indentured servitude in South Africa? Parks's strategic engagement with the past reflects a process bell hooks describes as common to black women: "Looking and looking back, black women involve ourselves in a process whereby we see history as counter-memory, using it as a way to know the present and invent the future."[40] With *Venus*, Parks both produces knowledge of Baartman for audiences in the present and invents her own future as a black artist. The spaces of repertoire and *lieu de mémoire* offer the ground on which Suzan-Lori Parks stands as a transgressive figure who turns neither away from race nor toward an uncritically celebratory, qualitative politics of representation to reimagine black performance's enabling potential.

VENUS AS LITERATURE

In addition to intervening in historical documentation of Saartjie Baartman's life, *Venus* provides new possibilities for black performance by challenging other textual productions of black female subjectivity. Within her own text, Parks recognizes the play *Hottentot Venus, or Hatred of Frenchwomen* (which Parks adapts and transforms into *For the Love of Venus*), the transcripts of Saartjie Baartman's London indecency trial, and the autopsy report that quantified Baartman's difference from the supposedly normative anatomy of white women as each playing a key role in the reconstitution of Saartjie Baartman as the Venus Hottentot. T. Denean Sharpley-Whiting refers to Saartjie Baartman's body as "the master text on black female sexuality for Europe's scientific community," which produced the "(mis)representation of black femininity embodied in Sarah Baartmann and carried on in fervor well into the twentieth century."[41] In other words, Saartjie Baartman was not only legible as a source of racialized knowledge about female sexuality, her body has become a citational site, available as the frame of reference through which other claims of black subjectivity may be read. However, Parks's use of historical artifacts reveals how the text exceeds Baartman's body and takes on an externalized life of its own. Parks's strategic use of the judicial, theatrical, and medical archives enables audiences to comprehend the extent of what W. B. Worthen refers to as "print's role in the spectacularization of Saartjie Baartman."[42]

The style of Parks's engagement with the textual tradition attached to Baartman's life story reflects what bell hooks terms the black woman's "oppositional gaze." Although hooks is attempting to theorize black female spectatorship of Hollywood films, these strategies of interpreting dominant representations are instructive in evaluating Parks's theatrical work as well. A way of see-ing that is specific to the black female's intersectional social location, the oppo-sitional gaze takes into account not just the gendered but also the raced as-sumptions that structure the traditional gaze postulated by feminist film theorists as a way of understanding how looking relations conspire to make white women the object of a (white) male gaze.[43] According to hooks, "Identi-fying with neither the phallocentric gaze nor the construction of white wom-anhood as lack, critical black female spectators construct a theory of looking relations where . . . visual delight is the pleasure of *interrogation*."[44] This inter-rogatory stance produces a critical distance that denies the spectator the possi-bility of total absorption within the text and instead derives pleasure from the very fact of existing outside of an equation of power that does not account for her.

Parks the author seems to have taken this oppositional stance toward Saartjie Baartman as the key object in a hegemonic historical narrative, and the formal structure of her text encourages audiences to do the same. This opposi-tionality helps to explain the liberties Parks feels free to take with her subject and the impunity with which she believes she can defy the rules of history and traditional formulations of desire. *Venus* seems emblematic of a practice of looking "from a distance, from that critical standpoint that did not want to be seduced by narratives producing her negation."[45] The multiple narratives that silence Baartman by reducing her to an abject victim are thwarted by Parks's depiction of the possibilities of black female resistance even from a disempow-ered space. We are both invited to look at the story of the Venus Hottentot in the traditional way, and at the same time criticized for doing so, sometimes by the world of the play, sometimes by the conscience bred in us by the opposi-tional perspective Parks embeds within the work.

This oppositional framework is created in *Venus* as a text for both reading and performance. Rather than conforming strictly to the codes of dramatic writing, which suggest that the text's primary function is to offer instructions for embodied performance (or conforming to codes of literature that devalue the added dimension of embodiment in the construction of meaning), Parks creates works that are uniquely and distinctly meaningful to readers and to the-ater audiences, refusing to privilege one over the other. The written edition of the text primes its audiences for the cultural work and contestation that *Venus* offers with two opening quotes that reveal Parks's own relationship to history as an (inter)discipline. The first, from a Jean-Luc Godard film, declares, "Hu-man work brings things back / from the dead."[46] The second, from Virginia

Woolf's *Between the Acts*, charges, "'You don't believe in history.'"[47] At the intersection of these two quotes, the claim of resurrective power braces us for the license that Parks will take with her subject and also induces us to think of history as a value system rather than as quantitative truth from which one may and sometimes must disengage. Parks demands that her audiences distrust the history that has embalmed Saartjie Baartman for nearly two centuries, and by doing so, help reanimate our relationship to her.

Additionally, Parks encodes the literary representation of her story with affective clues that manifest themselves differently in performance. Two of her unique conventions are the rest and the spell: in the former, actors "take a little time, a pause, a breather; make a transition," while the latter is "a place where the figures experience their pure true simple state." "Denoted by repetition of figures' names with no dialogue," the spell in particular has no known theatrical equivalent: Parks indicates that "no action or stage business is necessary, [but] directors should fill this moment as they best see fit."[48] By relying upon the relative stability of the text as literature (when coupled with the instructions from "Elements") Parks fixes her readers' attention, cryptically and concretely noting the existence of a "true simple state" that defies enunciation. As an example, consider "Scene 19: A Scene of Love (?)" which consists, in its printed entirety, of alternating names:

> *The Venus*
> *The Baron Docteur*
> *The Venus*
> *The Baron Docteur*
> *The Venus*
> *The Baron Docteur*
> *The Venus*
> *The Baron Docteur*
> *The Venus*[49]

The scene is a spell, staging the (im)possibility of love between two individuals who are diametrically opposed within the intersecting European hierarchies of race and gender. From the quotation marks in the title of the scene to the claim that textual representation can only demand—but not produce—the pure, simple state of the characters it employs, the scene displaces standard narratives of romance. It offers an absence that is both harrowing and liberating. As Jennifer Johung recognizes, this scene enables us "to recognize the very material concepts effected in Parks's specifically unspecific writerly marks, and so to understand that any practical decision should be only a momentary specification in order to invert the spell's suspension outside of dramatic conventions as a suspension contingently embedded within dramatic reinvention."[50] Readers, actors, directors, and viewing audiences must all work with only the most elemental of maps, aware of the failures and betrayals embedded in other texts that demand Parks's redressive formal moves. What previously passed for scenes of love, particularly when race and gender are in high relief, might better be understood as what Saidiya Hartman would term scenes of subjection, in which the terror of domination yielded pleasures only for those in power.[51]

At the same time, "A Scene of Love (?)" stages the conspicuous absence of text (i.e., the negation of black womanhood in narratives of love, similarly noted and condemned by Denzel Washington) in order to identify the space into which *Venus* will enter as a form of interrogation. The lack of words (but not content) in this scene presages Parks's own narration of the development of Venus's relationship with the Docteur. This love story (?) is juxtaposed with a play-within-the-play, *For the Love of the Venus*, which is Parks's adaptation of *The Hottentot Venus, or Hatred of Frenchwomen*,[52] an 1814 vaudevillian piece performed in Paris. In the original, a young woman is betrothed to her cousin only to find that he has sworn to abjure the company of Frenchwomen because his heart has been broken before. The young man's aunt, the Baroness, schemes to help her niece regain her fiancé's affection by dressing her as a Venus Hottentot. The ruse succeeds but is exposed, and nevertheless, the young man reaffirms his embrace of French cultural values through his embrace of and marriage to his French fiancée. In Parks's version, The Young Man grows weary of his Bride-to-Be because he feels he must "love something Wild" before settling down to a predictable life with his intended. The Bride-to-Be and the Young Man's mother scheme to pass her off as a Venus Hottentot, and, as in the original, their relationship is restored.

For the Love of the Venus is an act of repetition with difference: like its antecedent, it trades on an essentialized hierarchy of Western superiority and uncivilized non-Western inferiority, but Parks also manages to stage a critique of the very value system she represents with this play. Performed intermittently throughout the outer play, *For the Love of the Venus* creates the black woman's absence in order to demonstrate her simultaneous centrality and invisibility within the idealization of heterosexual desire. In both *Hatred of Frenchwomen* and *For the Love of the Venus*, the black woman as sex symbol never appears: when the young men in each story meet their fantasy women, these women are in fact the white women who are socially appropriate objects of their desire. The fantasy is revealed as immaterial (or, more precisely, as entirely material and not representative of any interiority), and the black woman's body is not strictly necessary to the self-knowledge each man acquires through his desire for cultural difference. "The Venus Hottentot" becomes a symbol of white ignorance that has nothing to do with the actual experiences or actions of black women.

The Hottentot as costumed persona gives materiality to the differences The Young Man and The Bride-to-Be want to place between white and black womanhood and sexuality. The white woman is allowed to experience Hottentot-ness as a temporary identity, and after she is assured of The Young Man's love, "She removes her disguise and again becomes The Bride-to-Be."[53] The Venus Hottentot becomes a literal fabric-ation, as we are privy to the "real" woman before she adds the layers of padding that transform her from a respectable woman into a fetish, and she is restored to her respectable self once the performance has fulfilled its purpose. But while *For the Love of the Venus* affords us the opportunity to see the difference between the actual white woman and the fiction she inhabits, we never receive the same opportunity to see the black woman shirk the fiction that the colonial gaze foists upon her. This reveals the very different standards of propriety that govern white and black femaleness: we must understand the white bride to be willfully, and temporarily, occupying an exoticized space, and conversely, we must understand the black woman as inescapably locked in the field of representation (in this instance, textual before embodied) as a sexual alien. However, this sentence to perpetual representation is ironic—she is written into the narrative by being written out of it, because of the assumption that there is nothing more that her physical presence can add to the dominant understanding of what she signifies.

For the Love of the Venus rehearses the textual strategies that constitute our knowledge of Saartjie Baartman, depicting a total absence of agency for the black woman in this text-based performance: it creates rules of representation that rely upon her erasure, upon the sufficiency of another's text to fix her identity. As Rokem suggests, "Even if the device [of performance within the performance] is by no means exclusive to the genre of performing history, it often serves a specific purpose when it is used in such performances, as a filter through which the 'truth' about the past can be examined and critiqued."[54] In this vein, The Bride-to-Be's impersonation recalls and anticipates the long history of blackface and other practices of misrepresentation through which the mandates for black performance practices have emerged, and establishes continuities between the misapprehension of (female) blackness in performances past and present. By reproducing this tradition of performed blackness, Parks exposes it to criticism, and also subverts it through the relationship she scripts elsewhere between Baartman and the Baron.

This attempted subversion of the black woman's lack of agency also occurs provocatively in the trial scene of the play, "Scene 20 A-J: The Venus Hottentot Before the Law."[55] As Parks tells it, when Saartjie Baartman was brought into court on charges of public indecency, some opposed her show on humane grounds, taking umbrage at the fact that three years after the abolition of the slave trade she was being displayed under abject circumstances that damaged English society, "contribut[ing] / to [their] growing social ills."[56] No place was made for this South African woman in the British civic imagination; quite to the contrary, her public display was wrong because it risked normalizing her unruly black presence. The show, however grotesque, gave Saartjie Baartman a place in the public sphere that demonstrated the imperfections in England's social and moral order. Rosemary Wiss suggests that "the assumptions upon which the abolitionist debate rested were as enslaving as the confinement and exhibition of Saartjie Baartman.... The very possibility of categorizing Saartjie Baartman in terms of bestiality and promiscuity exemplified the notions by which a civilized society could judge its own level of civilization while condemning others."[57] Therefore, the legal text produced through trial accounts remembers Baartman through racist condemnation. Like *For the Love of the Venus*, the promiscuity and bestiality that characterized even her defenders' description of Baartman rendered her useful only insofar as she confirmed the superiority of England as a civilized nation.

Parks traces the courtroom's descent from supposed altruism to selfishness in her dramatization of the proceedings. At the outset, the Chorus of the Court "ask[s] 2 questions: Is she or was she ever indecent? And at inny time against her will?"—indicating that they "do not wish to send her adrift into the world without asylum of a friend / a friend ready to receive and protect her."[58] The irony of the charge of indecency is clear: decency is a value judgment embedded within a particular cultural context; and yet to declare Baartman's display indecent would be to condemn the English hordes who turned her into the sensation she was. Therefore, the former question necessitated the latter: identifying Venus as a willing participant in her exhibition returned and isolated the question of decency to her and deflected it away from the audiences or other owners involved in her humiliating display. Thus even the fiction of concern for Baartman was necessary to produce the social order that they claimed her presence offended.

In Parks's version of events, when she enters the courtroom, the Venus's body gets the first word, so to speak, threatening to capitulate to the perception of Venus as a black woman lacking interiority, but Parks allows her to speak herself more traditionally into participation in the proceedings. Her first words, "Im called the Venus Hottentot,"[59] shock her audience of people who believed Baartman was incapable of speech in their civilized tongue. This moment of incredulity in the play forms a rupture between the theatrical present and the historical past. As Jean Young discusses, in the actual trial against Baartman and her owner, Baartman did not speak.

> Her silence was transformed into "assurances" that she was happy in England, that she had two Black boys to attend to her, that she went out in a coach for two or three hours on Sundays and, finally that "the man who 'shews' her never comes till she is just dressed, and then only ties a ribbon around her waist."
> . . . The silent "voice" of Baartman is misread, interpreted as acquiescence in this exchange or "discourse of domination." Baartman is never allowed to speak on her own behalf, her voice misinterpreted by the translators. Hence, the desire for freedom is silenced by a system that views Baartman as incapable of being a moral person by Victorian standards and by the decree of the courts.[60]

Parks violates history in allowing her Venus to speak at all, but she also takes on the particular tradition that requires Baartman's silence in order to level its critique against the social system in which she was trapped. Instead, Parks dismisses her silence as an ethical failure on the part of the archive, and writes against it to resist its invocation of Baartman as an object in order to deny her presence as a subject. The self-identification "Im called the Venus Hottentot" produces a distance between Baartman and the problematic presence the court has been convened to understand—Baartman is not the Venus Hottentot, even though she has been produced as such in spectacle and in print.

Her verbal proficiency provokes a host of offensive questions—devolving into "Were you ever beaten? / Did you like it was it good?"—all of which stage the indecency of her interrogators rather than of Venus herself: their prurient appetites make the courtroom scene necessary, providing a legitimate context for their illegitimate curiosity.[61] Once called upon to speak, Parks's Venus first tries to invoke the strategies of her white keepers (like the Mother Showman and the Baron Docteur, who were summoned to the court before, she attempts to be "unavailable for comment"), before trying to adopt the capitalist mindset. In saying she has come "to make a mint," this Venus seems prepared to manipulate the ideology of the period so that she can remain in England and make money.[62] Young sees this rhetorical trajectory as an affront to Baartman's memory, one that fails to recognize "the unequal power relationship as Saartjie, a kidnapped, colonized captive, is forced to speak on her own behalf against her 'keepers,' who have assumed absolute control over her body and person."[63] However, the resolution of Parks's narrative suggests quite the opposite: when Venus's fictionalized efforts to resist deportation are coupled with the subsequent events of her life as rendered by Parks (*bourgeois* house arrest with the Baron Docteur, forced abortions at the Baron's behest, sexual assault in the name of science by the Baron's professional colleagues), her success in evading prosecution as willfully indecent is rather hollow. Scripting the possibility of Baartman's agency in the legal proceedings brought against her is a way of scripting the impossibility of her agency within a discursive system that defines her as antithetical to its values.

Although *For the Love of the Venus* demonstrates the performance traditions through which blackness has been externally represented and the indecency trial uses text to chronicle the interracial politics to which Baartman was bound, the autopsy report read by the Baron Docteur is a text that defines Baartman as Venus at the most basic level. The Baron is merely the latest in the play's line of white men who want to secret away the Venus so they might use her outside of the orbital path of their society's mores, an echo of the desire typified by the Young Man from *For the Love of the Venus,* the men who sneak into Baartman's cage and rape her when the Mother Showman is away, and the Brother who brought Baartman to England from South Africa at the beginning of the play. However, the Docteur distinguishes himself from these other white men by claiming another, unimpeachable type of interest in Baartman: he wants to civilize her and then make her an object of scientific inquiry.

Parks introduces the Baron Docteur into the play in an unusual way: before he intersects directly with Venus, he is the sole audience for *For the Love of the Venus.* Actors perform the show for the Baron, and the spectacle triples as Venus watches him watch the show from afar. The Baron succumbs to the tremendous appeal of these misrepresentations of blackness, and when he buys Venus and takes her to France, his attitude toward her greatly resembles that of the Young Man, who relies upon his conquest of something culturally alien to produce his feelings of masculine power and privilege. Parks's controversial depiction of the sexual relationship between the Baron and Baartman as in any way consensual may not be historically defensible, but it repeatedly forces audience members to juxtapose the Venus produced through Parks's literary imaginings (alive, sexually proactive), with the lifeless, fragmented Venus that the autopsy report bequeaths contemporary audiences.[64]

The first time the autopsy report appears in the text, the Negro Resurrectionist reads from it while he "holds fast to The Venus's arm."[65] These stage directions allow Parks to stage the power of this text: the Negro Resurrectionist's grasp literalizes the hold this autopsy report has over our understanding of Baartman and her transformation into the Venus. The selection he reads from the report is relatively brief, describing her brain, liver, gallbladder, and intestines. The terse clinical language of the autopsy report ironically denies Baartman any interiority precisely by making her interior organs externally legible, underscoring the fact that our clearest textual memory of Baartman comes from a document utterly unconcerned with her humanity, and in fact, far more concerned with demonstrating her difference from normalized and humanized European bodies. The enduring circulation of this autopsy report demonstrates the perversely doubled truth of Harvey Young's assertion, "Those who record and preserve history have often overlooked the black body."[66] In the first sense, historians have indeed overlooked by ignoring the material conditions and social relations that black bodies make plain. However, in a second sense, these same historians (which here includes anatomists, as people involved in efforts to prove evolution as a part of human history) more literally over-look the black body, engaging in an obsessive spectatorship that traps blackness in the register of corporeality at the expense of morality, rationality, and subjectivity. The stage directions that follow the Negro Resurrectionist's reading make this over-looking of the black body clear: "He releases The Venus's arm. She flees but doesn't get far. She runs smack into the Mother Showman."[67] The hint of subjectivity, of agentic status displayed by the effort to escape before being acted upon, objectified, and abjected again, ends with the body. The physical collision with the Mother Showman makes Venus's body the culprit in her inability to escape the social and economic systems that rely upon her visibility.

Parks has the Baron Docteur read from the report at greater length during the intermission, which directly follows the scene in which the Baron purchases Venus from the Mother Showman. In this earlier scene, the Baron authenticates himself with Venus by differentiating his intentions toward her from those of the abusive men she has encountered in the past: when he meets her, he says, "Im yr biggest fan. / . . . / I find you fascinating. / . . . / Not like that, Girl. / Im a doctor. / 'Doctor.' / Understand.?"[68] Although these words deny the erotic potential of the scientific gaze, T. Denean Sharpley-Whiting's discussion of the actual Georges Cuvier disagrees: "Cuvier's gaze, it appears, is tempered with eroticism. . . . As he views Sarah Baartman displayed before him nude, the scientist is as captivated by the Venus's charms as the male spectators at her Rue St. Honoré exhibitions."[69] The autopsy report objectifies Baartman's sexuality and denies her subjectivity at the very same time that it documents and encourages the sexual appetites of those who study her. At the end of the intermission, the Baron becomes distracted from the objectivity of the report he reads, recalling, "Her shoulders back and chest had grace. / Her charming hands . . . *uh hehm.* / Where was I?"[70] With this line, Parks subverts the alleged disinterestedness of the autopsy text and implicates the Baron's (Cuvier's) sexualizing eyes (and hands) as central to the form the report takes, even though they are disavowed as extraneous to the production of racial knowledge.

Additionally, the title by which the Negro Resurrectionist introduces the Baron's document, "The Dis(-re-)memberment of the Venus Hottenot, Part I,"[71] calls into question both the motives and the truths to which the autopsy aspires. Rather than providing factual details about Saartjie Baartman, the autopsy and its performance "In the Anatomical Theatre of Tübingen" instead fragment our knowledge of Baartman, denying her subject status within her own historical narrative.[72] Again, Parks registers the overdetermining force of this document with the Docteur's acknowledgment that the audience's immediate presence is not required both because his "voice will surely carry beyond these walls" and because his "findings are published."[73] Parks calls attention to the multiple media that misrepresent and misremember black women, suggesting that there is nothing completely outside of the text of black female subjection. Any critical undoing cannot transcend these practices, but must transgress them from within.

Near the end of the play, after Venus has been expelled from the Baron's home and bed to die in the Negro Resurrectionist's care, Parks returns to the autopsy one final time: according to stage directions, "The Baron Docteur continues with great difficulty" and, in spite of the personal relationship he had with her, uses his scientific findings to exclude her from the human community:

The remarkable development of the *labia minora*
which heretofore is so general a characteristic of
the Hottentot or Bushman race
was so sufficiently well marked that it well distinguished itself
from those of any of the ordinary varieties of the human species.[74]

At the conclusion of his report, the Baron "stands there holding his notebook and hanging his head,"[75] physically communicating the shamefulness of the history he has just produced. Parks scripts our collective shame over the disservice done to Baartman's memory into her text, so that it documents the possibility of changing our relationship to the autopsy as a foundational document in the construction of gendered black racial realism. Robyn Wiegman asserts that

> part of the naturalness of any discourse of difference is its ability to marshal a history whose features seem inevitable and incontrovertible, freezing the future into a sequential unfolding of the dominant modes of knowledge. . . . If rethinking the historical contours of Western racial discourse matters as a political project, it is not as a manifestation of an other truth that has previously been denied, but as a vehicle for shifting the frame of reference in such a way that the present can emerge as somehow less familiar, less natural in its categories, its political delineations, and its epistemological foundations.[76]

Venus robs the autopsy text of its seeming neutrality, and also robs the Baron Docteur (Cuvier) of his seeming authority over black womanhood, teaching audiences to resist the inevitability and incontrovertibility of the texts through which Baartman has been produced as a sign of sexual and racial difference. This transgression of the textual past helps to alter the epistemological foundations of the present.

VENUS AS SHOW

Here, finally, we arrive at the raced, gendered bodies whose alternative signification through performance Parks has theorized with this text. In moving from history to literature to show, I have aspired to engage a sequential logic that funnels our attention, at last, to what happens at the turn of the twenty-first century when a black actress takes to a stage over which the transnational workings of history and the multidisciplinary force of textual discourse have cast very long shadows. *Venus* received its professional premiere at New York's Public Theater in a 1996 production directed by Richard Foreman. Critical assessments of the show varied, but one of the endorsements of the production came from none other than Robert Brustein, who praised Parks for "manag[ing] to portray the humiliation of blacks in white society without complaint or indictment."[77] As I hope to have made clear, Parks's alterations of historical narrative and her recontextualization of the print artifacts from which Baartman's life has been construed do in fact offer a sharp indictment of the narrative traditions that depend upon black humiliation to constitute a public sphere. However, Brustein's commentary does illuminate the fact that Parks refuses to adhere to anticipated modes of black complaint or indictment in performance. As she herself writes,

BLACK PEOPLE + "WHITEY" =
                        STANDARD DRAMATIC CONFLICT
                        (STANDARD TERRITORY)
i.e.
"BLACK DRAMA" = the presentation of the Black as oppressed
so that
WHATEVER the dramatic dynamics, they are most often READ to EQUAL an explanation or relation of Black oppression. This is not
only a false equation, this is bullshit.[78]

Parks's problem lies not with telling stories about characters who live under oppressive circumstances, but rather, with the practice of allowing that oppression to be the lens through which all dramatic possibility is filtered. *Venus*'s Saartjie Baartman is trapped within a system that denies her freedom, however, her struggle against "whitey" is not the center of the story: the exploitation Baartman suffered at the hands of her owners is clear, and therefore Parks chooses instead to examine the discursive processes through which her servile status is legitimated. *Venus* is not a story of oppression, but rather a meditation on the possibilities of black agency—and more specifically, black agency in performance. As a site of memory, Baartman's story—in its literary, historical, and performative dimensions—provides an opportunity to stage the mechanisms through which black subjectivity in the present moment can be understood as a bodily practice: an exterior mapping of internal possibilities.

Venus denaturalizes the black performing body in order to expose the falsity of the cultural traditions to which realistic black acting is supposed to correspond, even at a time when what Fredric Jameson refers to as our acute "historical deafness" attempts to make fictions such as color blindness a reality that untethers black actors from the relationship between realism and stereotype.[79] In so doing, Parks also attempts to reclaim performance as a site of intervention into the history of misrecognition inflicted upon Saartjie Baartman through her body and upon successive generations of black women. The power of embodied proof to supplant histories and texts of black female alterity reflects Allen Feldman's claim that the "cultural construction of the political subject is tied to the cultural construction of history. This intersection results in political agency as an embodied force."[80] The physical body (in this case, in performance) produces the potential for political action by hosting dissonant narratives of both History and self-making. Within Suzan-Lori Parks's work, the black body becomes self-referential, attuned to the histories of representation that produce blackness through a limited number of iterative possibilities yet unwilling to allow these histories to deny space to black performances that suggest alternate, self-determined forms of cultural practice.

Casting *Venus* opens up some of these possibilities. It would be easy, even obvious, to imagine the actress portraying Venus as the only black performer in this play that recruits and responds to the visualization of race as a vehicle for exploitation. However, Foreman's production cast a black actor as the Baron Docteur, prompting Jean Young to decry this choice for "suggest[ing] that Black men are the primary exploiters of Black women, further distancing white males from a recognition of Baartman's (i.e. the black woman's) exploitation and dehumanization."[81] This is a legitimate concern, indirectly echoed by Harvey Young's categorization of *Venus* as "one of the exceptional cases in which the original production actually creates an obstacle to a clear interpretation of the play text."[82] And yet if we linger with this casting choice for just a moment, it introduces an intriguing array of insights, all related to the fact that the play's transgressive potential is neither uncomplicated nor safe. Parks's actors must participate in the rites of possession that her words transcribe. According to Glenda Carpio, "In Parks's work, actors are surrogates for the bodies of the ancestors and, in this sense, become living effigies in the rituals of mourning and burial that [her] early plays effect."[83]

Following this argument, the black actor who takes on the Baron Docteur's role then implicitly identifies Georges Cuvier as an "ancestor," creating a kinship structure that accounts for the brutal heterogeneity of the black past, denying any pure, essential black identity that can be distinguished from the interrelational systems that colonial mobility produced. Furthermore, a black Baron Docteur stands in curious relation to historical records that suggest Saartje Baartman's original owner, Hendrick Cezar, was himself a free black in Southern Africa—a fact that serves as a caution against sentimentally using twenty-first-century African American diasporic sensibilities to flatten the complex racial classification systems of the eighteenth-century African continent (or that of today).[84] And finally, what haunting questions does "A Scene of Love (?)" pose when a black man and woman confront one another in their "pure true simple state" but devoid of verbal language? Disrupting an indexical understanding of the relationship between black performers and the figures they portray emphasizes the ritualized dimensions of Parks's work while demanding a skepticism toward the "truth" that representations can be expected to offer under any circumstances.

Spectatorship also plays a key role in black subjectification through embodiment within the play. Articulating new traditions of black performance requires cultivating audiences who are prepared to accept black bodies onstage engaged in transgressive acts, to resist the twin ideological calls of history and aesthetics in order to allow black performers to exceed or challenge their expectations. For instance, I attended a 1998 production of *Venus* that was staged in the round, a spatial move that foregrounded the gendered and racialized gaze as a mechanism that structures not only our access to pleasure through representation but also our participation in the social realm.[85] The directors chose to disrupt the safety of gazing as a private act and to force audiences to experience and contend with the consequences of bringing such a presumption of power to the world beyond these immediate representations. The circular enclosure of the playing space caused a proliferation of legible texts: both the enactment of Parks's script and the reactions of the spectators across the theater awaited decoding. As bearer and target of a gaze, audience members were afforded the opportunity to identify viscerally with Baartman, constituting and being (mis)constituted by others in the act of looking.

Deploying the gaze within the world of the play while also turning audience members into targets of the same looking process has the potential to cultivate bell hooks's oppositional gaze that challenges the erasure of black ocular power. Writing about the history of negative consequences attached to the black gaze, hooks asserts,

> all attempts to repress our/black peoples' right to gaze had produced in us an overwhelming longing to look, a rebellious desire, an oppositional gaze. By courageously looking, we defiantly declared: "Not only will I stare. I want my look to change reality." Even in the worse [sic] circumstances of domination, the ability to manipulate one's gaze in the face of structures of domination that would contain it, opens up the possibility of agency.[86]

Confronting the power of mutual apprehension disallows what Laura Mulvey refers to as the "imbalance[d]" total absorption into private pleasure upon which the traditional gaze is predicated.[87] On the symbolic level, exposing the scopophilic abuse of the black female body is the challenge that *Venus* as text and performance poses. Parks no longer allows the spectator to go ungazed upon, and instead (e.g., *For the Love of the Venus* being performed for the Baron Docteur as an audience of one, observed by Venus and also by the audience of *Venus*) suggests that we can in fact use looking practices to change reality by refusing the mandate that black women are little more than social ills made flesh.

Parks's text in performance invites audience members to rehearse the gaze that has subjugated Baartman for centuries, even as the production stages the disavowal of those processes of visual constitution. This occurs most clearly through the bodily presence of the actress who plays Venus: the idea of a separate, distinguishable Saartjie Baartman beneath the iconic Venus Hottentot is literalized by costuming the actress portraying Venus in a bodysuit that artificially provides her notorious backside. This disjuncture between the person and the image serves as a metaphor for the way that blackness has figured in the public imaginary for so many generations, obscured by artificial augmentations. The challenge that Venus's costume presents to spectators is to "interrogate not only the past history of abuses of spectatorship and voyeurism but also their material legacy in the moment of performance," to remain aware of the fiction of this rear end rather than to suspend our disbelief.[88] In specific relation to Baartman, this would mean emphasizing that certain narratives of History have assigned Baartman her qualitative bodily difference, just as the costumed steatopygia is/was given to the actress playing Venus in performance. Neither difference inheres naturally.

In pushing the boundaries of black performativity, this role and the costume that supports it offer a peculiar freedom to the black actress: her performance of Venus allows her to acknowledge the representational history to which she herself is beholden, and at the same time to disidentify with it. The bodysuit literally protects the black actress's body from the eroticized gaze of the spectators: she is hidden in plain sight, and encourages an act of displacement that forces the audience members to recognize their desire as a projection rather than a truth. Furthermore, the bodysuit allows the actress to perform her distance from the Venus Hottentot and her identification instead with Saartjie Baartman's semi-invisible interiority: her own body is not sufficient as an icon of deviance and sexuality, and must receive artificial supplementation.[89] Thus the normalized expectations of black bodies even in contemporary performance are undermined at the same time that their affective power is rendered devastatingly clear: as Harry Elam and Alice Rayner write, "When Venus stands alone in profile for the audience, the paying spectators of the Public Theater, no one can escape the discomforts of the Mother Showman saying 'What a bucket / What a bum! / What a spanker!'"[90] Denying the veracity of the spectacle does not allow us to deny the power that these racial displays continue to have today.

The transformation Baartman undergoes to become the Venus Hottentot literalizes the power of spectacle in the constitution of subjectivity. Although in discussing the play, I have used the names Baartman and Venus somewhat interchangeably, the moment when The Girl (Baartman) becomes the Venus Hottentot is staged with blazing lights and as much fanfare as the Mother Showman's menagerie can afford, underscoring its performative dimension. Her transformation makes plain the ontological emptiness of the prototypical black woman in many performance traditions: she serves instead as a key figure in someone else's tableau. The Mother Showman's chorus of human wonders culminates with the introduction of her newest acquisition: after each of the existing chorus members is introduced to the audience, the Mother Showman announces the Venus:

> we've got a new girl: #9
> "The Venus Hottentot."
> She bottoms out at the bottom of the ladder
> yr not a man—until youve hadder.
> But truly folks, before she showed up our little show was in the red
> but her big bottoms friendsll surely put us safely in the black!

> *The Girl stands in the semidarkness. Lights blaze on her.*
> *She is now the Venus Hottentot.*[91]

The Mother Showman's speech act produces The Girl as The Venus Hottentot, and its disinclination to follow Austin's rejection of "parasitic" "etiolations of language" is precisely the point.[92] Where gender, race, and performativity intersect, staged spectacle can almost always be found. Indeed, "real life" may be the parasite that feeds off of staged instantiations of black objecthood in performance, rather than the reverse.

Parks further emphasizes the central role of spectacle in constructing racial categories in the scene that shows the Mother Showman and Venus engaged in a (mock) fight: "The Mother Showman kicks The Venus repeatedly. The act has the feel of professional wrestling but also looks real."[93] This violence reduces Venus to an object whose bodily existence is entirely subject to the wills of her (unnatural) white Mother. At the same time, though, the artifice of the beating allows for resistant spectatorship, which recognizes the deployment of illusion and derives pleasure from the exposure of the charade rather than from the charade itself. Contemporary audiences of Parks's play are invited to understand the horror of the contrived circumstances of Baartman's subjugation, rather than to accept this violence as part of a natural social order. Within the context of *Venus* as a whole, the violence of this scene literally and symbolically stages the black female body as a target of discursive violence, and acts of domination are central to the way Venus is publicly constituted. Further, this violence allows Venus's body to become a political subject, inviting one to question "the degree to which the body [may be] a site of resistance to cultural discourse."[94] Just as the bodysuit protects the actress playing Venus from the full impact of the racializing gaze to which Baartman was subjected, the escape from true bodily harm performed by Venus and the Mother Showman also stages the unnaturalness of manufactured practices of black subjugation.[95]

Nevertheless, the staged violence provides a potent complement to Venus's refrain throughout the play: on many occasions, when asked if she consents to a significant change in her life, Venus responds with the question, "Do I have a choice?"[96] Hearing this question time and again, Parks's signature repetition is clear, but the revision is less so. Temporal progress revises the circumstances within which the question may be asked, but political progress—the possibility of a meaningfully different answer—is not. The stagnant question fuels Jean Young's criticism of the play as an exercise in reobjectification since to suggest that Baartman had the power to make a choice regarding the terms of her subjugation allows those responsible for it to escape critique. However, a different interpretation is possible, even necessary, if we accept that "Political agency is manifold and formed by a mosaic of subject positions that can be both discontinuous and contradictory."[97] In the mock fight, the Mother Showman's successful display of violence depends upon Venus's participation in the illusion, which has the ironic effect of staging the potential for the black body to escape certain types of physical violence while it remains susceptible to discursive violence. This discursive violence is emphasized in a later scene when Venus campaigns for a new performance in which she will "learn" to read before the spectators' eyes. Such a display would grant the black woman access to language and disrupt the excessive emphasis on the body as the locus of black value. Although the request is unsuccessful, Parks includes the scene of negotiation specifically to suggest the role that performance might play as a site of resistance to total subjugation. However, this resistance comes not through efforts to transcend past practices of racialization but by engaging deeply with them, and thereby requiring us to reconstitute our relationship to the past rather than trying simply to escape it.

While making the tropes of performance and spectatorship central to her reimagining of Baartman's history, Parks takes on a Western tradition of locating truth in the visual. However, this challenge to visual epistemes doesn't suggest (color) blindness as the appropriate redressive gesture. Instead, Parks asks us to look both differently and elsewhere for an understanding of black subjectivity. Rather than positioning them as simply to be looked at, *Venus* demands a synaesthetic response to black women in performance—looking and listening to and for the histories Saartjie Baartman's experience might reveal when we look at and listen to her as more than just evidence of white brutality and black suffering, when we complicate what Sara Warner identifies as "the global image of Baartman as victim cum national hero."[98]

In performance or in print, *Venus* invites new interpretations of both Baartman and the social systems that produced her enslaved condition. It intercepts the historical citational chain that helps to dictate what signifies as black and female in contemporary U.S. culture. By giving the character of the Venus Hottentot an acuity that complicates our received understanding of her place in her own life story, Parks manages simultaneously to reclaim Baartman as a woman and also to reimagine the black female performer's task of navigating a representational system that seems dependent upon her marginalization. If Parks truly is "interested in freeing Baartman not from the imperial gaze but from the burden of representation itself," the ritual that is *Venus* functions more as historiography than as history (or revisionist History), and thereby foregrounds the agency a black woman might negotiate for herself in performance.[99] Purging Baartman of the responsibility to represent anything external to herself offers a black actress a rehearsal of the same freedom, which produces instead the possibility of voluntary, improvisational interactions with the past as well as the performance present. Through *Venus,* Parks practices radical love, which, Chela Sandoval suggests, "can transit all citizen-subjects toward a differential mode of consciousness."[100] From Baartman's stage name to Parks's constant injection of love into the story to her own dedication of the print edition of the play "with love," Suzan-Lori Parks works for a transformation of the public sphere—of performance and civic life—that recalculates the value of black performance possibilities.

CHAPTER 5

Are We There Yet? Race, Redemption, and *Black. White.*

The majority of this book has looked back at the 1990s to understand how the culture wars' vocabulary and ideals affected black performance during that decade. The twenty-first century, however, has forged its own relationship to the still-unresolved controversies over race, culture, and national character, as California's Racial Privacy Initiative and other reinvigorated state-level fights over affirmative action programs have demonstrated. In the current millennium, new terms such as *postrace* have emerged that eclipse the now-quaint terminology of multiculturalism, particularly in light of the rapid acceleration of globalization, the post-9/11 cultural climate both in the United States and throughout the world, and the obsessive commodification of "reality" that currently characterizes U.S. mass culture. The last of these has especially affected black people and black performance by giving credence to simulacra that function like a hall of mirrors, in which prior, often fictive representations of blackness become the authenticating referents for behavior in these "real" televisual situations, obscuring the manufactured origins of a blackness that now travels throughout the world. I am thinking, for example, of MTV's reality series *Making the Band,* particularly its second season, in which music mogul Sean Combs attempted to create the next hip-hop supergroup. Some of the young adults he selected for the project immediately adopted the swagger and the hard-partying ways of rappers in videos they idolized, but were less keen to take on such disciplines as regular rehearsal, responsible collaboration, and punctual attendance at meetings that can contribute to becoming successful performers, even though (or, because) these aspects are rarely represented to the public. In other words, the instructive lure of representation is so strong that a media behemoth like MTV finds itself creating reality programming that tries only to re-create the contrivances of its nonreality content.[1] This chapter, by way of a conclusion, will examine a few twenty-first-century instances of black cultural production in an effort to understand the complexly interarticulated relationships between the increasing appeal of postracial discourses, the mainstreaming of blackness via hip-hop culture, the explosion of reality television, and the possibilities for black performance in light of these other conditions.

In some ways, the move toward a postracial understanding of identity can be understood as an extension of the postmodern and poststructuralist theories that transformed the academy, especially its Anglophone and Francophone wings, in the second half of the last century, rejecting the absolute ontology of what conventional wisdom had previously deemed stable identity categories.[2] In this context, the concept of postraciality is not just a prescriptive assignation, but a descriptive one as well. Rather than encouraging us to develop a postrace sensibility, it suggests that we already have. Titles such as *The End of Blackness, Post-Ethnic America, Against Race,* and *After Race* reflect scholars' efforts to clarify the conditions of belonging that actually structure contemporary relationships on both intimate and broadly social scales.[3] In general, they point to factors such as shifting political and historical circumstances, as well as patterns of migration and intermarriage, to argue that the old definitions of race to which we cling no longer reflect the lived loyalties of "hyphenated Americans." For example, Paul Gilroy has spent over a decade refining his claims that the technologies that emerged as a part of modernity created and relied upon race as a social and biological category but have since been eclipsed by new technologies that trouble our continued fealty to the "dermal" by moving to the nanopolitical level, "oblig[ing] us to ask on what scale human sameness and diversity are to be calibrated."[4] The potential danger of postrace philosophies is that they repeat the shortcomings of multiculturalism: while emphasizing elective culture over supposedly inert racial categories, they substitute a quantitative focus on representation for a sustained commitment to political and material change in American society (e.g., we have elected a president who only happens to be black, therefore race and racism must be over).

By arguing that the social conditions of identity have evolved, much postracial discourse is meant to see the social constructionist viewpoint to its logical conclusion, suggesting that our society is no longer meaningfully constructed along racial lines. In this way, postraciality conforms to the logic employed in arguments for color blindness and transcendence, encouraging us to get over our own reflexive employment of outdated terminology and social relations. However, the more specific term *postblackness*—borrowed from the art world—offers a different way of thinking chronologically about the meanings of race, one that falls squarely within the framework of racial transgression. In her essay introducing the 2001 "Freestyle" exhibition catalog, Thelma Golden, who had by then left the Whitney for The Studio Museum in Harlem, defined *postblack* as a "clarifying term . . . [with] ideological and chronological dimensions and repercussions" referring to "artists who were adamant about not being labeled as 'black' artists, though their work was steeped, in fact deeply interested, in redefining complex notions of blackness."[5] While postblack artists challenge the constitutive power of language (i.e., the discursive dimensions of race) to impose certain interpretive frames or market values on their art, they do not deny the continued and complex experiential relevance of blackness in the twenty-first century. Furthermore, the moniker of postblackness does what postrace does not: it names and thereby keeps blackness alive even while demanding that its significance to the public sphere be renegotiated.

"Freestyle" opened at a moment of unique national innocence. The fatalistic paranoia associated with the potential Y2K technological meltdown had subsided, and the epic trauma of the September 11, 2001, terrorist attacks was still months away. Golden saw the show as specifically diagnostic, clearly distinct from the identity politics that characterized the end of the twentieth century, intimating possibilities that answered the question, "After all of this [theory-driven multicultural art of the 1980s and the late globalist expansion of the 1990s], what's next?"[6] The works featured in the show explain *postblackness* as a critical term that takes exception not to blackness but to the ways it has been framed and limited both by dominant Western culture and sometimes from within black culture as well. For example, Kori Newkirk's large-scale curtainlike tapestries made of hair beads repurposed black hair accessories with fraught connotations into high art, racing and to some extent gendering postmodern art practice.[7] David Huffman's *TraumaBots* took black interiority (often denied in mainstream representations of blackness) as the site for his meditation on stereotypical imagery, the constitution of black humanity, memory, and cultural bricolage. Senam Okudzeto emphasized the diasporic dimensions of blackness in order to reflect upon the market forces that both facilitate and undermine the maintenance of personal relationships on a global scale. Jennie Jones used found objects to rewrite the racialized history of the suburbs, pulling "an unknown suburban black girl" into prominence, the potency of the gesture deriving from its capitulation to and triumph over her invisibility in what we know as the suburbs.

This domestication of blackness is perhaps one of the most quietly powerful acts of transgression contained within the show. Engaging the public and the private spheres in which race is produced and regulated, *Homage to an Unknown Black Girl* denies the racial purity of either domain both in the past and in the present. The image of a young girl with a full afro in a knit white dress, sitting on a low coffee table, is not staged in the present to comment on the past; instead it highlights a fragment of some nearly forgotten archive. As posited by Jones, the transformation of a found object into a work of art rejects traditional languages of authenticity that would deny any black girl a place in the suburbs or any suburban girl a place within some black community that could not be defined solely in spatial terms. The girl in the photo may be unknown, but Jones's archaeological gesture allows us to know both the suburbs and blackness differently than we otherwise might, at the intersections of race, class, gender, and place.

The exhibition also included artist Rico Gatson, whose larger body of work takes on the overlapping discourses of race, domesticity, and representation. Although not a part of "Freestyle," two of his video installations, *Picket Cage* (1998–99) and *Fenced In* (2000), suggest the claustrophobic effects of televisual representation.[8] In the first, audiences enter what amounts to a phone booth-sized enclosure made of white picket fence material and housing a television screen. The door to the space is open and inviting, but the scale of the fencing overwhelms spectators, denying them mastery of the space and revealing the seductive magnitude of literally dominant representations of home life. The small video screen suggests that the apparatus responsible for these images is also a victim of its success, no longer able to control the power of the representations it produces. By contrast, *Fenced In* features Gatson frantically darting to and fro in front of the camera. His manic running, as if in an attempt to escape something, is made comical by having the action take place within a tightly limited space—a patch of green lawn enclosed by a white picket fence. As Maria Villeseñor notes, "Gatson's focus on the forced 'sunniness' of the scene emphasizes the hypocrisies of television and the unreal, homogenized narratives it so often enforces."[9] This time, an inversion of scale repeats and revises a message about the absurd, mythic power of the suburban utopia implied by the picket fence. In *Fenced In,* the picket fence is trapped within the screen rather than the reverse, yet the sense of confinement is equally acute.

The homogeneity of the narratives that television enforces can be measured in racial, sexual, and classed terms. Heterosexual, nuclear, monoracial families living in spacious, comfortably furnished homes continue to be representationally idealized and normalized in a nation where at least half of all marriages end in divorce, single-parent households are on the rise, interracial and same-sex partnerships and parenting relationships have increased, wages fail to keep up with escalating costs of living, and the gap between the economic resources of the wealthy and the poor continues to grow. In spite of this experiential dissonance, representations of successful domestic units that approximate these homogenizing values of the mainstream as closely as possible remain important tools in minority struggles that choose (or feel the need) to engage with the politics of respectability. For example, in an atmosphere where dominant representations of black women continue to emphasize wanton sexuality and irresponsible oversight of "pathological" family units, representations that de-emphasize black sexuality, or emphasize heteronuclear stability actually do transgress the racial common sense that otherwise marginalizes them. Nevertheless, an oft-unintended consequence of such representations is the temporary production of curious and sometimes troubling alliances and exclusions among minority communities, placing "respectable" black women (for example) in ideological league with cultural conservatives whose other political positions might not match their own. Likewise, Dwight McBride has cautioned that "the politics of black respectability . . . can be seen as laying the foundation for the necessary disavowal of black queers in dominant representations of the African American community."[10] By overemphasizing respectability on terms defined outside of the black community and its concerns, African American cultural politics have sometimes ended up reproducing and strengthening oppressive hierarchies that in fact damage multiple black constituencies, regardless of class position, sexual orientation, or gender.

While tactical respectability is often framed relative to domestic roles and relationships, it is just as often a cultural move that aspires to increasing the legibility of valued commodities—a rebranding, if you will. In particular, the mainstreaming of hip-hop has been partly achieved through a synergistic frenzy that capitalizes upon current celebrity culture. To an unprecedented degree, singers now star in movies, actors make records, and athletes write books, endorse clothing, and star in movies. Reality programming stars show up at public events to be photographed drinking whatever new beverage is handed to them while they wait for recording contracts. Many hip-hop celebrities earn mainstream success by flagrantly enacting our dystopic fantasies about race, sex, and money. They enable consumers to purchase transgression of social norms, obscuring the fact that the commodification of outlaw culture is actually central—not counter—to American mass market values to such an extent that "when hip hop dominated the music scene, you didn't necessarily have to name things as Black because they were mainstream."[11] With this mainstream status came the opportunity for hip-hop as a cultural sensibility and form to move into territory where it previously couldn't have been imagined. Though he was never the most hard-core rapper in the industry, Will Smith forged an early path for rappers in television (outside of MTV, at a time when MTV was still strongly identified as a rock network, to the specific exclusion of black music) by starring in *The Fresh Prince of Bel-Air* in 1990. In the gentlest of ways, this sitcom enacted and foreshadowed the penetration of a hip-hop sensibility into the "sunny," respectable spaces of idealized domestic environments. Will Smith played a young man named Will Smith who moved from gritty West Philadelphia to live with the Banks family (his maternal uncle et al.) in the elite Los Angeles enclave of Bel Air, where Ronald and Nancy Reagan would have been neighbors. The situation's comedy derived from Will's efforts to acclimate to his new environment, from which he felt estranged by both class and race—not only were the Bankses the only black family around, they were barely black themselves in any way that Will understood. Over the course of seven seasons, the narrative of this extended nuclear family relaxed its loyalties to essentialized understandings of the rigid racial and classed demarcations of black life, and thereby provided the social proxy for rap's total absorption into the fabric of respectable American culture.

"THE NIGGA YOU LOVE TO HATE" BECOMES A FAMILY MOVIE STAR

During the same year in which the Fresh Prince moved to Bel Air, O'Shea Jackson, better known to his fans as Ice Cube, left the pioneering gangsta rap group NWA to launch a solo career. As the self-proclaimed "Nigga Ya Love to Hate" on his first CD, *AmeriKKKa's Most Wanted,* Cube[12] in some ways emblematized the provocative masculinity that Thelma Golden probed four years later with the Whitney exhibition *Black Male*. Since that time, however, Ice Cube has completed a remarkable expansion, if not transformation, in the branding of his celebrity, the apotheosis of which might be his starring role in the 2005 Columbia Pictures family film *Are We There Yet?* From boy in the hood to surrogate dad in the SUV, Ice Cube has both profited from and furthered the resignification of blackness in the public sphere. Intrinsic to this process have been both the cultural logic of late capitalism, which has relentlessly expanded the "center" of the public sphere, along with a national investment in the idea that race is endlessly malleable at the individual level. By supplementing the soundtrack of his estrangement from white middle-class cultural norms with the visual image of his aspirations toward them, Ice Cube has made himself legible to a broader audience of Americans, deftly manipulating the "postracial"—if not postblack—moment in which he finds himself.

In addition to his work as a solo recording artist, Ice Cube made his acting debut in John Singleton's 1991 film *Boyz n the Hood*, which borrowed its title from NWA's song of the same name. Ice Cube played the role of Doughboy, a young man whose family lives and dies by the codes of gang violence ruling South Central Los Angeles. His casting capitalized on the synergy with his prior reputation as one whose music chronicled the lifestyle that the film portrayed, adding—in a way that actors Laurence Fishburne, Morris Chestnut, and Cuba Gooding, Jr. did not—a seeming authenticity to the film's depiction of a world that the growing popularity of gangsta rap was publicizing sonically. In fact, Ice Cube wasn't the only rapper to star in a film that summer: an article in *USA Today* heralded the advent of the "rap pack" (following packs rat and brat) because of the simultaneous appearance of LL Cool J and Ice-T that summer in *The Hard Way* and *New Jack City*, respectively.[13] Ice Cube was lauded for displaying "particularly impressive passion" in "an unexpectedly good screen debut," setting the stage for future roles in both black and mainstream films.[14] After his success in *Boyz*, he began to take roles in many more action films, enabling him to assume the "buddy" status typical of black crossover performances in Hollywood, while still maintaining his appeal to specifically black audiences with films such as the *Friday* series and *Barbershop*. The oscillation between vernacular and mainstream performances allowed Ice Cube to expand his fan base rather than simply trading one for another.

It was no accident that this increase in Cube's commercial viability coincided with the rise of hip-hop as the emblem of youth culture and the engine of many marketing campaigns. Ice Cube helped to blur the distinctions between hip-hop as a constellation of formal practices (e.g., the four elements: MC-ing, Bboying, DJ-ing, and tagging) and hip-hop as a commercially legible lifestyle brand, thereby emphasizing—in all of their racialized dimensions—the crises over racial authenticity and appropriation that form the underside of hip-hop culture's rise to prominence and dominance.[15] For some, hip-hop is the ultimate postblack (as in postracial) art form—as evidenced by the ease with which certain consumers and critics blithely ignore its earliest racial and class politics and equate it simply with youthful rebellion. For others, it taps into the strategic subtext of Golden's postblack formulation, giving those objects it describes a distinct status in the marketplace that challenges prior valuations of black culture.[16]

In light of these competing frameworks of postblackness, Ice Cube functions as something of a ligament uniting two intersecting vectors of racial possibility: the new, conditional refiguring of racial politics, and the anxiety over when, where, and at whose hand notions of authentic blackness go to die. His film *Are We There Yet?* practices a double-voicedness that reflects Cube's own awareness of the tensions between the marketability and the viability of the particular brand of postblackness he seems to represent. Not only does the film's title locate it within the familiar genres of comedy, family film, and travel narrative, it also implicitly asks us as audience members to assess our progress on the national journey to postblackness. Have we yet arrived at a place where we can see Ice Cube as the harried yet ultimately loveable curmudgeon at the center of a heterosexed family unit, rather than as the fierce rapper whose entire musical genre provoked the ire of the National Congress of Black Women and helped to spur the creation of the Parents Music Resource Center? Given the long-standing irrepresentability of the responsible black father figure—lest he challenge the racialized patriarchy that much of Hollywood's output seems designed to honor—what cultural moves are necessary to insert Ice Cube into this narrative without welcoming in a host of unfavorable frames of reference that damn the black family as a pathologically broken social unit, one that few people would pay to see depicted?[17]

The film performs a delicate chronological balance in its efforts to "post" blackness. Invoking old patterns of representing black masculinity largely in an effort to revise them, Ice Cube's character Nick Persons may drive a brand-new Lincoln Navigator with spinners, and he does wear his "bling" proudly, but he drives his shiny car to the sports collectibles shop that he owns, rewriting blacks' relationship to the multi-billion-dollar sports industry as more than just "forty million dollar slaves"[18] or potentially criminal billboards for a favorite team.[19] Our introduction to Persons—whose last name offers him up as an everyman with whom audiences are invited to identify across racial lines—inverts the expectations that televisual representation has traditionally cultivated. The car and the jewelry are the fruits of respectable, middle-class, entrepreneurial labor, and criminality—which Ice Cube's character thwarts—is contrapuntally embodied by young white boys trying to steal a Celtics card, replacing the usual black suspects. Throughout the film this pattern continues, acknowledging the blackness of the characters at the center of the narrative while rejecting any negative connotations that might otherwise cling to them.

Are We There Yet? centers on Nick Persons's efforts to win the heart of Suzanne Kingston, a divorcée with a young son and daughter, in spite of his intense dislike of children. Against his better judgment, Nick offers to escort Suzanne's children from their home in Portland to her job site in Vancouver on New Year's Eve. Because the children are suspicious of and hostile toward any man who vies for their mother's affection, they sabotage this road trip both intentionally and inadvertently, making it a longer and more treacherous journey than Nick could ever have imagined. Nevertheless, by the end, the children reach their mother safely, the children and Nick develop a deep attachment to one another, and Nick and Suzanne declare their love for one another, paving the way for the sequel (a home improvement comedy, *Are We Done Yet?*) that followed in 2007.[20] The process of integrating both the performer Ice Cube and the character Nick Persons into this narrative of familial belonging relies upon denuding his black male image of some of its intensity and granting a different legibility to Ice Cube's performing body. Within this film, race is both visually incontrovertible and a decoy, allowing for a performative signifying that implies a chronological departure from the strict genealogy of menace that usually overdetermines the black male body in performance.

Ice Cube's brand of postblack swagger allows his character, by the end of the film, both to survive the loss of his iconic Lincoln Navigator and spinners and to voluntarily surrender his jewelry as a declaration of love for the children that he hated a mere eight hours earlier. The film predictably and flagrantly abandons any pretenses of temporal plausibility in order to achieve its narrative payoff, which explains reviews calling it a "vulgar, grating alleged family comedy" that was "phony and formulaic from start to finish."[21] However, Nick Persons's accelerated emotional transformation within the film in some ways mirrors the concerted effort to complete the social transformation of Ice Cube the artist that Columbia Pictures effects by placing him within this story. Both reviews and supplementary entertainment news coverage took note of Ice Cube's "15-year transformation from pariah to family entertainment hero."[22] Films like *Friday* and *Barbershop* allowed him to remain legible as a black performer while moving him away from his synonymity with violent urban angst, but *Are We There Yet?* represented Cube's most aggressive push toward the mainstream to date. Here we have an enactment of Golden's chronological implications of postblackness: rather than relying upon the existing timetable for racial reconciliation that is bound up in the ways that law and public policy move with "all deliberate speed," popular culture (like some postblack artists) initiates a rupture with the status quo. This rupture is not inherently benevolent or progressive, as it measures success in terms of commercial viability, but it nevertheless refuses the protracted narrative of post–civil rights patience and progress, opting instead for the almost instantaneous creation of the unproblematic racial landscape the film wishes to occupy. In this view, distinctions between whiteness and blackness become practically irrelevant, as evidenced by the fact that *Are We There Yet?* was actually written as a star vehicle for Adam Sandler, into which Ice Cube could be inserted with only minor cosmetic changes that capitalized upon his particular celebrity genealogy. At the time of the film's release, Ice Cube discussed the role as a strategic move to appeal to a mass audience with a PG-rated film, a move that was earned after a steady history of confounding audience expectations, saying, "To me, it's been a nice progression to show maturity, to show growth. Not to be stuck in the same thing. Let people know where you start, you don't have to end in the same place."[23]

I do not mean to suggest that Ice Cube the artist completely surrenders his racial self-knowledge within *Are We There Yet?* Instead, there are several subtle moments when blackness is self-consciously reconfigured within the context of the film. The first occurs when Nick and Suzanne have a conversation about their pasts and how they came to be in the same city. When asked if he grew up locally, Nick returns the question, "A black man from Oregon?" prompting a laugh of recognition from Suzanne. Cube is acknowledged as being out of his element, geographically and culturally, and yet the development of his character suggests that the displacement was a successful one. In another scene, at the beginning of his road trip with the kids, Nick appeals to the heavens, saying, "Lord, these kids are ethnically challenged" when instead of respecting his determination to "keep it real" by listening to rapper 50 Cent, they want to listen to Hampton and The Hampsters, Justin Timberlake, or Clay Aiken. Nick goes on to articulate the links between music and a community-regulated racial authenticity by saying, "In my old neighborhood, asking for that kind of music could get you shot," deftly confirming both his proficiency with and spatiotemporal distance from those manifestations of blackness. Ironically, playing 50 Cent in the racially coded Pacific Northwest actually places his character in the cultural mainstream, given whites' status as the majority consumers of rap music.[24]

A final example of this racial awareness comes when Nick assumes the stance of an angry black man in order to intimidate a pharmacist into giving him the inhaler he desperately needs for Suzanne's asthmatic son. When describing his intimidation tactic to young Kevin, who has looked on in admiration of Nick's power over white recalcitrance, he refers to it as "The Look," which is actually an echo of the celebrity Ice Cube's previous persona, described by one reporter as "the scowl he always wore under that black Raiders cap back in the hard days."[25] In the scene, Nick moves from mere description to an acting lesson in black masculinity. Nick scowls and Kevin makes his best efforts to perfect this mask that has demonstrated use value but that seems most unnatural for a prepubescent "asthmatic in the accelerated program," who is as un-"ghetto" (his word) as they come. Naming "The Look" as a discrete practice that can be learned regardless of one's temperament is strategically critical, as it names and puts to rest any lingering questions about Ice Cube's legitimacy in the role. Aggression, by both Nick (or, implicitly, Ice Cube) and his young charge, is exposed as action rather than essence in order to denaturalize the performance of race. This lets the air out of the proverbial balloon of rap stars as sociological curios, unmasking them as entertainers hidden in plain sight, and recenters Ice Cube as a performer capable of lending his charismatic persona to any number of contexts. The multigenerational gesture of having him move away from The Look even as he introduces a young black boy to it helps to identify both black performative agency and the structures within which such agency can and can't be wielded.

MAINSTREAMING BLACK. WHITE.

The popular success of *Are We There Yet?* confirmed the breadth of Ice Cube's appeal, earning over $82 million in domestic box office receipts on $32 million in production costs, and demonstrated the ways in which blackness can remain legible as such while being rendered ostensibly neutral within popular cultural representations.[26] A year after the film's success, Cube parlayed his likability into a reality television program that attempted to place race relations at the forefront of popular culture by capitalizing on the phenomenal success of the reality genre. Ice Cube served as one of the producers of *Black. White.*, a six-episode series that revised and expanded the project of John Howard Griffin's 1959 racial odyssey as chronicled in the book *Black Like Me:* rather than a single person responding to the question, "How else except by becoming a Negro could a white man hope to learn the truth?," this 2006 project featured two families, one black, the other white, who agreed to live together in Los Angeles for six weeks while participating in racial masquerade.[27] Through the magic of Hollywood makeup artists, the black and white families would each "trade" races, passing for the other. In any instance, such an experiment would be worthy of critical contemplation, but *Black. White.* offers especially useful insights into the limits of a language of performance in our national conversations about race. With often-conflicting racial politics, the series attempted to highlight both the centrality and the irrelevance of race to Americans today, and in so doing, it exposed the failures of the type of color blindness that was the inadvertent precondition of the experiment. My close reading will focus on the narrative structure of *Black. White.* in order to interrogate the definitions of race and racism that animated the project, and thereby to demonstrate that the racialization of the series' narrative mitigated the individual agency—which proponents of color blindness relentlessly espouse—that was supposed to enable each participant to shed his or her real racial identity to become black or become white.

Before I begin this close reading, however, it is important to locate reality television as a genre within the representational landscape and to question its specific relation to ideas of black performance and its transgressive potential. MTV's *The Real World* is generally understood to be the grandfather of the genre as it is currently used to appeal to the young adult demographic.[28] Its extraordinary popularity with both viewers and network producers is the result of a perfect storm of turn-of-the-century media conditions: as Herman Gray notes, the decentralization of "network television" away from the big three networks has resulted in a proliferation of smaller networks needing content that works ever more specifically to "make identifications" that "can relentlessly dis-aggregate and re-aggregate [viewers] through whatever categories [advertisers] so desire."[29] Reality television is an efficient form of content—without having to pay expensive actors and a full writing staff, build sets or design costumes, production costs per episode are significantly decreased while the appeal of the shows justifies higher ad rates that in turn produce incredibly attractive profit margins.[30] On the consumer end, audiences seem drawn to the voyeuristic opportunities that watching reality television provides, and thousands upon thousands of viewers line up for their opportunities to star in future seasons of their favorite shows, providing a virtually inexhaustible labor force for the industry.

As reality programming has transformed the televisual landscape, it has come under critical scrutiny, particularly over the truth claims embedded in the name of the genre.[31] What makes reality television real at all? The unscripted nature of the participants' interactions with one another is typically the core of the genre's designations as true—this is how people "really" behaved in these circumstances—yet the contrivance of circumstances calls even this premise into question: how "real" is it for seven strangers who are not independently wealthy to move into a home together in a new city, with no pressure to provide for themselves but plenty of time to chat, barhop, and travel internationally? Questions about contrivance extend to the editing practices that reduce hundreds of hours of footage into twenty-two- or forty-four-minute units of entertainment that are paced to unfold over multiepisode season arcs. Chronological accuracy is one of the first representational "truths" to be sacrificed: events are re-presented in an order that aids the story editors' narrative ends.[32] Because these narrative objectives tend to be borrowed from preexisting genres, the participants in reality television situations are often interpellated into roles that precede and exceed their actual social interactions, roles that conform to raced, classed, and gendered logics that may not reflect participants' personal histories. Thus "authenticity" becomes another critical term that influences both participation and reception of reality television programming. Many participants make a great effort to preserve personal authenticity, to suggest that camera surveillance is not influencing their behavior.[33] But even beyond the notion of individual authenticity come concerns about cultural authenticity, particularly as people of color engage in complicated negotiations of the reality genre. On one hand, reality TV provides the chance for the individual's reality to be documented, while on the other, the burden of representation might cause under- and misrepresented minorities to curtail their behavior in order to shoulder the burden of providing a more "authentic"—which ends up meaning respectable—representation of their culture as a whole.[34]

These tensions between individual and cultural authenticity are especially acute for black people at a time when the appropriation of black culture—emblematized by corporate ownership of hip-hop—made the phrase *keeping it real* first a necessary and then a meaningless articulation of ownership on both the individual and the cultural levels. What are the implications of this devaluation of the real for black performance? Katrina Bell-Jordan, following the language of Herman Gray, identifies reality television in particular as "a site of struggle over the meaning of race and racial issues."[35] There is a certain irony to this simultaneous obsessive interest in reality television and intense skepticism as to its truth claims: just as bell hooks wryly noted the disappearance of the "subject" precisely when previously objectified people of color were finally coming into voice as subjects, the "corrective" potential of reality TV gets called into question even as it becomes one of the few ways to get a black show on television. In the case of *Black. White.*, black performance and concepts of reality are rendered even more complex as the show relies upon deception and fluid subject positions in order to do its work. Which black performance, we are forced to ask, is real: the concerted, studied charade of the Wurgel/Marcotulli family, or the involuntary, unstudied presence of the Sparkses? The Sparks family becomes the stable referent against which the success of the white family's charade can be measured (and vice versa), and this capitulation to a supposedly factual, experiential binary clearly reflects the complicated relationship between notions of authenticity and sincerity as they pertain to the social dimensions of racialized subjectivity.

In *Real Black: Adventures in Racial Sincerity,* John L. Jackson asserts,

> Racial sincerity and authenticity are both ways of thinking through how we find these shortcuts for knowing ourselves and others—for locating *the real* in (and the intentions of) everyone around us. The difference is that authenticity theorizes this as an unbalanced relationship between the powerful seer and the impotently seen, the latter being a mere object of the seer's racial gaze and discourse. ... Sincerity, however, is an attempt to talk about racial *subjects* and subjectivities. Race is not singularly and exclusively about authenticating others—or, more specifically, it is about authenticating others who concomitantly escape solitary confinement within the pre-scripted categories that others impose."[36]

For Jackson, authenticity is too often beholden to an essentialist vocabulary that sincerity, on the other hand, acknowledges as incomplete. The authentic and the sincere are not mutually exclusive impulses, though, and this is where the tensions that a series like *Black. White.* documents tend to emerge. The premise of authentic racial subjectivity, that what is real can be seen and adjudicated by an outsider with superior knowledge, makes this experiment possible. It places the show's audiences in that superior position of adjudicator, and also creates a level of suspense that sustains the length of the experiment: what is compelling about watching the participants move through the world in inauthentic racial garb is the possibility that they will be found out. Despite this voyeuristic narrative rationale, the possibility of racial sincerity as an intersubjective experience is a progressive goal of the project. The participants are supposed to make a sincere effort to understand the racialized other: performing what race looks like from the outside may be an impulsive aspiration toward authenticity, but if the participants are to experience any growth and transformation over the course of the six episodes, they must move past that reflex and instead strive to be sincerely inauthentic, refusing easy, appropriated stereotypes for a deeper engagement with a different social location. And while Jackson suggests that reality television represents "a certain replacement of actorly authenticity with purportedly non-acted sincerities," *Black. White.* stands out in its genre—and ultimately, failed to catch on with viewers—precisely because it engages each of these modes simultaneously rather than restricting itself to one apparent moral register.[37]

The fact that the show was beholden to these distinct racial imperatives is reflected in the many reality genres that were blended to create the project for television: it simultaneously draws at least upon the traditions of the makeover show (external transformations that are meant to yield internal and interpersonal ones, e.g., *The Swan, The Biggest Loser*), the surveillance show (*Big Brother, The Real World*), and the instructional program (*What Not to Wear*).[38] The surveillance framework, in which cameras are unobtrusive flies on the wall of the participants' social interactions, allows audiences to believe that actorly authenticity might be renounced for nonacted sincerity, while the titillating makeovers seem automatically to confound that belief by requiring the participants to aspire to actorly behaviors. *Black. White.* premiered, to much media hype, on the FX cable network on Wednesday, March 8, 2006. The first episode of the series begins with a series of self-introductions, the first of which is a forty-seven-year-old white man addressing the camera saying, "My name is Bruno and I became a black person."[39] This very utterance invites questions about the experience it purports to describe: how does one "become" black? The next image is a still photo of Bruno in black makeup with the word "WHITE" stamped across the bottom of the screen. This moment visualizes the crisis of meaning that a competition between embodiment and discursivity can produce through individual bodies that must be categorized racially. Are we to understand from this earliest moment that the discursive claims of race cannot be controverted by the seeming truth of the visual? The assertion "I became a black person" works to arouse a degree of suspicion in its audience that foreshadows the limits of any understanding of embodiment that detaches bodies from their sociohistorical context, as *Black. White.* was inevitably required to do. Bruno's claim to blackness as a temporary and entirely anterior state of being runs counter to everything we think we know about how blackness as a social location is experienced (typically, once you go black, you [can] never go back). Even those who choose to "pass" into or out of racialized communities must maintain carefully calibrated performances of affiliation and disavowal, requiring the constant articulation of a racial present in an effort to delineate a racial past that remains firmly put.

After Bruno's introduction, we meet his partner, Carmen, her teenaged daughter Rose, and the black Sparks family, forty-year-old Brian, thirty-eight-year-old Renee, and their teenaged son, Nick. The Wurgel and Sparks families were deliberately chosen as appropriate racial counterparts to one another: nuclear(ish), middle-class families with fairly typical values, aside from their different placement within the embodied politics of race.[40] This lateral symmetry is complicated by the vertical integration of two generations' potentially different experiences of race, providing the opportunity to explore what Farai Chideya calls "the color of our future."[41] Nick Sparks's and Rose Wurgel's participation provides the opportunity to test current hypotheses about the obsolescence of racial frameworks. If changes in popular culture truly do presage a revolution in racial tolerance, in the context of this project Nick and Rose should perhaps have more in common with one another than with their nuclear and racial families. Organizing the participants along comparative vertical axes invites a historical rootedness (in the interest of allowing for its obsolescence) that the horizontal relationships across racial and familial lines are supposed to disallow.

Beyond mapping out the participants' relationships to one another, the opening episode works narratively and rhetorically to represent the participants as both authentic and sincere spokespersons for their racial groups. Bruno, as the son of an immigrant who "came here with nothing" (BW), firmly believes in bootstraps and personal accountability, of which he sees his father as an exemplar. Brian, on the other hand, has a keen awareness of how racism manifests itself on both sides of the color line: as a light-skinned black man with green eyes growing up in Michigan in the 1970s, he felt ostracized as both too black and not black enough. Carmen, a blue-eyed blonde, claims a progressive legacy for herself, saying that because her parents were involved in the civil rights movement she "feels compassion for anyone who has suffered" (BW). Renee declares her inheritance of nonconfrontational, middle-class values when she reveals, "I was raised by two hardworking parents who taught me not to use race as an excuse" (BW). The four testimonials are meant to reflect the (narrow) range of racial attitudes held by mainstream Americans on both sides of the color line. Brian and Bruno appear at the outset, and are confirmed throughout the series, to possess the extremes of the racial sentiments within the project. However, these extremes are carefully denuded of their full intensity: Bruno distances himself from generations of inherited wealth and white privilege by pointing to his humble—and most importantly, recently transplanted—origins, a tactic that entitles him to whatever frustrations he may feel toward (racial) others who have unrealistic expectations of American society, who misrecognize the fruits of white labor as the fruits of white skin alone. Brian, on the other hand, is defused as an angry black man both visually and politically: his physical traits mark him as atypical among blacks (having both light skin and green eyes), and his frustration with racism is societal, rather than merely personal, as demonstrated by his indictment of both inter- and intraracial prejudice. Both men's racial politics are rationalized through their experiences. Rather than needing recourse to external, abstract theories about what race means, they extrapolate theories from their own experiences of assimilation and marginalization.

Those authenticating moments help to articulate the definitions of race that structure this experiment, both the contrived experiences and their edited presentation to audiences. Race is what you look like, what you make of it, a political and ethical position with which one can affiliate, and a potential encumbrance that one must work to overcome. However, in addition to these perspectives on race that are born of the participants' personal histories, there is also an implicit belief in at least the possibility of color blindness (or, race as an irrelevant social category) animating the experiment. As it is practiced in American society, color blindness involves an acute awareness and subsequent disavowal of the significance of another person's racialized material presence, difference, and reality, rather than simply the inability to recognize them. In the case of Black. White., however, race has to be real enough for audiences to accept and distinguish between different people's racialized sense of themselves, yet permeable enough that the charade to which the series aspires is not offensive or impossible to imagine succeeding. The disavowal of difference in this scenario involves reducing it to something inhabitable by or transferable to another. To put it differently, we need race to make this series possible, but we need it not to be an intractable feature of the participants' identities: the presumption of subdermal similarity both enables and anticipates the desired outcome of the project. To that end, the series structures its explorations of race according to very specific narrative threads: the intersection between visuality and interiority; the participants' positionality relative to systems of belonging (social location, access to experience); and the participants' individual and collective relationships to racism.

The first axis, intersections between visuality and interiority, provides the gimmick that drew many viewers to the show. How exactly would they turn a black man into a white man? Hollywood makeup artists spent up to four hours per participant each day creating the transracial facades that allowed the families to pass into the opposite race, and the "reveals," to use reality-makeover show parlance, provided an early opportunity for participants to declare the connotations that the opposite race held for them. In a two-step process, the participants were first revealed to themselves as racial opposites (they had no access to mirrors during the transformation process), then allowed to reveal their transformed selves to others. The Sparks family approached the transformations with a sense of humor that was probably enabled by the recent and supposedly humorous use of whiteface in films such as *White Chicks,* in which black people good-naturedly impersonate whites not strictly for access to the general social privileges of whiteness, but as part of a task-specific enterprise like solving a crime. Once they "became" white, Brian first adopted surfer slang and intonation, while Renee simply experienced bemused shock. Confronting one another as Others (and yet also as the Same) sent the interaction directly to the realm of desire—or the lack thereof. One of the requirements of a successful charade was to transfer their emotional lives to their new selves, including their heterosexual attraction to their mates. Renee had difficulty with this, confessing that as a white man, Brian did not "look anything like a person [she] would be attracted to" (BW). Brian, on the other hand, playfully revealed the persistence of his black sensibility under the white makeup. Since Renee was transformed into a blonde, he dropped the surfer accent and danced over to her crooning, "C'mon, white girl, c'mon white girl" (BW), displaying the black man's supposedly instinctual desire for white women. Conversely, the Wurgels' reintroduction to one another was a mutually libidinal encounter. Once the shock of (mis)recognition subsided, Bruno looked at Carmen desirously, telling her of her beauty, and Carmen was effusive: in a direct-address camera confessional moment she declared, "It's nice. I mean, black, I love, visually and somehow heartwise; there's that warmth."[42] To Bruno directly she added, "You look like a *really* nice man" (BW).

These reactions occurred in moments of racial simultaneity, in which what the participants temporarily looked like grated against what they still felt like inside. Each couple's romantic repartee reflected a racial common sense gleaned from a lifetime spent on the opposite side of the color line, where whites are taught that blacks are effortlessly sensual, and blacks are taught that white men are uptight, but white women are the elusive objects of everyone's desire. The exterior transformations were supposed to initiate and facilitate an abrupt and voluntary disengagement from the histories of race that otherwise structured the participants' understandings of themselves in/and the world. However, from the outset, the participants' internal understandings of themselves and others through racialized histories of desire and belonging proved extremely durable, and impervious to the fictions that latex and artificial pigment attempted to impose. I do not mean to suggest that these interior, ostensibly agential conceptions of the self and other are inherently real, true, or stable, but rather that they have a depth that radical shifts in the visual field cannot entirely or immediately upend. Whatever the participants' or the producers' intentions, the performances of racial inversion that the Sparks and Wurgel families undertook were dictated not solely by a coercive force in the social field based upon one's presumed phenotyical "fit" in one community or another, nor by the self-directed assumption of learned, "opposite" racial characteristics. Instead, acts of racial subterfuge, like all performative understandings of race, occur at the complex intersection of the powerful routinizations of race through behavior and what these performances have looked like and demanded of us through our past experiences. Performing another race is always to some extent a performance of what that other race looked like to you from the outside.

The theme song for the show, written and performed by Ice Cube, adds another perspective to *Black. White.*'s manipulation of race as relational trompe l'oeil: just as this artistic term refers to paintings that trick the eye into imbuing artifice with depth, with greater dimensionality, so too do contemporary racial discourses in general and the cosmetic virtuosity of the show in particular involve an embrace of the surface as a route to the depths of how people self-select and are positioned into groups today. Cube's first command in the song is, "Please don't believe the hype; everything in the world ain't black and white. Everybody ain't a stereotype, just because I look wrong, I'm about to do right" (BW). While the song refuses to deny that race has any significance whatsoever, it resists the overdetermination of its influence on individual identity and broader social relations. In fact, it offers performance as a site of resistance to racialization: "*Just because* I look wrong, I'm about to do right" (BW, emphasis added). A twenty-first-century deployment of double consciousness, this line acknowledges the quintessential problematization of blackness as one of misrecognition while positing that misrecognition as the very thing inciting action that triumphs over the limitations of externally reproduced (i.e., stereotypical) social controls. If the soundtrack is as much a plea for less prejudging on the part of viewers out in the real world as it is a description of what happens within the show, we are supposed to understand the participating families as having abandoned racial enmity in favor of restorative performances of blackness and whiteness, in which people "[did] right" by being true to themselves, thereby proving the similarities that the project intended to emphasize.

Beyond the theme song's conceptual invocation of performativity, the series explicitly engages with a theatrical tradition at the intersection of performance and performativity: blackface minstrelsy. This form of popular entertainment (the mass culture of yesteryear) involves parody, illicit liberation, and the definition and maintenance of racial order through discourses of embodiment. Because minstrelsy stands most prominently in popular memory as a phenomenon in which white performing bodies temporarily inhabited blackness, I will pay particular attention to the white performance of blackness that occurred within *Black. White.*[43] I am especially interested in understanding to what end the producers recruited one of American performance history's most reviled traditions. Within the context of the show, Bruno and Carmen served not only as performers but also as their own white audiences for their racial masquerades. Racial simultaneity persisted as they rehearsed and granted themselves distance from white fascination with black culture. Furthermore, because their masquerades were typically only immediately understood as such by themselves, they also functioned as the authenticators of their performances, adjudicating the realness of their cultural performance.[44] The black people with whom they interacted had no reason to suspect the impersonations taking place; even their imperfections could be absorbed into an antiessentialist racial logic that affirms the heterogeneity of blackness, leaving only Bruno and Carmen as their own most scrupulous audiences for their performances, attentive to the nuances of their efforts to enact blackness.[45]

But what was the reward for success under these circumstances? One of the traditional understandings of minstrelsy's efficacy for whites was that it provided a defensible outlet for all of the traits that whites recognized as existing within their society but from which they wanted to dissociate themselves: blacking up offered white performers the chance to escape the strictures of whiteness by expressing themselves in satisfying ways that they could leave behind when they removed their makeup. Carmen, in her eagerness to inhabit what she believed blackness to be, certainly fell into this pattern. On one occasion, she and Renee went clothes shopping as two black women, and Carmen was drawn to the vibrantly colored and patterned "traditional African" attire because it made her feel "proud and beautiful" (BW). (Incidentally, her shopping partner, Renee, who accompanied her sans makeup, found it curious that Carmen was drawn to the most extreme clothing choices, those that marked blackness as falling outside of American cultural and sartorial norms.) Additionally, Carmen revealed that her more intimate costume, her new skin color, "[did] for some reason give [her] permission to be more outrageous in ways, and [she] like[d] that. [She] like[d] stepping into that" (BW). For Carmen, makeup erased—or better, effaced—her long-standing sense of her "true" white self, allowing a new conception of self to emerge within that void as confident, beautiful, and proud.

Bruno indulged in a similar cultural license when, in a black Baptist church, he worked himself into a sweating frenzy, clapping and singing along to the gospel music, vocalizing with the congregants who were moved by the sermon. As the church service was depicted in the episode, Bruno outperformed the most devout churchgoers, overlooking the less ostentatious performances of blackness taking place simultaneously to which he could instead have conformed. Bruno's rapturous display certainly calls to mind E. Patrick Johnson's discussion of the work of the mostly white Australian gospel choir, Café of the Gate of Salvation, whose members selectively appropriate the symbolic import of gospel music as an expressive form rooted in the experiences of African Americans during and after slavery. Rather than a religious experience, Bruno's behavior at the worship service is a temporary moment of mimicry that seems, in the edited footage, to be responding not to the actual service he is attending, but to the broader stereotypes of black religious experience that position it as one of the most productive sites of racial difference, and thus as one of the most appealing sites for cultural voyeurism.[46] Both the clothing choices and the display of religious ecstasy were obvious departures from the behaviors that Bruno and Carmen usually displayed, and seemed to affirm Harryette Mullen's recognition of a change in race relations whereby "The black begins to be seen less as the dark body contrasted with the enlightened mind and more as the repressed and emotional soul of a white social-cultural-political-economic body."[47] In the twenty-first century, appropriative black performance works both to articulate and attempt to bridge difference, but this articulation now mourns the dissipated innocence and optimism of a civil rights discourse of interracial sociality. The extreme nature of Bruno and Carmen's black performances insists upon the profound distance between the two races, rather than some mid-point of similarity or reconciliation. In this context, blackness appears as/at the limit of white comprehensibility rather than at the center of its own cultural logic.

Turning our attention now to the series' construction of communities of belonging into which the participants earned their way or felt excluded from allows us to ponder more carefully yet another type of social performance, the racial pass, which provides the premise of at least half of the experiences the Wurgels and Sparkses undertake. Traditionally, racial passing has been understood to involve masquerade in the interest of gaining privileges that systemic inequality would otherwise hold out of one's reach, "an attempt to move from the margin to the center of American identity."[48] Furthermore, as I discussed in my analysis of attempts to position Denzel Washington's film career, the racial pass is most productively framed as a triangulated negotiation between the primary actor, the dupe, and a member of the primary actor's marginalized group who recognizes a peer's efforts to cross over.[49] The phenomenon of racial passing in *Black. White.* tends to affirm the sensibilities of the perpetrator, while also positing the television audience as the in-group clairvoyant fluent in racial difference, and who therefore recognizes the performance as such. Producers give audiences the tools of racial literacy at the very beginning of the series, when the families are put through a racial boot camp that addresses the exterior and the interior of race: language coaches educate the participants on the differences between black and white idiomatic expression and styles of delivery, and the participants have the opportunity to observe racially homogeneous panels in which black and white focus groups discuss their experiences of and attitudes toward race.

The series' narrative is propelled by the various instances when each member of the family tries to gain entry into a transracialized cultural space: young Nick attends etiquette class with rich white teens in Bel-Air, while Rose participates in a poetry slam workshop—one that was specifically crafted as a racially homogeneous space for the purposes of the show.[50] Brian gets a job at a bar in a middle-class white suburb that one resident proudly describes as one of the last preserves of well-meaning white people who have been unaffected by the waves of social migration, immigration, and decay that have touched the rest of the metropolis, while Bruno is escorted to a dominoes party and also spends some time walking through Leimert Park (a central public space in black Los Angeles) as the ultimate race traitor: a black man with a blonde white woman (i.e., Carmen, sans makeup). Lastly, Carmen is "adopted" by a black woman with a local radio show on issues affecting the black community, and Renee moves from Bible study to knitting to scrapbooking in her quest for white sisterhood. It is important to note how many of the participants' immersive scenarios involve explicit instruction in a cultural form whose racial connotations are assumed. With this given circumstance, the performance objective for the participants allows for a certain degree of incompetence that might excuse their imperfect transformations. If Nick struggles with the socioeconomically coded behaviors of the (white) elite, his presence is justified by the classroom setting even as his failures might be read as the irruption of an actual racial self that is incompatible with the demands of whiteness. The classroom model allows the producers to articulate the rules of white masculinity and femininity, and their black corollaries, even as it subtly suggests that racial difference is little more than the activities people undertake in their leisure time.

Making performance-as-competency the standard by which inclusion or exclusion from racialized communities is earned turns race once again into a profoundly autonomous category—a group may need to affirm the success of your enactments of race, but it can neither take credit for that success nor be held liable for your incompetence. This emphasis on localized behavior manages to de-emphasize the social and political force of racialization by ignoring the scalar model of power as differently wielded by individuals than by a racialized aggregate. Katrina Bell-Jordan recognizes this as a common strategy on reality television, where show after show "personalize[s] racism by privileging individual solutions to complex social problems."[51] Throughout *Black. White.*, various participants engage in diagnostic exchanges that are meant to validate the racial pass externally while also suggesting its irrelevance. The "coming out" encounters that Carmen, Renee, Rose, and Nick experience provide opportunities for ethical cleansing: the perpetrators hope to alleviate their guilt over beginning relationships with people that are rooted in deception, and the dupes have the opportunity to assuage that guilt by liking the perpetrators in spite of their racial difference.[52]

The confessional moments are structured so that the perpetrators reveal, while still in makeup, that they are not "natural" members of the racial community into which they have been welcomed. In each instance but one, the "dupes" respond graciously, saying that the difference doesn't matter and thereby affirming the mission of the series by proving that one's physical exterior may sometimes offer automatic invitation to or exclusion from systems of belonging, but ultimately, how one chooses to behave determines whether or not an individual is truly welcome within a community. These reveals overemphasize the power of individual agency as a dimension of racialization in their efforts to conform to the color-blind aspirations of the project by de-emphasizing race as a historical project functioning simultaneously at the social and individual levels. When Renee comes out to her white friend from scrapbooking class, the woman says, "Why would I care?," insisting that the other commonalities they have—shared Catholic faith, parenting adolescents, a fondness for scrapbooking and shopping—form the grounds for their relationship. In a voice-over, Renee states with wonder and pleasure, "I made a friend in California and she didn't care if I was black or white" (BW).[53]

White, teenaged Rose has the only televised experience that compromises this liberal humanist message. When she revealed herself to the black students in her poetry class, one young man commended her for her courage, and others politely agreed with noticeably varying levels of intensity, but another young man, Chazz, interrupted the encounter to declare, "You haven't even begun to apologize to me. . . . So cry, so I can see part of your white skin because I don't know who you are" (BW). Chazz's reaction seizes upon the difference between Rose's black mask and white self, and begins to hint at the complex grounds for inclusion in a racial community. Beyond the issue of trust being compromised by the revelation that her authentic blackness was merely an actorly facade, Rose also risks symbolic expulsion from the community because her earnestness, ironically, prevents her from being sincere. Her abiding anxieties initially about being found out, and later about being emotionally compelling enough to share the stage with her colleagues, keep Rose from experiencing total acceptance, and hint at the different stakes and strategies of the pass into versus out of blackness. Passing out of blackness means mastering the external behaviors of a whiteness that is predicated on a concerted ignorance of histories that would call attention to the violence through which privilege and whiteness become equivalent terms. On the other hand, successfully passing into blackness requires some conscious and informed relationship to the history of racial contestation in America, and the attitudes and behaviors that history has produced.[54] This difference produces the trap—or teachable moment—that the producers of *Black. White.* contrive with their experiment. The whiteness that the Sparks family is invited to inhabit must be reduced to scrapbooking and good manners in order to hide the assumed naturalness of its relationship to power and resources, but blackness cannot be reduced to writing poetry—even this mode of communication must be located in a historical appreciation for the role that expressive culture and specifically orality/orature have played in the constitution of black communities and blacks' place in a broader public sphere.

The Sparks's son Nick is the quietest member of the cast, but he is featured in one of the most controversial racialized moments in the entire series. After Nick has his coming out moment with the white students in his etiquette class—which prompts cries of "That's so cool!" (BW)—they are eager to help him refine his performance of whiteness, encouraging him to enunciate more clearly, to carry himself more vertically, to talk about the stock market, and to leave the heavy jewelry at home. Their advice emphasizes the aspirational qualities of the racial pass. While there are certainly many young adult white men who adopt the swagger of hip-hop culture (i.e., Nick's performance of a certain type of whiteness might be successful as it is), the teens suggest that the form of whiteness worth making an effort to master is associated with wealth, discretion, and control. Even though Nick's peers aren't bothered by the presumption of racial difference upon which the experiment relies, they recognize it as real: experienced both in the body and ideologically, elite whiteness is a skill they (or their parents) are committed to mastering for themselves and willing to share with others like them (or, willing to share temporarily with others who can never be like them). In fact, the white teens are far more interested in the entire project than Nick is. Confessional voice-overs depict him as one who repeatedly declares that he cares nothing about race or racism. He's bored by the project, and simply wants to finish and return home. In his mind, race and racism seem to be synonymous, and since he pays no attention to racism, he need not pay any attention to race either.

Just how racially transcendent Nick believes himself to be is revealed when the classmates are all in a shuttle together—postdisclosure—and one of the white young men throws a bottle at another and punctuates the toss by saying, "Nigger," as if it's a playful warning to mind his manners. The young women in the car are shocked, but Nick attempts to defuse the controversy by indicating that he isn't offended: "It's OK, I let him," he says, as if this privilege actually does reside with him (BW). But under what circumstances can we imagine Nick having the ability to grant such permission to a young white man to use a racist slur? The temporal elasticity of the verb to let—in which present and past tenses can be grammatically indistinguishable from one another—complicates any effort to explicate the dynamics of the moment. When Nick says, "I let him," is his "let" in the past or the habitual present? Had he offered an isolated instance of permission to use the term, or is permission to use the term in fact one of the terms of Nick's relationship to the other young men? Whatever the tense of his declaration, the tension it attempts to dissipate instantiates the inescapably communal investments in language as a social currency, of race as a discursive—rather than purely, ontologically physical—construction, in which discourse proscribes the values that define a culture, the limits of how it is willing to know itself and to articulate that knowledge. Dropping the n-word tested the limits of color blindness by daring everyone in the shuttle to disavow what that action had forced them to know: that a white person had used a racial slur in the presence of a black person, which risked giving evidence and credence to blacks' racial pessimism about America's values.

Rather than stoking any sort of pessimism, though, Nick's indulgence allows the white youth to feel vindicated, as if he is participating in a bonding exercise, in which the ritual of transracial (or color-blind) inclusion is functioning in both directions: despite their knowledge of Nick's brown skin beneath the makeup, the white guys are behaving just as they would in a monoracial environment of trust, and Nick is welcoming them into the community of people—usually presumed to be black—who have permission to say the word in an ostensibly nonviolent context. However, the manipulations of trust and agency in this scene are much more complicated. The "acceptable" reclamation of *nigger* usually presupposes its use as a term of kinship that reverses its use as a term of dehumanization, but its use in this moment instead legitimated the young man's aggressive behavior: act like a nigger and you'll be treated like one, subject to reprisals for unacceptable behavior. The exchange issues an implicit challenge to Nick, in which accepting the use of this slur without comment would be the real proof of his successful performance of whiteness as privilege.[55] Nick's consent to this speech act does far more to shore up whiteness than to demonstrate the deracinated equivalence of blackness with cool.

By denying the historical weight attached to the term *nigger,* particularly when uttered by a white person in the presence of a black person, the young men reinscribe the white privileges of unmarkedness and unaccountability that are the worst fears of color blindness's opponents. Denying the possibility that their use of the n-word could be construed as hate speech, and could incite fear in their audiences, the series shows the young men refuse individual responsibility for the long social history attached to the term. Additionally, this encounter exposes the intersections of race and gender: after the youngster who uses the word receives ablution from Nick, one of the girls says, "It doesn't matter if it doesn't bother him; it bothers *us*" (BW). Such as it was, the resolution of this controversy suggested that gendered understanding trumps racial hypersensitivity. The manner in which the young men dismissed the young women's concerns highlights another potential consequence of color blindness, a reinvigorated sexism in which men of different races focus on their similarities (especially gender) and unite to castigate women who challenge their authority.[56]

This encounter forms the bridge to the final axis of racial definition that is important to the development of *Black. White.*'s narrative, that of the participants' individual relationships to racism. One of the series' most striking dynamics is the intense hunger, shared by Bruno Marcotulli and Brian and Renee Sparks, for Bruno in particular to experience racism. Bruno wants the opportunity to be dignified in the face of oppression, while Brian and Renee want him to experience the irrefutable truths of overt and covert racism that, from their perspective, continue to structure black life. Brian's secondary objective in the project is to be the fly on the wall of white society, to see how close real life comes to the famous *Saturday Night Live* skit in which Eddie Murphy goes undercover and learns of the spectacular celebration of kinship and racial exclusivity that white people undertake the minute they are all alone. In spite of their shared desire to see racism in action, Bruno and Brian diverged in their estimations of what counted as such. For Bruno, who offered an obligatory affirmation of the persistence of racism in some contexts at some times, racism is comprised of individually motivated, intentional, conscious acts of hatred—whether through speech or other forms of intimidation—that reflect one's antipathy toward members of another race. For Brian, racism is the accretion of patterns of looking and moving through the world that perpetuate practices of segregation and inequality. Both men looked for manifestations of racism largely on the individual level, but Bruno required the added qualification of conscious intent, while Brian saw the inadvertent ways in which people have been socialized to suspect blacks of wrongdoing, or to reject them from social spaces.

With these objectives, both men approached the project looking to conduct audits of racism. Very early in the project, Bruno says, "It'll be interesting, and I'm sure it will happen, where I'll be in black and I'll get some attitude from some prick white guy. And I won't have all the history of resentment that a black man has, and I'll be able to fuck with him, oh just, you know, mentally spar with him and go, you know, he says 'Hey nigger,' you know, I won't get angry, I'll just kind of smile to myself and go, 'Wow, why'd you say that?'" Brian responds, "No one's gonna just straight say, strictly come up and say, you know, 'Hey nigger,' or anything like that, because that kind of racism is really not there today. Now it's more of we won't get the positions that we're qualified for, or we won't get the service that everybody else gets" (BW). This is a distinction that Bruno refuses to see, rooted as it is in durable histories of intergroup hostility and resource allocation. Brian's understanding of racial hostility is located more broadly in structures of interaction eliciting certain behaviors that conform to a collective racial unconscious that relies upon hierarchies of privilege. On the other hand, Bruno fervently believes that the post–civil rights epoch offers a radical break from racism of the past, and that race—and therefore racism—is an individual rather than societal phenomenon, which causes him to move through the project with a deep resentment of people who, in his view, allow their anticipatory hypersensitivity to racism serve as an "excuse" for their lack of social mobility.

Brian deserves an equal level of scrutiny: his two goals are to see Bruno and Carmen experience racism and thereby realize that blacks in twenty-first-century America aren't simply crying wolf, and to confirm the racism that he knows lurks beneath the surface of all white skin. Brian's definition of racism combines both a systematic production of inequality and the more individual acts of aggression in social settings that Stephen Small refers to as "racialized hostility"—an important distinction that is not always grasped.[57] These intentions unite Brian and Bruno in unusual ways: Brian constantly complains of the "Bruno block," Bruno's unwillingness to see the racism that is right in front of his face, but the arrogance that allows Bruno to do this is also present in Brian. He adopts the same Teflon attitude, and becomes impervious to anything that challenges the way he wants to see white interactions with and attitudes toward blacks. Anything that fails to confirm his hypothesis is transformed into ancillary evidence or dismissed.

In their efforts to gather evidence supporting their views on the function of race in everyday life, both families undertook racial audits that were not especially careful in their extrapolation of larger social truths. For example, both Renee and Bruno went looking for racism in classed contexts that would confirm the hypotheses with which they entered the project. Renee asked questions about race in a bar where people's attire suggested them to be working-class or lower-middle-class whites, and did in fact hear a man speak at length about how "America was founded by white people . . . and [if you don't want to assimilate to that culture, you should] go somewhere else" (BW). Likewise, Bruno conducted his audit in a wine bar in upper-middle-class Pasadena, where a white man spoke of the comfort level between the races, the noncontroversial nature of interracial relationships, and the fact that he would be willing to marry a black woman. Both conversations confirm Michael Brown's assertion in *Whitewashing Race* that assessing the prevalence of racism by asking people whether or not they harbor racist beliefs doesn't offer a very complete picture of how racism works.[58] Furthermore, in the interrogations conducted by both Renee and Bruno, the different results extracted from white respondents may also reflect the classed dimensions of racial etiquette: regardless of his actual feelings, the upper-middle-class white man has learned not to speak negatively about blacks in public spaces (especially to strangers, even white ones), while the working-class white man hasn't necessarily received the same training in hiding his negative opinions of blacks (or understands that he has less to lose from expressing them). Importantly, neither man believes himself to be a racist while describing what he understands of the world, but neither person draws from experiential evidence of the actual instances in which he may have had the opportunity to perpetuate or intervene against social and political practices that maintain imbalanced power relations between blacks and whites.

Taken together, these axes of racial exploration return us to the questions of individual agency versus aggregate racial characteristics or concerns that make explorations of black performance socially and politically urgent. The challenge within *Black. White.* is for the participants to see the liberatory potential of performance, to experience connections to people whom they would otherwise dismiss or fear being dismissed by, and thereby be empowered to do their individual part to dismantle racism in American culture by transcending racial particularism in favor of commonality. For the most part, this is not what happens. Instead, performance is deployed to sometimes oppressive ends: Bruno's ahistoricized ability to "mentally spar" with those who would use hate speech in his presence becomes his proof that blacks are responsible for dismantling racism by refusing to empower it with overheated responses. Bruno's hunger to experience racism is actually a hunger to be interpellated into the opportunity to redefine blackness through performance, on his terms. The most literal example of this comes when he shares with his housemates a video he has filmed of himself performing a rap song he has penned. The song takes a racialized expressive form and repurposes it to express his white frustration with those who fail to perform blackness appropriately, including those who use this musical form to produce unhelpful manifestations of blackness. However, by taking this stance, Bruno performs whiteness as much as, if not more than, he performs blackness, through his inability to shake loose the privilege of anticipating respect and kindness that forty years in white skin in America seem to have taught him. Because of this privileged way of inhabiting his body, Bruno will be the black man that others can't seem to, thereby offering a different citational possibility to blacks who want to improve themselves. His performance of blackness is an invitation to blacks to join the rest of America in the land of individual responsibility and agency, where "you get out of life what you put into it."

Ultimately, *Black. White.* functions as a discursive response to D. W. Griffith's *The Birth of a Nation:* the 1915 film also took nuclear families as the symbols of national fragmentation, and staged the redemption of the union through expulsion of racial others and the reconstitution of the heteronuclear family to span North and South, healing old divides through a shared commitment to white supremacy.[59] The television series of 2006 attempted to rewrite that narrative through the experiences of the Sparks and Wurgel families: on the evening before their departure, the families host a party to which all of the people who aided their racial charade are invited: this is the opportunity for black and white to share intimate domestic space, to challenge heteronuclear norms by reconfiguring the notion of family to include those to whom one feels committed and connected not solely by blood (authenticity), but also by choice (sincerity). The redemption that the series offers to its audience—if not to the participants of the project—is managed by bringing the various factions of black and white Los Angeles together for our viewing pleasure, giving us a host of racial proxies with which to identify in this simulation of multiracial sociality. It is only in these final minutes that the producers even begin to complicate the definitions of community within which race is experienced and potentially transgressed.

Heard differently by the end of this six-episode arc, Ice Cube's lyrics now sound like a prediction of the limitations of the project: indeed, "Everything in the world ain't black and white," and the narrowness with which the project defines black and white, and the constricted performances of race (and class and gender) that such definitions enable, teach us only that the microcosmic aspirations of the series cannot but fail to deliver, because they are premised on the transcendent deployment of bodies out of time, and out of place. *Black. White.* does not offer us black performance as transgressive potentiality because it refuses its place in a complex, intersectional world, and traps its actors within a depthless environment in which the interior and the anterior are always, frustratingly, out of reach. Nevertheless, *Black. White.* also teaches, through its shortcomings, lessons about performance, transgression, and race. It reminds us that transgressive efforts to redefine blackness through performance must be resolutely social, not solitary, gestures. To transgress on any scale with affective force is to engage both the public and private spheres, to negotiate a shared understanding of the past that works through contradictions rather than suppressing them. Using performance as the cultural site and expressive medium for dialogue about race that refuses to disparage it as mere problem or succumb to a reductively quantitative politics of representation, transgressive theories of black performance enable us both to imagine and to enact more just configurations of the past, the present, and the future.

Notes

CHAPTER 1

1. Jon McKenzie, *Perform or Else: From Discipline to Performance* (New York: Routledge, 2001), 166.

2. Herman Gray, *Cultural Moves: African Americans and the Politics of Representation* (Berkeley: University of California Press, 2005), 2.

3. Saidiya Hartman, *Scenes of Subjection: Terror, Slavery, and Self-Making in Nineteenth-Century America* (Oxford: Oxford University Press, 1997), 23.

4. California Secretary of State, http://vote96.sos.ca.gov/BP209yesarg.htm (accessed August 1, 2008).

5. W. E. B. Du Bois, *The Souls of Black Folk: Authoritative Text, Contexts, Criticism*, ed. Henry Louis Gates, Jr., and Terri Hume Oliver (1903; New York: W. W. Norton, 1999), 5.

6. California Secretary of State, Official Voter Information Guide, http://vote2003 .sos.ca.gov/propositions/2-3-4-text.html (accessed May 2009).

7. Tanya Schevitz, "Prop. 54 Defeated Soundly: State Initiative on Racial Privacy Raised Issues about Health, Education," *San Francisco Chronicle*, October 8, 2003, A12.

8. Ibid.

9. Exile as privacy is not only a visual strategy: one can also connect these concerns about choosing or being forced to hide one's culturally marked traits to the discourses surrounding racial ventriloquism. Racial ventriloquism focuses on linguistic patterns rather than visuality as a key to racial identification and therefore often (but not always) refers to written work (such as some modernist poetry) or cross-racial performances that obscure the performing body, whether through the medium of transfer (e.g., white actors Freeman Gosden and Charles Correll as stars of the 1920s–40s radio program *Amos 'n Andy*) or through cosmetic tools such as blackface and whiteface costuming (e.g., minstrelsy, which is assumed to be a theatrical practice located exclusively in the past, with only a few egregiously racist exceptions). Patricia J. Williams decried the persistence of racial ventriloquism when she noted the fractured English of the character Jar Jar Binks in the Star Wars franchise installment *The Phantom Menace*, a film that in her estimation is "filled with hierarchies of accent and class status" across fictive species lines that offer disturbing proxies for recognizable Anglophone racial categories ("Racial Ventriloquism," *Nation*, June 17, 1999, http://www.thenation.com/doc/ 19990705/Williams [accessed January 2009]). Likewise, radio advertisements rely heav-

ily upon associations between colloquialisms, intonation, and specifically racialized demographics. Even in the practice of everyday life, we might also consider strategies such
as "dialect coaching" and "accent reduction workshops" to be part of a similar practice
that recognizes the power of raced and classed associations between language patterns
and identity to limit or expand social and professional opportunities. Lynette Clemetson
wrote an essay for the *New York Times* in which she and other "articulate" black Americans admitted to "get[ting] a little testy when white people call them 'articulate'" because of the implicit assumption that such linguistic competence marks them as exceptional among members of their racial group, and the fact that such acclaim requires
overlooking the skills that ought to be assumed as normal for people of their class standing and educational attainment (Lynette Clemetson, "The Racial Politics of Speaking
Well," *New York Times*, February 4, 2007, http://www.nytimes.com/2007/02/04/weekin
review/04clemetson.html?scp=1&sq=the%20racial%20politics%20of%20speaking%
20well&st=cse [accessed January 2009]).

  10. John L. Jackson, Jr., *Racial Paranoia: The Unintended Consequences of Political
Correctness* (New York: Basic Civitas, 2008), 7.

  11. Lani Guinier and Gerald Torres, *The Miner's Canary: Enlisting Race, Resisting
Power, Transforming Democracy* (Cambridge: Harvard University Press, 2002), n308.
Guinier and Torres cite this comment made by R. Emmett Tyrell in order to disavow it
by "redefining racism so that it does not encompass all discussion of race."

  12. I use the word *incorporation* here deliberately: unlike other words that might fit
here (e.g., *assimilation, integration*), incorporation locates race as a problem of bodies
both social and individual and clarifies the outsider status that clings to American understandings of black subjectivity. I am suggesting that blacks existed as/at the limits of
the civic imaginary, necessary to the articulation of value implicit therein.

  13. David Hollinger, *Postethnic America: Beyond Multiculturalism* (New York: Basic
Books, 1995). The former of these assumes the intrinsic separation of cultures yet works
to preserve them, while the latter recognizes the more complicated dynamics of voluntary cultural membership that the end of the twentieth century offered to individuals
via forces including technology, shifting political circumstances, and the economic and
cultural consequences of globalization.

  14. Robin D. G. Kelley, "People in Me," *Colorlines: Race, Culture, Action* (Winter 1999):
6–7.

  15. James Kyung-Jin Lee, *Urban Triage: Race and the Fictions of Multiculturalism*
(Minneapolis: University of Minnesota Press, 2004).

  16. Paul Gilroy, *Postcolonial Melancholia* (New York: Columbia University Press,
2005), xv.

  17. The Wooster Group has used blackface in other productions, but their 1981 production of *Route 1 and 9* cost them some of the state arts funding they had received to
support their work.

  18. Michele Wallace, "The Culture War within the Culture Wars: Race," in *Art Matters:
How the Culture Wars Changed America*, ed. Brian Wallis, Marianne Weems, and Philip
Yenawine (New York: New York University Press, 1999), 169.

  19. Abigail Derecho (DeKosnik), "Illegitimate Media: Race, Gender, and Censorship
in Early Digital Remix Culture" (diss., Northwestern University, 2007).

20. Israel Zangwill, *The Melting Pot: Drama in Four Acts* (Norwood, MA: Norwood Press, 1909), 37–38.

21. Ibid., 199.

22. David Wiles, "Burdens of Representation: The Method and the Audience," in *Method Acting Reconsidered: Theory, Practice, Future*, ed. David Krasner (New York: St. Martin's Press, 2000), 170.

23. For these purposes, "mainstream theaters" refers to those theaters that have regular producing seasons and sustainable budgets and tend to receive the lion's share of governmental and philanthropic foundation grants. Furthermore, while this employment platform emerged in relation to the theater, it has since been used in relation to both television and film as well.

24. Harry Newman, "Holding Back: The Theatre's Resistance to Non-Traditional Casting," *TDR* 33.3 (1989): 23.

25. Newman's description of the origins of nontraditional casting is accurate though truncated: AEA notes its abiding conviction that American theater should be more integrated than it is and touts a history of action on its website that dates back to the 1950s, when AEA refused to allow its actors to perform to segregated audiences and actually convened an Integration Showcase in 1959 in New York, well before the subcommittee's articulation of nontraditional casting per se in 1986. http://www.actorsequity.org/aboutequity/timeline/timeline_1950.html (accessed July 2007).

26. The Non-Traditional Casting Project has since changed its name to Alliance for Inclusion in the Arts, the better to describe their multiple advocacy platforms, but because they were known as the Non-Traditional Casting Project throughout the 1990s, I will continue to refer to them as such here.

27. Non-Traditional Casting Project, "Mission," http://www.ntcp.org/missionframe .htm (accessed January 2002).

28. Ibid.

29. Casting practices at the symposium were diverse, but playwright selection was not: according to *Beyond Tradition*, all of the scenes performed during the symposium were from plays by white authors, reinforcing the notion of white neutrality contained within subsequent criticisms of nontraditional casting, which I will discuss later.

30. "Paul Robeson, Jr. on Non-Traditional Casting," in *Beyond Tradition: Transcripts from the First National Symposium on Non-Traditional Casting*, ed. Clinton Turner Davis and Harry Newman (New York: Non-Traditional Casting Project, 1988), 65.

31. Margaret Wilkerson, "Non-Traditional Casting: What Tradition?" in *Beyond Tradition: Transcripts from the First National Symposium on Non-Traditional Casting*, ed. Clinton Turner Davis and Harry Newman (New York: Non-Traditional Casting Project, 1988), 19.

32. Davis and Newman, *Beyond Tradition*, no page.

33. Ibid., no page.

34. Richard Schechner, "Race Free, Gender Free, Body-Type Free, Age Free Casting," *TDR* 33.1 (1989): 9.

35. In Davis and Newman, *Beyond Tradition*, 3.

36. Quoted in Bruce Weber, "On Stage, and Off," *New York Times*, April 1, 1994, C2.

37. Charles Mee, "A Note on Casting," http://www.charlesmee.com/html/cast.html (accessed August 2007).

38. Quoted in Weber, "On Stage, and Off," C2.

39. Quoted in Helen Epstein, *Joe Papp: An American Life* (New York: Little, Brown), 291.

40. Josephine Lee, "Racial Actors, Liberal Myths," *Xcp: Cross Cultural Poetics* 13 (2003): 95–98.

41. Angela C. Pao, "Changing Faces: Recasting National Identity in All-Asian(-) American Dramas," *Theatre Journal* 53.3 (2001): 394.

42. Ibid., 405.

43. Ibid., 407.

44. Likewise, Stephanie Batiste's research on "imperial performances" by black American performers—including the "Voodoo" *Macbeth* and *Haiti* productions during the years of the Federal Theater Project—indicates that acts of racial appropriation (whether of supposedly neutral texts like Shakespeare's *Macbeth* or of people of African descent in a differently racialized country) both enable readings of black performing bodies as passive objects upon which primitivist stereotypes may be placed and at the same time "[demonstrate] an African American investment in relationships of power and the politics of identity" that rejects those very assumptions of passivity (Stephanie Batiste, "Epaulettes and Leaf Skirts, Warriors and Subversives: Black National Subjectivity in *Macbeth* and *Haiti*," *Text and Performance Quarterly* 23.2 [2003]: 157).

45. William H. Sun, "Power and Problems of Performance across Ethnic Lines: An Alternative Approach to Nontraditional Casting," *TDR* 44.4 (2000): 87.

46. Harry J. Elam, Jr., "The Black Performer and the Performance of Blackness: *The Escape; or, A Leap to Freedom* by William Wells Brown and *No Place to Be Somebody* by Charles Gordone," in *African American Performance and Theater History: A Critical Reader*, ed. Harry J. Elam, Jr., and David Krasner (Oxford: Oxford University Press, 2001), 289.

47. *Race: The Floating Signifier*, videocassette, dir. Sut Jhally (Media Education Foundation, 1996).

48. Robyn Wiegman, *American Anatomies: Theorizing Race and Gender* (Durham: Duke University Press, 1995), 24.

49. Shannon Jackson, *Professing Performance: Theatre in the Academy from Philology to Performativity* (Cambridge: Cambridge University Press, 2004), 183.

50. Michael Omi and Howard Winant, *Racial Formation in the United States: From the 1960s to the 1990s* (New York: Routledge, 1994), 55–56.

51. Ibid., 55.

52. Judith Butler, *Gender Trouble: Feminism and the Subversion of Identity* (New York: Routledge, 1990), 33.

53. Ann Pellegrini, *Performance Anxieties: Staging Psychoanalysis, Staging Race* (New York: Routledge, 1997), 11.

54. E. Patrick Johnson, *Appropriating Blackness: Performance and the Politics of Authenticity* (Durham: Duke University Press, 2003), 2.

55. Andrew Parker and Eve Kosofsky Sedgwick, eds., *Performativity and Performance* (New York: Routledge, 1995), 3.

56. Harry J. Elam, Jr., "The Device of Race: An Introduction," in *African American*

Performance and Theater History, ed. Harry J. Elam, Jr., and David Krasner (Oxford: Oxford University Press, 2001), 13.

57. Hal Foster, *Recodings: Art, Spectacle, Cultural Politics* (Port Townsend: Bay Press, 1985).

58. Michael Brown, et al., *Whitewashing Race: The Myth of a Color-Blind Society* (Berkeley: University of California Press, 2003).

59. Michel Foucault, *Language, Counter-memory, Practice: Selected Essays and Interviews,* ed. Donald F. Bouchard, trans. Donald F. Bouchard and Sherry Simon (Ithaca: Cornell University Press, 1977), 30.

60. In this way, my championing of the utility of the term *transgression* follows Rebecca Schneider's feminist rejection of the end of transgression. In *The Explicit Body in Performance,* she writes: "the timing of this claim [that transgression is defunct] is suspiciously gender-, race- and preference-marked, coming at a moment when the terms of transgression, the agents of transgressive art, had radically shifted" (*The Explicit Body in Performance* [New York: Routledge, 1997], 4).

61. *Oxford English Dictionary,* www.oed.com (accessed June 2007).

62. *Oxford English Dictionary,* www.oed.com (accessed June 2007).

63. Steven Shaviro, *The Cinematic Body* (Minneapolis: University of Minnesota Press, 1993), 10.

64. Christina Maslach, "Welcome from the Vice Provost for Teaching and Learning," http://americancultures.berkeley.edu/ (accessed August 2009).

65. Lisa Claustro, "Haysbert Says *24* Role Paved the Way for Presidential Hopeful Barack Obama," http://www.buddytv.com/articles/24/haysbert-says-24-role-paved-th-15880.aspx (accessed January 2009).

66. These presidents were, respectively, characters in *The Man* (1972, played by James Earl Jones), *Deep Impact* (1998, played by Morgan Freeman), *Head of State* (2003, played by Chris Rock), *Idiocracy* (2006, played by Terry Crews), and the eponymous ship in James Schevill's 1965 play.

67. *NBC Nightly News,* November 4, 2008.

68. Pew Research Center, "A Year After Obama's Election: Blacks Upbeat about Black Progress, Prospects" (Washington, D.C.: Pew Research Center, 2010), 2. The same report indicates that one year after Obama's election, assessments had shifted, with 54% of blacks and 32% of whites believing that race relations actually had improved during the Obama administration.

69. NBC News, "White House Disputes Carter's Analysis; Gibbs: Obama doesn't believe he's being criticized for his race," September 16, 2009. http://www.msnbc.msn.com/id/32869276 (accessed August 2010). FoxNews.com, "Video Shows USDA Offical Saying She Didn't Give 'Full Force' of Help to White Farmer," July 20, 2010. http://www.foxnews.com/politics/2010/07/19/clip-shows-usda-official-admitting-withheld-help-white-farmer (accessed August 2010).

70. See Michele Elam's essay "Obama's Mixology" for a discussion of the ways in which Obama's racial signification became a site of struggle for various pro and anti-Obama factions during the campaign, most of whom deployed his blackness in ways that ran counter to his own self-presentation (http://www.theroot.com/views/obamas-

mixology [accessed January 2009]). See also the introductory chapter of Tavia Nyong'o's *The Amalgamation Waltz: Race, Performance, and the Ruses of History* (Minneapolis: University of Minnesota Press, 2009) for a discussion of how anxieties about Obama's racial legitimacy that were deeply inflected by the fact of his mixed heritage expose "how easily hybridity causes us to slip between race and racism" (6) and render us unsure as to whether we believe that amalgamation holds the key to the transcendence of race or threatens to enmesh us within it more securely.

71. Monica Davey, "The Speaker: A Surprise Senate Contender Reaches His Biggest Stage Yet," *New York Times* July 26, 2004. http://www.nytimes.com/2004/07/26/us/the-speaker-a-surprise-senate-contender-reaches-his-biggest-stage-yet.html (accessed August 2009).

72. Barack Obama, "Out of Many, One," July 27, 2004. http://www.washingtonpost.com/wp-dyn/articles/A19751-2004Jul27.html (accessed August 2010).

73. Ibid.

74. Marvin McAllister, *White People Do Not Know How to Behave at Entertainments Designed for Ladies and Gentlemen of Colour: William Brown's African and American Theater.* Chapel Hill: University of North Carolina Press, 2003.

75. Jason Horowitz, "Biden Unbound: Lays into Clinton, Obama, Edwards," *New York Observer* 4 February 2007, http://www.observer.com/2007/politics/biden-unbound-lays-clinton-obama-edwards (accessed September 2009).

76. Barack Obama, "A More Perfect Union," March 18, 2008. http://my.barack obama.com/page/content/hisownwords (accessed July 2010).

77. Daphne Brooks, *Bodies in Dissent: Spectacular Performances of Race and Freedom, 1850–1910* (Durham: Duke University Press, 2006), 5.

CHAPTER 2

First epigraph: Stanley Crouch, "Race Is Over," *New York Times,* September 29, 1996, sec. 6, 170.

Second epigraph: Patricia J. Williams, *Seeing a Color-Blind Future: The Paradox of Race* (New York: Noonday Press, 1997), 4, 6.

1. August Wilson, "The Ground on Which I Stand," *American Theatre,* September 1996, 72.

2. Ibid., 72.

3. Robert Brustein, "Subsidized Separatism," *American Theatre,* October 1996, 26ff.

4. Michael Eric Dyson, *Race Rules: Navigating the Color Line* (Reading: Addison-Wesley, 1996), 156.

5. Crouch, "Race Is Over," 170.

6. Ibid.

7. Williams, *Seeing a Color-Blind Future,* 7.

8. Andrew Kull, *The Color-Blind Constitution* (Cambridge: Harvard University Press, 1992), 182.

9. *Plessy v. Ferguson,* 163 U.S. 537 (1896), http://supreme.justia.com/us/163/537/

case.html (accessed December 2008). Furthermore, Harlan's belief in the colorblindness of the Constitution was coupled with a belief in the superiority of white people: he argued, "The white race deems itself to be the dominant race in this country. And so it is in prestige, in achievements, in education, in wealth and in power. So, I doubt not, it will continue to be for all time if it remains true to its great heritage and holds fast to the principles of constitutional liberty" (ibid.).

10. *Oxford English Dictionary,* www.oed.com (accessed December 10, 2008).

11. Constitution of the United States, http://www.archives.gov/exhibits/charters/con stitution_transcript.html (accessed December 2008).

12. Neil Gotanda, "A Critique of 'Our Constitution Is Color-Blind,' " in *Critical Race Theory: The Cutting Edge,* ed. Richard Delgado and Jean Stefancic, 2nd ed. (Philadelphia: Temple University Press, 2000), 35.

13. Wilson, "Ground," 72.

14. Ibid., 16.

15. Ibid., 16.

16. Ibid., 73.

17. Ibid., 14.

18. Glenn C. Loury, *The Anatomy of Racial Inequality* (Cambridge: Harvard University Press, 2002).

19. According to Brustein, "Wilson's vacillating use of the word 'we' [. . .] betrays his ambivalent sense of American identity" (Brustein, "Subsidized Separatism," 26).

20. Ibid., 71.

21. Ibid., 16.

22. Ibid., 72.

23. Harry J. Elam, Jr., *The Past as Present in the Drama of August Wilson* (Ann Arbor: University of Michigan Press, 2006), 228.

24. Ibid., 72.

25. Ibid., 16. Wilson's formulation of race as a singular and primary identity category includes within it a masculinist notion of racial meaning: if the world of *men* is the one in which race holds such sway over human behavior, how does race figure differently within the world of women? While Wilson would certainly disavow any intentions of sexism with this comment, it reveals how impossible it is to disarticulate race from gender, rendering the essentialist definitions upon which Wilson relies problematic.

26. Ibid., 72.

27. August Wilson, "August Wilson Responds," *American Theatre,* October 1996, 102.

28. Wilson, "Ground," 14.

29. Ibid., 16.

30. Incidentally, Wilson himself is a living demonstration of the intersection of genetics and self-affiliation in the production of racialized subjectivity: although he is of mixed racial heritage, having a black mother and a white father, he conforms to American principles of racial categorization and identifies himself as black, tracing his cultural identity through his mother alone.

31. Ibid., 14.

32. Ibid., 16.

33. Wilson, "August Wilson Responds," 103.

34. In the Obama era, any invocation of "white culture" is now ghosted by Fox News personality Glenn Beck's assertion that "the President has a deep-seated hatred of white culture," a statement that he stands by but also refuses to clarify by defining "white culture."

35. Wilson, "Ground," 72.

36. Ibid., 72.

37. Loury, *The Anatomy of Racial Inequality*, 5.

38. That is, people are held socially accountable for the virtual properties of their blackness even when these differ greatly from their actual blackness.

39. Loury, *The Anatomy of Racial Inequality*, 59.

40. This is not a claim that is meant to dehistoricize racial cultures, but rather an assertion that the fundamental dynamics of racial inequality persist, while the contexts within which they are experienced change.

41. Loury, *The Anatomy of Racial Inequality*, 69.

42. Ibid., 59, 67.

43. Ibid., 61.

44. Wilson, "Ground," 72.

45. Loury, *The Anatomy of Racial Inequality*, 83.

46. Brustein, "Subsidized Separatism," 26.

47. However, Brustein also suggests that, far from being colorblind, white foundations are actually engaged in the shallowest type of multiculturalism, as I will discuss later in this chapter.

48. Wilson, "Ground," 16.

49. Wilson, "Ground," 73. In fact, this meeting does take place at Dartmouth College in 1998, as Sandra Shannon describes in *August Wilson and Black Aesthetics* (New York: Palgrave Macmillan, 2004).

50. Loury, *The Anatomy of Racial Inequality*, 97. However, one might still ponder how much blacks, as targets of racial stigma that explains the persistence of their unequal status in American culture, are empowered to significantly alter the racial disparities by which they are marginalized; that is, there seem to be severe limitations upon the racial egalitarianism pro-black discrimination in contact could produce.

51. "Casting: Colorblind or Conscious?" *American Theatre*, September 1996, 20.

52. Loury, *The Anatomy of Racial Inequality*, 97.

53. Harry J. Elam notes that Wilson's language specifies colorblind rather than nontraditional casting, but my point here is to trouble our sense of this distinction as absolute and also to point to the difference between casting decisions and performance practices.

54. Ibid., 203. As Erika Munk points out, the concerns Wilson expresses in "I Want a Black Director" form the basis of his "The Ground on Which I Stand" address: I have just quoted Wilson as wondering "whether we as blacks are going to have control over our own culture and its products," and in his later keynote address Wilson again says, "We cannot allow others to have authority over our cultural and spiritual products" ("Ground," 72).

55. Ibid., 201–2. The conclusion of this paragraph provides yet another example of Wilson's monolithic formulation of "the culture of black Americans."

56. Ibid., 204. These were Wilson's words within the essay; they remained true at the time of his death in 2005.

57. Ibid., 202, 200.

58. Wilson, "Ground," 16.

59. Ibid., 15.

60. However, it must be noted that while Wilson was criticizing the demographics of LORT, the absented institutional presence in question at the time of his speech was more specifically the membership of Theatre Communications Group, a much larger (but differently organized and differently influential) association of theater workers, which does include more diverse membership.

61. Elin Diamond. "The Violence of 'We': Politicizing Identification," *Critical Theory and Performance*, ed. Janelle G. Reinelt and Joseph R. Roach (Ann Arbor: University of Michigan Press, 1992), 391.

62. Wilson, "Ground," 15.

63. Audre Lorde, "Learning from the 60s," *Sister Outsider: Essays and Speeches* (Freedom, CA: Crossing Press, 1984), 142.

64. Wilson, "Ground," 71, 72.

65. Ibid., 74.

66. In "Subsidized Separatism," Brustein notes that "almost alone among white critics, [he has] expressed reservations about Wilson's plays . . . a lot of his writing has seemed to [him] weakly structured, badly edited, prosaic and overwritten" (27).

67. This is not to single out Robert Brustein: he is no different from the head of any other reputable actor training program, in that students who matriculate through these programs are expected to develop technical facility with canonical works that makes them qualified to step into the production seasons of any mainstream repertory theater.

68. Brustein, "Subsidized Separatism," 27.

69. William Bennett, *The De-Valuing of America: The Fight for Our Culture and Our Children* (New York: Summit Books, 1992), 25.

70. Ibid., 29.

71. Bennett, *The De-Valuing of America*, 35. See Goldberg's excellent essay "Multicultural Conditions" in his *Multiculturalism: A Critical Reader* (Cambridge: Harvard University Press, 1994) for a discussion of the emergence of monoculturalism as an "institutional ideology" that grounded American public life.

72. Robert Brustein, "Diversity and Unity," in *Dumbocracy in America: Studies in the Theatre of Guilt, 1987–1994* (Chicago: Ivan R. Dee, 1994), 195.

73. Robert Brustein, *Reimagining American Theater* (New York: Hill and Wang, 1991), 5.

74. Robert Brustein, *Cultural Calisthenics: Writings on Race, Politics, and Theatre* (Chicago: Ivan R. Dee, 1998), 4.

75. Robert Brustein, "Coercive Philanthropy," in *Cultural Calisthenics: Writings on Race, Politics, and Theatre* (Chicago: Ivan R. Dee, 1998), 13.

76. Ibid., 14.

77. Bush used this phrase in his July 2000 speech at the NAACP's national conven-

tion, specifically in reference to addressing the educational achievement gap between whites and students of color. http://www.washingtonpost.com/wpsrv/onpolitics/elec tions/bushtexto71000.htm (accessed August 2008).

78. Brustein, "Subsidized Separatism," 26.

79. Ibid., 27.

80. Brustein, "Race, Art and Inclusion," *American Theatre*, November 1996, 62.

81. Bennett, *The De-Valuing of America*, 188.

82. Wilson, "Ground," 16.

83. Brustein, "Subsidized Separatism," 100.

84. Ibid., 100.

85. Ibid., 26.

86. Ibid., 26.

87. Elsewhere, Brustein does suggest a separate but equal racially identifiable funding structure that might benefit black theater: "At a time when the black middle class is growing by leaps and bounds, you would think that the impulse to start such a [black] theatre would begin with a visionary artistic director, supported financially by the wealthier members of the black community, perhaps including Wilson himself" ("Race, Art, and Inclusion," 63). Nevertheless, this admonition preserves the race-consciousness that runs counter to his alleged belief in the colorblindness of contemporary American theater culture.

88. And beyond this, on the broader relationship between art and commerce, the source of some of his struggles with Bart Giamatti, the president of Yale who called for his dismissal.

89. Arguably, Brustein's unfavorable reviews of Wilson's work form another, a fact alluded to by Brustein when he suggests that Wilson "smart[s] under adverse criticism, even in a relatively small-circulation periodical such as *The New Republic*" ("Subsidized Separatism," 27).

90. Brustein, "Coercive Philanthropy," 9.

91. Brustein, "Subsidized Separatism," 100.

92. Ibid., 27.

93. Ibid., 27.

94. E.g., the advertisement on p. 5 of *American Theatre*'s January 1997 issue, which featured a head shot of each participant.

95. However, I suspect Brustein would contest this allegation, saying instead that he represented a universal artistic tradition.

96. Robert Brustein, "On Cultural Power," in *Cultural Calisthenics: Writings on Race, Politics, and Theatre* (Chicago: Ivan R. Dee, 1998), 31.

97. Ibid., 31.

98. E.g., Wilson's claim that "Inside all blacks is at least one heartbeat that is fueled by Africa" and Brustein's "nostalgi[a] for a community of dancers that didn't acknowledge race ('like the community of Bill Robinson dancing with Shirley Temple')" (Stephen Nunns, "Wilson, Brustein & the Press," *American Theatre*, March 1997, 18).

99. Nunns, "Wilson, Brustein & the Press," 18.

100. Ibid., 18.

101. In this regard, even her gender serves the meaning of the event: distanced from both men by gender, and from one by race, Smith nevertheless demonstrates through her own performance work that differences can be real and meaningful without being obstacles to identification.

102. Nunns, "Wilson, Brustein & the Press," 17.

103. Richard Schechner, "In Praise of Promiscuity," *American Theatre,* December 1996, 59.

104. Lou Bellamy, "Race, Art and Inclusion," *American Theatre,* November 1996, 62.

105. Erika Munk, "Up Front," *Theater* 27.2–3 (1997): 5.

106. Robbie McCauley, "Working around Power," *Theater* 27.2–3 (1997): 34.

107. Wilson, "Ground," 72.

108. Brustein, "Subsidized Separatism," 27. Brustein's conviction is sincere, as he was one of Joseph Papp's "staunchest supporters" among the press during the early years of the New York Shakespeare Festival (Epstein, *Joe Papp,* 184), concurrent with the push for desegregation of American public culture.

109. Brustein also mentioned that Wilson's platform would bar white South African actor/playwright Athol Fugard from "tak[ing] a colored role in his own plays" (27).

110. I specify this essay because in later writings, Brustein makes more of an effort to acknowledge the difficult conditions under which black theater operates.

111. Larry Neal, "Black Arts Movement," in *A Sourcebook of African American Performance: Plays, People, Contexts,* ed. Annemarie Bean (New York: Routledge, 1999), 55.

112. Clinton Turner Davis, "To Whom It May Concern," *Theater* 27.1–2 (1997): 32.

113. Gitta Honegger, "On Cultural Power: 13 Commentaries," *American Theatre,* May–June 1997, 16.

114. Davis, "To Whom It May Concern," 30.

115. Ibid., 31.

116. Robert Brustein, "Resident Theatre Hopes," in *Cultural Calisthenics: Writings on Race, Politics, and Theatre* (Chicago: Ivan R. Dee, 1998), 147.

117. Ibid., 147. This comment was made in relation not only to Parks's subject matter but also to the fact that an ensemble of black and white actors took on roles that deviated from their actual racial identities.

118. Ibid., 147.

119. Alan Nadel, "August Wilson and the (Color-Blind) Whiteness of Public Space," *Theater* 27.2–3 (1997): 39.

120. Ibid., 40.

121. Una Chaudhuri, "On Cultural Power: 13 Commentaries," *American Theatre,* May–June 1997, 61.

122. Zelda Fichandler, "On Cultural Power: 13 Commentaries," *American Theatre,* May–June 1997, 58 (emphasis added).

123. Schechner, ""In Praise of Promiscuity," 59.

124. Goldberg, "Multicultural Conditions," 27.

125. http://lort.web.officelive.com/members.aspx (accessed May 2010). Of the member theaters listed one, the Pasadena Playhouse, perhaps comes closest to this goal. Under the direction of Sheldon Epps, it strongly emphasized making opportunities for

African American artists by producing several—rather than one—African American plays per season, even though it does not restrict itself to producing plays by or exclusively featuring African Americans. However, in July 2010, it emerged from chapter 11 restructuring and its future programming profile remains to be seen.

126. Sandra Shannon and Dana Williams, "A Conversation with August Wilson," in *August Wilson and Black Aesthetics*, ed. Sandra Shannon and Dana Williams (New York: Palgrave Macmillan, 2004), 188. Incidentally, in this same interview, Wilson said that if he had to do it again, he would not mention his disapproval of nontraditional casting, because of the ways that it overshadowed the rest of his institutional critique.

127. League of Resident Theatres, http://www.lort.org/mission.htm (accessed July 2007).

128. Wilson, "Ground," 16.

129. Quoted in Campbell Robertson, "The World of Black Theater Becomes Ever Bigger," *New York Times*, February 12, 2007, http://www.nytimes.com/2007/02/21/theater/21urba.html?_r=1&pagewanted=all (accessed July 2009).

130. Ibid.

131. Goldberg, "Multicultural Conditions," 18.

132. Claudia Moscovi, *Double Dialectics: Between Universalism and Relativism in Enlightenment and Postmodern Thought* (New York: Rowan and Littlefield, 2002), 6.

133. It is worth noting that the Classical Theater of Harlem aspires to the type of multiracial collaboration that Wilson says is missing in most encounters between black actors and "the classics." Founded by two white directors in 1999, the company produces not only American and European canonical texts in which black actors are cast against type but also classic work from the African American theatrical tradition. They do not have LORT status, a fact that underscores that we must look beyond just the regional theater circuit to assess the prospects for cultivating black performance practices that challenge our views of the potential inherent within black performing bodies.

CHAPTER 3

Epigraph: Richard Dyer, *White* (New York: Routledge, 1997), 20.

1. Elizabeth Alexander, *The Black Interior* (St. Paul, MN: Graywolf Press, 2004), 151–52.

2. Michael Kimmelman, "Constructing Images of the Black Male," *New York Times*, November 11, 1994, C1.

3. James Gardner, "Lost in the Male—Whitney Museum of American Art, New York, New York; Various Artists." *National Review*, February 6, 1995, 76.

4. Thelma Golden, "My Brother," in *Black Male: Representations of Masculinity in Contemporary American Art*, ed. Thelma Golden (New York: Whitney Museum of American Art, 1994), 22.

5. Dyer, *White*, 25.

6. This remains true even as more Americans break out of the heteronuclear family paradigm: with assisted reproductive technologies such as sperm banks, egg donor programs, and surrogate parenting agreements that allow not just heterosexual couples but also single parents and queer parents to produce children with whom they share ge-

netic material, race remains a valued category of inclusion and exclusion as people make choices about the races from whom they do and do not wish to accept reproductive assistance.

7. E.g., August Wilson's allegations of the ideological permanence of "white" theater, regardless of the number of blacks who are invited to participate in it. The institutional aims and the distribution of power that are central to Wilson's definition of white theater can remain intact even when people of color are present.

8. Cedric Robinson, *Forgeries of Memory & Meaning: Blacks and the Regimes of Race in American Theater and Film before World War II* (Chapel Hill: University of North Carolina Press, 2007), 108.

9. These are my subjective narrations of scenes from *The Birth of a Nation*. Griffith's text is directly quoted only through intertitles.

10. Richard Dyer has suggested that the "cult of true womanhood" to which characters like Elsie Stoneman belonged was both appealing and off-putting to audiences: in addition to making white women feel at once prized and imprisoned, "It provided white men with an object of inspirational devotion, but one which might also provoke resentment of moral superiority and *sexual unavailability*" (emphasis added) (*White*, 130).

11. D. W. Griffith. *The Birth of a Nation* (Biograph Film, 1915). All subsequent intertitle quotations are from the same text.

12. Flora's suicide is itself a repetition with difference of a virgin suicide scene from the novel *Last of the Mohicans*. The familiarity and portability of this trope can be connected as well to the many tragic mulatta narratives in which a "nearly white" woman commits suicide or is otherwise undone, in part to keep her from or punish her for a miscegenated relationship, e.g., Dion Boucicault's classic, *The Octoroon*. As Sterling Brown writes about white writers' fascination with the tragic mulatto, "Their favorite character, the octoroon, wretched because of the single drop of midnight in her veins, desires a white lover above all else, and must therefore go down to a tragic end" (*Negro Poetry & Drama and the Negro in American Fiction* [New York: Atheneum, 1969], 145). See also Jennifer DeVere Brody's own *Impossible Purities* for her reading of Boucicault's *Octoroon* and her development of the term "mulattaroon to suggest this figure's status as an unreal, impossible ideal whose corrupted and corrupting constitution inevitably causes conflicts in narratives that attempt to promote purity" (Jennifer DeVere Brody, *Impossible Purities: Blackness, Femininity, and Victorian Culture* [Durham: Duke University Press, 1998], 16). This connection between the threat of miscegenation and the plight of the miscegenated will become important later in the chapter.

13. Robinson, *Forgeries of Memory & Meaning*, 92.

14. While the code was nominally adopted in 1930, provisions for its enforcement were implemented in 1934.

15. Motion Picture Association of America, *A Code to Govern the Making of Motion Pictures: The Reasons Supporting It and the Resolution for Uniform Interpretation* (New York, 1930–55), 1.

16. Ibid., 6.

17. Mark A. Reid, *Redefining Black Film* (Berkeley: University of California Press, 1993), 12.

18. Donald Bogle, *Toms, Coons, Mulattoes, Mammies, and Bucks: An Interpretive History of Blacks in American Films*, 4th ed. (New York: Continuum, 2003), 176. The generalization of "black America" is intentional here and meant to reflect the very real burden of representation attached to Poitier's status as the first black American movie star, and the hopeful expectation that his successes would be seen as indicative of the potential of all black Americans.

19. While Sidney Poitier's celebrity is widely recognized as a turning point in black film history, Henry Louis Gates, Jr.'s, *Thirteen Ways of Looking at a Black Man* (New York: Random House, 1997), includes chapters on both Poitier and his friend Harry Belafonte, another black performer with crossover appeal to whites. Belafonte himself wonders if part of the reason Poitier enjoyed such marquee success is that his sexuality was more easily sublimated than Belafonte's own. Belafonte starred in the controversial yet financially successful 1957 film *Island in the Sun*, which represented interracial sexuality as dangerously romantic. Beyond his on-screen roles, Belafonte also points to his more overtly politicized identity as a difference between the two that may have kept him from being equally bankable as a high-profile black star during an era that sought ambassadors of peaceful integration who would not aggressively challenge white privilege. Additionally, both Poitier and Belafonte were from Caribbean families: each man was born in the United States but spent a significant portion of his childhood in the Caribbean (the Bahamas and Jamaica, respectively). These multinational politics of location, mobility, and identity pose challenges to the burden placed on either man to represent black American masculinity, both demonstrating the ethnic and cultural variability within the aggregated community of blacks in America and exposing the competing identificatory claims that other countries and cultures might place on the same performer.

20. Bogle, *Toms, Coons, Mulattoes, Mammies, and Bucks*, 181, 182.

21. Although the film was commercially successful, film historian Ed Guerrero recounts that black audiences were disappointed in Poitier's performance in a film that was so conspicuously divorced from the social context that actually produced the enmity over which John and Joey triumphed in the narrative (Ed Guerrero, *Framing Blackness: The African American Image in Film* [Philadelphia: Temple University Press, 1993], 76). Rather than opting for transgression, which would entail a deep engagement with this social context, Kramer aspired to transcendence that protected white privilege—in this instance, the privilege of being able to ignore racist social and sexual history—and invited Poitier to reap its benefits.

22. To be clear, limiting is not eliminating. In films including *Mississippi Masala, Ricochet, Mo Better Blues*, and *Devil in a Blue Dress*, Washington has had onscreen dalliances with female costars, the first of which was in fact a film about an interracial romance with an Indian woman in the southern United States.

23. Hazel Carby, *Race Men* (Cambridge: Harvard University Press, 1998), 176.

24. Academy of Motion Picture Arts and Sciences, http://www.oscars.org/74acade myawards/specialawards/honorary01.html (accessed July 2008). The president of the academy went on to say, "When the Academy honors Sidney Poitier, it honors itself even more" (ibid.). The president's claim can be read at least two ways: while it might mean that the academy feels honored to have benefited from Poitier's involvement in the pro-

fession, it might also be a self-congratulatory claim priding the academy on its ability to recognize the accomplishments of people of color, as evidence of its color-conscious colorblindness.

25. Academy of Motion Picture Arts and Sciences, http://www.oscars.org/74acade myawards/winners/04leadingactress.html (accessed July 2008).

26. Academy of Motion Picture Arts and Sciences, http://www.oscars.org/74acade myawards/winners/02leadingactor.html (accessed July 2008).

27. Ibid.

28. Reid, *Redefining Black Film*, 52.

29. Douglas Brode, *Denzel Washington: His Films and Career* (Seacaucus: Birch Lane Press, 1997), xxviii. It is important to note that Brode's book does not include citations that indicate the sources of his information, and so this declaration of Washington's colorblind aspirations could be entirely Brode's conjecture. However, I cite it as part of the public collection of interpretations of and responses to Washington's work. In other words, whether accurately or not, Brode has recruited Washington as a symbol of Hollywood's colorblind potential, supporting my claims about Washington's significance to understanding the racial politics and performance of black masculinity at the turn of the twenty-first century.

30. E! Online, "One Hundred Years: Heartthrobs," http://www.eonline.com/Fea tures/Specials/Century/Feb/05.b.html (accessed May 2003). The different career trajectories that lead to and follow from this racialized distinction between Snipes, Fishburne, and Washington are worth investigating in another context.

31. Internet Movie Database, http://www.imdb.com/title/tto107798/business (accessed June 10, 2007).

32. David Ansen, "No 'Brief' Pelican," *Newsweek*, December 20, 1993, 121.

33. Perhaps it helps that Washington enters the plot once the action has moved from the conspicuously miscegenated locale of New Orleans to the more urbane Washington, DC.

34. Allison Samuels, "Will It Be Denzel's Day?" *Newsweek*, February 25, 2002, 60.

35. Stanley Crouch, "Who's Zooming Who?" *Theater* 27.1–2 (1997): 22.

36. Linda Williams, *Playing the Race Card: Melodramas of Black and White from Uncle Tom to O.J. Simpson* (Princeton: Princeton University Press, 2001), 300.

37. Amy Robinson, "It Takes One to Know One: Passing and Communities of Common Interest," *Critical Inquiry* 20.4 (1994): 715–36.

38. Ibid., 721.

39. Ibid., 716.

40. This omission—and its racial undertones—was not lost on a few of the film's critics. Janet Maslin's *New York Times* review noted that John Grisham "did close his book with a clinch and a promise of romance between Darby and Gray. The film, which thrives on the comfortable chemistry between its two stars, isn't quite gutsy or colorblind enough to do the same" (Janet Maslin, "Presenting Nancy Drew for the 90s," *New York Times*, December 17, 1993, C1).

41. While *The Pelican Brief* rationalizes this slight in part through Washington's costume, Cornel West writes of a similar experience in New York City when, at the corner

of 60th Street and Park Avenue, he watched ten taxis pass him by. A professional man in a suit and spectacles, an esteemed professor at an Ivy League institution, West was on his way to a photo shoot for the cover of his book, *Race Matters,* published in the same year of *The Pelican Brief*'s release. See West, *Race Matters* (Boston: Beacon Press, 1993), x–xi.

42. *The Pelican Brief,* dir. Alan Pakula (Warner Brothers, 1993). Subsequent citations of the film will be noted as *Pelican Brief* (film).

43. Robinson, "It Takes One to Know One," 716.

44. Ibid., 716.

45. John Grisham, *The Pelican Brief* (New York: Island Books, 1992), 253.

46. Ibid., 254–55.

47. Indeed, Janet Maslin refers to the film as "a celebration of liquid brown eyes and serious star quality" ("Nancy Drew for the 90s," C1).

48. *Pelican Brief* (film).

49. In effect, their relationship replicates the Shirley Temple/Bill "Bojangles" Washington dynamic in which the sexual viability of the black man is elided by focusing instead on his watchful, loyal qualities. Of course, in the Shirley Temple/Bill Robinson example, the neutralization is also effected through the disparity in age between the two performers. See Ann DuCille's "The Shirley Temple of My Familiar" for a discussion of the racial dynamics of the seemingly benign movies starring Temple in *Transition* 73 (1997): 10–32.

50. *Pelican Brief* (film).

51. Ibid.

52. Grisham, *Pelican Brief,* 354–55.

53. Phillip Brian Harper, *Are We Not Men? Masculine Anxiety and the Problem of African American Identity* (New York: Oxford University Press, 1996), 119.

54. Willie Horton was a Massachusetts prisoner serving a life sentence for murder whose temporary social freedom came through the state's prison furlough program that allowed prisoners unsupervised weekend passes as part of an effort to rehabilitate rather than simply punish them. In 1986, Horton received a weekend pass, became a fugitive, and in 1987 raped a white woman and stabbed her fiancé. After being apprehended, he was sentenced to consecutive life sentences in prison. O. J. Simpson's social mobility came through his wealth and his crossover celebrity appeal.

55. Samuels, "Will It Be Denzel's Day?" 61.

56. Ed Guerrero, "Devil in a Blue Dress," *Cineaste* 22.1 (1996): 41.

57. Director's commentary, *Devil in a Blue Dress,* DVD version. Subsequent citations of footage and commentary from the film will be noted as *Devil in a Blue Dress* (film).

58. While social policies often treat Mexican Americans (and all other people labeled Hispanic) as a subset of the white race, the bigotry directed toward them reveals the marginal nature of that racial status. Within *Devil in a Blue Dress,* Terrell's actions seem to exoticize his adopted sons as racial others. It is also important to note that director Carl Franklin changed the name of Matthew Terrell's character from Mosley's original Matthew Teran, because "it sounded Middle Eastern and didn't make a lot of sense that he'd be running for mayor."

59. Dyer, *White,* 219–20. Terrell's access to patriarchal authority comes through non-traditional means and therefore his raced and immorally sexualized position within this hierarchy might instill terror within the white community at large.

60. Rachel F. Moran, *Interracial Intimacy: The Regulation of Race and Romance* (Chicago: University of Chicago Press, 2001).

61. See Harper, *Are We Not Men?* for a discussion of this photo illustration and the controversy it generated.

62. Ralph Wiley, "White Lies: HBO Gets It Half Right," November 14, 2002, http://espn.go.com/page2/s/wiley/021113.html (accessed February 2006).

63. Williams, *Playing the Race Card,* 43.

64. The parenthetical construction in this sentence is crucial because even as Simpson was remanded to blackness, victims' rights advocates were at great pains to make their explicit condemnations all about a disarticulated gender binary. Nicole B. Simpson's fate reflected the tragedy of unchecked, escalating violence against women, an epidemic that transcended—i.e., had nothing to do with—class and racial categories. This allowed the media to narrate the crime in raced and gendered terms that preceded, ran concurrent with, and followed these principled condemnations.

65. Williams, *Playing the Race Card,* 266.

66. Ibid., 266.

67. Kimberlé Williams Crenshaw, "Color-Blind Dreams and Racial Nightmares: Reconfiguring Racism in the Post–Civil Rights Era," in *Birth of a Nation'hood: Gaze, Script and Spectacle in the O.J. Simpson Case,* ed. Toni Morrison and Claudia Brodsky Lacour (New York: Pantheon Books, 1997), 99.

68. *Devil in a Blue Dress* (film).

69. *Devil in a Blue Dress* (film), director's commentary. In fact, Franklin seems so uncomfortable with the sexual trauma in the scene that, in the moment when Albright orders the young white man to his knees, Franklin chooses to mention that the kneeling actor is a very nice man and an excellent swing dancer, rather than to offer commentary that would illuminate the racial confrontation within the scene.

70. Walter Mosley, *Devil in a Blue Dress* (New York: Pocket Books, 1990), 53.

71. Ibid., 54.

72. Ibid., 55.

73. See E. Ann Kaplan, *Women in Film Noir* (London: BFI Publishing, 1980). We might say that if the concept of whiteness includes within it terror over reproductive inadequacy, the femme fatale produces and/or exposes the terror within masculinity over productive inadequacy, the inability to provide materially for a woman in ways that she could not for herself.

74. Such coverage often notes the fact that Beals resisted efforts to make her racial identity the primary feature of her public biography: e.g., "Beals avoids answering questions about her personal life, especially those on grades, boyfriends and whether she faced racial problems while growing up in Chicago with a black father (who died when she was nine) and a white mother" (Richard Lormand, "Jennifer Beals Finds Success Courting Her," *Globe and Mail* (Canada), August 29, 1985, https://www.lexisnexis.com/us/lnacademic/results/docview/docview.do?docLinkInd=true&risb=21_T5441520570&format=GNBFI&sort=DATE,A,H&startDocNo=26&resultsUrlKey=29_T5441520554&ci

sb=22_T5441532043&tree Max=true&treeWidth=0&csi=303830&docNo=26).

75. It is also worth noting that class figures into this sense of power to regulate access: even though his job in the service sector marks him as belonging to the working class, his role as an enforcer of segregationist policy (and his ability to betray it) grants the bellhop a degree of influence that is seemingly at odds with his class status.

76. Mosley, *Devil in a Blue Dress*, 95.

77. *Devil in a Blue Dress* (film), director's commentary.

78. I am reminded of Kim Hall's work in *Things of Darkness: Economies of Race and Gender in Early Modern England* (Ithaca: Cornell University Press, 1995), in which she notes the representational strategy of placing a white women in portraits with black servants (usually boys) who emphasized through contradistinction the white woman's race and gender. In that context, proximity was a privilege of "pure" whiteness that could pass the test of comparative scrutiny, but Beals has to manage literal and figurative distances between herself and Washington carefully in order to sustain her temporary pass within the film. We might even say that instead of needing proximity to a black boy to emphasize her desired racial identity, she needs proximity to a white man to normalize her presence as white. The fact that the film is implicitly about the pursuit of this visual and narrative proximity—but never succeeds in achieving it—further demonstrates the failure of Franklin's retroactively colorblind paradigm.

79. Dinitia Smith, "Novelists Get Back at Hollywood, Mostly Gently," *New York Times*, September 25, 1999, http://query.nytimes.com/gst/fullpage.html?res=9402E5D7133FF936A1575AC0A96F958260&sec=&spon=&pagew anted=all (accessed August 2008). In the same article, Mosley bluntly declared his willingness to sacrifice narrative consistency across media as long as he was properly compensated for his work as a writer. Also worth noting is the fact that the descriptions of Beals and Washington are reduced to skin color rather than attached to race, lest they be forced to account for the complications that Beals's light skinned body poses for racial categories.

80. Mosley, *Devil in a Blue Dress*, 187.

81. I.e., technically, her relationships with white men are actually the transgressive ones, but they do not seem to be so because of her physical appearance.

82. Williams, *Playing the Race Card*, 29.

83. Mosley, *Devil in a Blue Dress*, 204.

84. Domestic receipts for *Devil in a Blue Dress* were recorded as $16 million, versus the $23.9 million and $91.3 million recorded for *Virtuosity* and *Crimson Tide*, respectively, Washington's other two 1995 releases (The Numbers, Box office receipts: Denzel Washington. http://www.the-numbers.com/people/DWASH.html [accessed March 13, 2003]).

85. Ed Guerrero, "Devil in a Blue Dress," *Cineaste* 22.1 (Winter 1996): 41.

86. In *Ricochet* (1991), Washington portrayed a character who involuntarily kisses a white woman when he is framed by a criminal who constructs an elaborate plot to destroy his career. After kidnapping and drugging Washington's character Nick Styles, his nemesis films him having sex with a prostitute from whom he contracts a venereal disease. As already mentioned, Washington had the kiss removed from *The Mighty Quinn* and apparently also vetoed any on-screen romance between himself and Kelly Lynch in *Virtuosity* (1995) and again between himself and Radha Mitchell in *Man on Fire* (2004).

Washington has come to be known for these refusals, and yet, a black colleague says, "Hanging this around Denzel's neck isn't fair. This is a system that everybody knows about. A black man kissing a white woman in movies—you know who makes it the kiss of death? Studio executives. They think they're reflecting what the general populace thinks it wants to see. White men made these rules" (*Entertainment Weekly* online, "Washington Square?" http://www.ew.com/ew/article/0,,298675,00.html [accessed July 25, 2008]). However, many Washington fans have also noted the absurdly sublimated sexual energy between Washington and costar Angelina Jolie in *The Bone Collector* (1999), in which he plays a quadruplegic former police detective. After mentoring Jolie through a search for the killer, the consummating physical gesture of their relationship in the film comes when she touches the one of his fingers that is still mobile, near the end of the film. The director and cinematographer work to extract maximum emotional significance from this gesture. Likewise, black/Latina pairings continue to be acceptable, as in his Oscar-winning performance opposite Eva Mendes in *Training Day* (2001) and again opposite Mendes in *Out of Time* (2003).

87. Bruce Kirkland, "They're Hot about His Kiss: Denzel Washington's Passion in *He Got Game* Ignites Racial Anger," *Toronto Sun*, May 4, 1998, E42.

CHAPTER 4

1. Suzan-Lori Parks, "Possession," in *The America Play and Other Works* (New York: Theatre Communications Group, 1994), 4.

2. Parks, "Possession," 4, 5.

3. Freddie Rokem, *Performing History: Theatrical Representations of the Past in Contemporary Theatre* (Iowa City: University of Iowa Press, 2000), xiii.

4. Michele Pearce, "Alien Nation: An Interview with the Playwright (Suzan-Lori Parks)," *American Theatre*, March 1994, 26.

5. Suzan-Lori Parks, "An Equation for Black People Onstage," in *The America Play and Other Works* (New York: Theatre Communications Group, 1994), 20.

6. *Saartjie* is a diminutive form of *Sarah*, and some scholarly writings refer to her as Saartjie while others refer to her as Sarah. Unless I am citing the words of another critic, I will refer to her as Saartjie, in keeping with the name Suzan-Lori Parks uses for the woman she has chosen to re-member with her work. Likewise, other spellings of her last name include Bartman and Baartmann.

7. Sander L. Gilman, "Black Bodies, White Bodies: Toward an Iconography of Female Sexuality in Late Nineteenth-Century Art, Medicine, and Literature," in *"Race," Writing, and Difference*, ed. Henry Louis Gates, Jr. (Chicago: University of Chicago Press, 1985), 231.

8. Pierre Nora, "Between Memory and History: *Les Lieux des Mémoire*," in *History and Memory in African-American Culture*, ed. Genevieve Fabre and Robert O'Meally (New York: Oxford University Press, 1994), 284–300.

9. Ibid., 288.

10. Diana Taylor, *The Archive and the Repertoire: Performing Cultural Memory in the Americas* (Durham: Duke University Press, 2003), 20.

11. Ibid., 22.

12. Zine Magubane, "Which Bodies Matter? Feminism, Poststructuralism, Race, and the Curious Theoretical Odyssey of the 'Hottentot Venus,'" *Gender & Society* 15.6 (2001): 817.

13. Tavia Nyong'o, "The Body in Question," *International Journal of Communication* 1 (2007): 30.

14. Nora, "Between Memory and History," 287.

15. Ibid., 289.

16. Ibid., 289.

17. Harvey Young, "Touching History: Suzan-Lori Parks, Robbie McCauley and the Black Body," *Text and Performance Quarterly* 23.2 (2003): 134.

18. According to T. Denean Sharpley-Whiting, "There is some confusion as to her date of death. Records at the museum list the date as January 1, 1816, while Cuvier maintains it was December 29, 1815" (T. Denean Sharpley-Whiting, *Black Venus: Sexualized Savages, Primal Fears, and Primitive Narratives in French* [Durham: Duke University Press, 1999], 167).

19. Lynn Duke, "South Africans Seek to Bring Home Bones of a Bitter Past; Tribes Say Colonial-Era 'Trophies' Don't Belong in European Museum Collections," *Washington Post*, February 7, 1996, A01.

20. I note "multiple European socio-racial hierarchies" because Magubane reminds us of Baartman's "very different interpellation into French versus British medicine and science" ("Which Bodies Matter" 818), denying the ahistorical essentialization of "Europe," not just of blackness.

21. Part of the Griqua's political motive in waging high-profile repatriation campaigns such as Baartman's was garnering recognition of their tribe as separate from both black and mixed race South Africans in the classificatory schema of postapartheid South Africa: a historically contingent identity, it is enmeshed in politics that Baartman could of course neither anticipate nor choose to endorse.

22. Jon Jeter, "After 186 Years, Human Rites; S. Africa Buries Woman Caged and Humiliated by European Colonialists," *Washington Post*, August 10, 2002, A14.

23. Suzan-Lori Parks, "Elements of Style," in *The America Play and Other Works* (New York: Theatre Communications Group, 1994), 9, 10.

24. Ibid., 10.

25. Ibid., 9.

26. Suzan-Lori Parks, *Venus* (New York: Theatre Communications Group, 1997), 155.

27. Ibid., 155.

28. Ibid., 155.

29. Ibid., 155.

30. Ibid., 155.

31. Ibid., 157.

32. Ibid., 159.

33. Scene 1 is, in fact, a reannouncement of her death, as the ensemble has already announced her death in the overture that begins the play. Thus scene 1 provides repetition with revision: the death announced at the beginning of the play takes on new meaning when reinserted as the culminating piece of information in our understanding of Baartman's life.

34. Jean Young, "The Re-Objectification and Re-Commodification of Saartjie Baartman in Suzan-Lori Parks's *Venus*," *African American Review* 31.4 (1997): 699–708.

35. Ibid., 699–700.

36. Nora, "Between Memory and History," 300.

37. Taylor, *The Archive and the Repertoire*, 263.

38. Admittedly, in the early twenty-first century, other women of color are also included in this emphasis on a single body part as an icon of sexualized, racialized difference. And beyond that, individual women of all races have entered the popular cultural imaginary in a piecemeal fashion (e.g., Dolly Parton = breasts; Marilyn Monroe = lips).

39. Nora, "Between Memory and History," 294.

40. bell hooks, "The Oppositional Gaze," in *Black Looks: Race and Representation* (Boston: South End Press, 1992), 131.

41. Sharpley-Whiting, *Black Venus*, 17, 11.

42. W. B. Worthen, "Citing History: Textuality and Performativity in the Plays of Suzan-Lori Parks," *Etudes Theatrales/Essays in Theatre*, 181, 15.

43. The heterosexism within the conceit of the gaze is not explicitly interrogated by hooks in her deconstruction, although it is a feature of other writings.

44. hooks, "The Oppositional Gaze," 126 (emphasis added).

45. Ibid., 126.

46. Parks, *Venus*, vi.

47. Ibid., vi.

48. Ibid., v.

49. Ibid., 80.

50. Jennifer Johung, "Figuring the 'Spells'/Spelling the Figures: Suzan-Lori Parks's 'Scene of Love (?),'" *Theatre Journal* 58 (2006): 52.

51. Hartman, *Scenes*, esp. chap. 1.

52. Reprinted in Sharpley-Whiting, *Black Venus*, 127–64, in an English translation by the author.

53. Parks, *Venus*, 154.

54. Rokem, *Performing History*, 203.

55. Parks, *Venus*, 62.

56. Ibid., 64.

57. Rosemary Wiss, "Lipreading: Remembering Saartjie Baartman," *Australian Journal of Anthropology* 5.1–2 (1994): 11–41.

58. Parks, *Venus*, 64.

59. Ibid., 74.

60. Young, "Re-Objectification," 703–4.

61. Parks, *Venus*, 74.

62. Ibid., 75.

63. Young, "Re-Objectification," 704.

64. Just as Denzel Washington's heterosexual contact with white women invites some audience members to recall traditional definitions of black men as the sexual tormentors of white women, for some audience members, the union of Venus and the Baron repeats the sexual practices of American slavery, in which white owners routinely raped

their black female slaves. This practice challenges the idea that consensual sex is possible for women who are legally considered property.

65. Parks, *Venus*, 28.

66. Young, "Touching History," 142.

67. Parks, *Venus*, 28.

68. Ibid., 85–86.

69. Sharpley-Whiting, *Black Venus*, 24–25.

70. Parks, *Venus* 98.

71. Ibid., 92.

72. Ibid., 92.

73. Ibid., 92.

74. Ibid., 148, 149.

75. Ibid., 149.

76. Robyn Wiegman, *American Anatomies: Theorizing Race and Gender* (Durham: Duke University Press, 1995), 35.

77. Robert Brustein, "Resident Theatre Hopes," in *Cultural Calisthenics: Writings on Race, Politics, and Theatre* (Chicago: Ivan R. Dee, 1998), 147.

78. Parks, "Equation," 20.

79. Fredric Jameson, *Postmodernism, or, The Cultural Logic of Late Capitalism* (Durham: Duke University Press, 1991), xi.

80. Allen Feldman, *Formations of Violence: The Narrative of the Body and Political Terror in Northern Ireland* (Chicago: University of Chicago Press, 1991), 2.

81. Jean Young, "Re-Objectification," 703.

82. Harvey Young, "Touching History," 137.

83. Glenda R. Carpio, *Laughing Fit to Kill: Black Humor in the Fictions of Slavery* (Oxford: Oxford University Press, 2008), 200.

84. In *African Queen: The Real Life of the Hottentot Venus* (New York: Random House, 2007), Sarah Holmes draws this conclusion, but Janell Hobson instead believes "Cezar was probably Dutch" in a way that conflates national and racial identities (*Venus in the Dark: Blackness and Beauty in Popular Culture* [New York: Routledge, 2005], 40).

85. *Venus*, Stanford University Department of Drama, October 1998, codirected by Irma Mayorga and Shannon Steen.

86. hooks, "The Oppositional Gaze," 116.

87. Laura Mulvey, "Visual Pleasure and Narrative Cinema," in *The Critical Tradition: Classic Texts and Contemporary Trends,* ed. David H. Richter, 2nd ed. (Boston: Bedford/St. Martin's, 1998), 1448.

88. Carpio, *Laughing Fit to Kill,* 228.

89. However, not all productions of *Venus* costume the title character in prosthetic buttocks, a choice that further damns spectators who literally place that burden upon the actress's body where it does not even artificially exist.

90. Harry J. Elam, Jr., and Alice Rayner, "Body Parts: Between Story and Spectacle in *Venus* by Suzan-Lori Parks," in *Staging Resistance: Essays on Political Theater,* ed. Jean Colleran and Jenny Spencer (Ann Arbor: University of Michigan Press, 1998), 271.

91. Parks, *Venus*, 35.

92. He famously declared, "a performative utterance will, for example, be *in a pecu-liar way* hollow or void if said by an actor on the stage . . . Language in such circum-stances is in special ways—intelligibly—used not seriously, but in ways *parasitic* upon its normal use—ways which fall under the doctrine of *etiolations* of language" (J. L. Austin, *How to Do Things with Words*, ed. J. O. Urmison and Marina Sbisa, 2nd ed. [Cambridge: Harvard University Press, 1962], 22).

93. Parks, *Venus*, 45.

94. Elam and Rayner, "Body Parts," 266.

95. This is not to suggest that the material consequences of this symbolic violence are benign, but rather that the justifications for them are contrived.

96. For example, in the beginning of the play, The Girl asks The Brother, "Do I have a choice? Id like to think on it" (17), after his proposal that she travel with him to Europe to perform.

97. Feldman, *Formations of Violence*, 4–5.

98. Sara L. Warner, "Suzan-Lori Parks's Drama of Disinterment: A Transnational Exploration of *Venus*," *Theatre Journal* 60 (2008): 183.

99. Ibid., 197.

100. Chela Sandoval, *Methodology of the Oppressed* (Minneapolis: University of Min-nesota Press, 2000), 140.

CHAPTER 5

1. And badly, to boot: Da Band, the product of Combs's first *Making the Band* ven-ture, was dissolved as a failure because the bandmates couldn't work together effectively. Subsequent seasons of the show have led to similar outcomes with different groups: while Danity Kane is to date the most successful *MTB* group, its members were fired one at a time until one unattached singer remained, and the male group Day26 has experi-enced a tumultuous journey as well.

2. Of course, one could argue that the identity implications of postmodern theory and its "discovery" of the constructed and contingent nature of identity are somewhat like Christopher Columbus's discovery of the Americas, in which what is discovered/ex-posed is more the limitations of one worldview than the sudden presence of other epis-temologies.

3. Debra Dickerson, *The End of Blackness: Returning the Souls of Black Folk to Their Rightful Owners* (New York: Anchor Books, 2005); David Hollinger, *Post-Ethnic America* (New York: Basic Books, 1995); Paul Gilroy, *Against Race: Imagining Political Culture be-yond the Color Line* (Cambridge: Harvard University Press, 2000); Antonia Darder and Rodolfo D. Torres, *After Race: Racism after Multiculturalism* (New York: New York Uni-versity Press, 2004). It is worth noting that Gilroy's text is titled "Against Race" for its U.S. readership in order to resonate with this trend. It was first released in the UK, with the title *Between Camps: Nations, Culture, and the Allure of Race* (London: Allen Lane, 2000).

4. Gilroy, *Against Race*, 47.

5. Thelma Golden, "Post . . . ," in *Freestyle*, ed. Thelma Golden (New York: Studio Museum in Harlem, 2001), 14.

6. Ibid., 14.

7. E.g., Venus and Serena Williams in the beginning of their tennis careers, when their braided, beaded hair was the sign of their atypical and potentially disruptive physical presence on hallowed courts from the All England Lawn Tennis Club to Roland Garros. Indeed, in describing Newkirk's piece, Holland Cutter of the *New York Times* asserted, "urban violence, the Sublime, and Venus Williams meet" ("Art Review; A Full Studio Museum Show Starts with 28 Young Artists and a Shoehorn," *New York Times,* May 11, 2001, E36).

8. *Frames,* also a video installation, was his contribution to *Freestyle.*

9. Maria Villeseñor, "Rico Gatson," in *Freestyle,* ed. Thelma Golden (New York: Studio Museum in Harlem, 2001), 30–31.

10. Dwight McBride. *Why I Hate Abercrombie & Fitch: Essays on Race and Sexuality* (New York: NYU Press, 2005), 38.

11. Thelma Golden, introduction to *Frequency* (New York: Studio Museum in Harlem, 2005), 14. According to Golden, this is one of the conditions that produces the postblack sensibility.

12. Following habitual use of his name, I sometimes refer to Ice Cube simply as Cube, "just Cube, never Ice—fair warning" (Sean Daly, "The Warm and Fuzzy Side of Ice Cube," *Washington Post,* January 19, 2005, C01).

13. James T. Jones, IV, "Yo, Hollywood: Rappers Are Here," *USA Today,* May 13, 1991, 6D.

14. David Klinghoffer. "No Bad Rap for Preachy 'Boyz'; Uneven Film Impossible to Dismiss," *Washington Times,* July 12, 1991, E3.

15. See Jeff Chang's *Can't Stop, Won't Stop: A History of the Hip-Hop Generation* (New York: Picador, 2005) for a detailed discussion of this development.

16. I am indebted to Huey Copeland for this insight; in a casual conversation with me, he mentioned the fact that *postblack* quickly became a very handy marketing term in the art world and noted that when *Freestyle* debuted, most of the artists in the show had no representation, but all had acquired agents within a short time after the show closed, now that there was an attractive shorthand for work that would otherwise be hard to explain.

17. *The Cosby Show,* of course, stands as the paradigmatic exception to this representational rule.

18. William C. Rhoden, *Forty Million Dollar Slaves: The Rise, Fall, and Redemption of the Black Athlete* (New York: Crown Publishers, 2006).

19. I am thinking, for example, of the Starter Jacket crime wave of the early 1990s in which many youngsters were violently robbed of their gear, linking this sportswear line in the public eye to the provocation and perpetration of crime.

20. In June 2010, the television series *Are We There Yet?* premiered on TBS. Ice Cube is an executive producer and has a recurring role, but the main characters are played by different actors than the ones in the films.

21. Lou Lumenik, "Road Kill—Ice Cube Hits Dead End in 'Are We There Yet?'" *New York Post,* January 21, 2005, 39; Michael O'Sullivan, "Ice Cube's Rocky Road Trip," *Washington Post,* January 21, 2005, T43.

22. Daly, "The Warm and Fuzzy Side of Ice Cube," C01.

23. Rebecca Murray, "Ice Cube Discusses His First Family Film, 'Are We There Yet?'" http://movies.about.com/od/arewethereyet/a/areweico11605_2.htm (accessed September 2008).

24. Carl Bialik, "Is the Conventional Wisdom Correct in Measuring Hip-Hop Audience?" *Wall Street Journal*, May 5, 2005, http://online.wsj.com/public/article/SB111521 814339424546.html (accessed January 2007).

25. Daly, "The Warm and Fuzzy Side of Ice Cube," C01.

26. http://www.imdb.com/title/tt0368578/business (accessed July 1, 2007).

27. John Howard Griffin, *Black Like Me* (1962; New York: Signet Group, 1996), 7.

28. Television studies scholars trace an even longer genealogy that includes both the 1970s series *An American Family* and the 1960s show *Candid Camera*.

29. Herman Gray, introduction to *Watching Race: Television and the Struggle for Blackness* (1995; Minneapolis: University of Minnesota Press, 2004), xx.

30. The economics of reality TV are unquestionably changing in the United States, as the stars of the most popular reality shows are often quite handsomely compensated for their continued participation once the shows are proven successful. While most production companies will not disclose the salaries their participants draw, estimates usually range from $30,000 to $75,000 per episode for the stars of the most successful shows.

31. Of course, these debates over the truth of reality TV echo the charges leveled at photography and also at documentary regarding objectivity versus mediation.

32. See Laura Grindstaff's *The Money Shot: Trash, Class, and the Making of TV Talk Shows* (Chicago: University of Chicago Press, 2002) for a discussion of the ways in which preexisting cultural "myths" provide the templates into which reality footage is reinscribed through editorial practices.

33. I make these claims as someone who has watched a meaningful amount of reality television: unless the show is a contest—and even sometimes when it is—participants often insist on the consistency of their behavior, and the formal conceit of the confessional (participants' direct address to the camera out of context, commenting upon the situations in which they have already been filmed) is often specifically recruited to affirm participants' authenticity, as they explain their behavior or attitudes in an effort to ensure a "true" and multifaceted representation of their personalities.

34. As an example, the Bravo *Real Housewives* franchise—which features wealthy women in major metropolitan areas—presented a season focused on Atlanta's elite and recruited the first black women to appear as cast members. When asked during a reunion show if they had felt any pressure to represent black people well, at least one housewife said yes, because this was an opportunity to complicate television's reductively classed representations of blacks.

35. Katrina E. Bell-Jordan, "*Black.White.* and a *Survivor* of *The Real World:* Constructions of Race on Reality TV," *Critical Studies in Media Communication* 25.4 (2008): 355.

36. John L. Jackson, Jr., *Real Black: Adventures in Racial Sincerity* (Chicago: University of Chicago Press, 2005), 17.

37. Ibid., 29.

38. Of course, the distinctions between these narrative genres are not absolute, as some of the shows mentioned above actually combine narrative conventions. (e.g., *Biggest Loser,*

which exists at the intersection of makeover, instructional, and competition).

39. *Black. White.* FX Network, 2006. All subsequent quotes from this series will be noted parenthetically in the text as BW.

40. A *Boston Globe* article notes that this was intentional: "The producers selected two middle-class families with 'mainstream' points of view. 'We didn't want to put somebody from Idaho with people from Compton,' says Cube. 'The show would have lost its texture over economic and other hang-ups'" (Suzanne C. Ryan, "New FX Series Has Families Trading Races," *Boston Globe*, March 24, 2006, http://www.boston.com/news/globe/liv ing/articles/2006/03/04/new_fx_series_has_families_trading_races/ [accessed June 2009]).

41. Farai Chideya, *The Color of Our Future: Our Multiracial Future* (New York: William Morrow, 1999).

42. This sense of warmth that Carmen imputes to Bruno in blackface is short lived, as she subsequently becomes frustrated with Bruno for his insensitivity to others' opinions.

43. However, works like Louis Chude-Sokei's 2006 *The Last "Darky": Bert Williams, Black on Black Minstrelsy, and the African Diaspora* (Durham: Duke University Press, 2006) are directing critical attention to the complicated function of black performers in blackface minstrelsy.

44. Aside from the times when the Sparks family accompanied the Wurgels on excursions, the two families typically interacted sans makeup when they were in the shared house.

45. Of course, I am focusing on the performative dimensions of the social encounters captured on film rather than the roles that the Wurgels and the Sparkses were ultimately performing for mass audiences that would see their "experiment" on TV. In this regard, I am taking reality television at its word in its supposition that the presence of the camera does not alter participants' behavior by becoming the primary audience that the participants must please.

46. In *Appropriating Blackness,* Johnson discusses his work with Café and other gospel choirs in Australia and notes the relative speed with which he became a local celebrity because of his presumed ability to imbue the choirs' performances with a degree of authenticity that their white choir directors could not. Additionally, he discusses the publicity activities that became part of his Australian experience and his complicated responses to the ways that various interviewers craved on the spot performances of black religious flair, expectations that clearly failed to locate this "flair" in the context of the religious communion that produced them. Rather than needing to be caught, "the spirit" was understood to be an essential feature of blackness, always accessible by blacks (and always available for white appreciation if not appropriation). For additional insights into the specific role that the black church plays as a supposed site where the differences between whiteness and blackness are in high relief, see Patricia J. Williams's discussion of gospel brunch tours in Harlem, in *Seeing a Color-Blind Future.*

47. Harryette Mullen, "Optic White: Blackness and the Production of Whiteness," *Diacritics* 24.2–3 (1994): 84.

48. Mullen, "Optic White," 77.

49. Robinson, "It Takes One to Know One."

50. Greg Braxton, "Is It Really That BLACK & WHITE?" *Los Angeles Times*, March 4, 2006, E1.

51. Bell-Jordan, "*Black.White.*," 357.

52. It is worth pondering why the adult men in the series are not shown confessing their racial charades and experiencing ritualized acceptance or rejection.

53. Renee's surprise makes particular sense when you recall that she comes from Atlanta, which may be the self-proclaimed capital of the New South but remains extremely segregated.

54. This is true not just for Rose but also for members of the African diaspora in the United States who do not identify as African American and find it difficult (or undesirable) to navigate the systems of inclusion that frame the black community in the United States. See Jean Mutaba Rahier and Percy Hintzen, *Problematizing Blackness: Self Ethnographies by Black Immigrants to the United States* (New York: Routledge, 2003), for examples of this phenomenon.

55. I am, of course, reminded of Adrian Piper's "race cards," with their exposure of the ordinariness of racist speech in environments that are presumed to be free of people of color.

56. Many feminists saw precisely this dynamic at work in mainstream media coverage of the race for the 2008 Democratic presidential nomination, in which male (and a few female) politicians and pundits tripped over themselves to enfold Barack Obama in a colorblind embrace while making very sexist criticisms of his opponent Hillary Rodham Clinton.

57. Stephen Small, "The Contours of Racialization: Structures, Representation, and Resistance in the United States," in *Race, Identity and Citizenship*, ed. Rodolfo D. Torres, Louis F. Mirón, and Jonathan Xavier Inda (Malden, MA: Blackwell Publishers, 1999).

58. Brown et al., *Whitewashing Race.*

59. The transfer of this project of national imagination from film to television serves as a reminder of the mutually constitutive relationship between public and private spheres. In its origins, television viewership was meant to "form the basis for a feeling and (electronic) experience of national identity and belonging," and in particular, "the middle class ideal of Americanness was staged in the theater of domesticity" (Gray, *Cultural Moves*, 97). However, Gray goes on to suggest that this ideo-representational strategy has reached the limits of its own potential and now "expresses the failure of a liberal pluralist vision of a national imaginary achieved through the management of cultural differences" (105). This management requires a consolidated authority to determine the types and proportions of difference that a national imaginary might contain, but the resolute decentralization of social networks and media content delivery systems makes pretensions to holding such authority difficult to sustain.

Bibliography

Black. White. FX Network, 2006.

"Casting: Colorblind or Conscious?" *American Theatre*, September 1996, 20.

Constitution of the United States. http://www.archives.gov/exhibits/charters/constitu
tion_transcript.html (accessed December 2008).

Academy of Motion Picture Arts and Sciences. http://www.oscars.org (accessed July
2008).

Actor's Equity Association. "Actor's Equity Timeline: The 1950s." http://www.actors
equity.org/aboutequity/timeline/timeline_1950.html (accessed July 2007).

Alexander, Elizabeth. *The Black Interior*. St. Paul, MN: Graywolf Press, 2004.

Ansen, David. "No 'Brief' Pelican." *Newsweek*, December 20, 1993, 121.

Austin, J. L. *How To Do Things with Words*. 2nd ed. Ed. J. O. Urmison and Marina Sbisa.
Cambridge: Harvard University Press, 1962.

Batiste, Stephanie. "Epaulettes and Leaf Skirts, Warriors and Subversives: Black National
Subjectivity in *Macbeth* and *Haiti*." *Text and Performance Quarterly* 23.2 (2003):
154–85.

Bean, Annemarie, ed. *A Sourcebook of African American Performance: Plays, People, Contexts*. New York: Routledge, 1999.

Bellamy, Lou. "Race, Art and Inclusion." *American Theatre*, November 1996, 62.

Bell-Jordan, Katrina E. "*Black.White.* and a *Survivor* of *The Real World:* Constructions of
Race on Reality TV." *Critical Studies in Media Communication* 25.4 (2008): 353–72.

Bennett, William. *The De-Valuing of America: The Fight for Our Culture and Our Children*. New York: Summit Books, 1992.

Bialik, Carl. "Is the Conventional Wisdom Correct in Measuring Hip-Hop Audience?"
Wall Street Journal, May 5, 2005. http://online.wsj.com/public/article/SB1115218
14339424546.html (accessed January 2007).

Bogle, Donald. *Toms, Coons, Mulattoes, Mammies, and Bucks: An Interpretive History of
Blacks in American Films*. 4th ed. New York: Continuum, 2003.

Braxton, Greg. "Is It Really That BLACK & WHITE?" *Los Angeles Times*, March 4, 2006,
E1.

Brode, Douglas. *Denzel Washington: His Films and Career*. Seacaucus: Birch Lane Press,
1997.

Brody, Jennifer DeVere. *Impossible Purities: Blackness, Femininity, and Victorian Culture*.
Durham: Duke University Press, 1998.

Brown, Michael, Martin Carnoy, Elliott Currie, Troy Duster, David B. Oppenheimer, Marjorie M. Schultz, and David Wellman. *Whitewashing Race: The Myth of a Color-Blind Society*. Berkeley: University of California Press, 2003.

Brown, Sterling. *Negro Poetry & Drama and the Negro in American Fiction*. New York: Atheneum, 1969.

Brustein, Robert. *Cultural Calisthenics: Writings on Race, Politics, and Theatre*. Chicago: Ivan R. Dee, 1998.

Brustein, Robert. *Dumbocracy in America: Studies in the Theatre of Guilt, 1987–1994*. Chicago: Ivan R. Dee, 1994.

Brustein, Robert. "Race, Art and Inclusion." *American Theatre*, November 1996, 62–63.

Brustein, Robert. *Reimagining American Theater*. New York: Hill and Wang, 1991.

Brustein, Robert. "Subsidized Separatism." *American Theatre*, October 1996, 26–27, 100–107.

Bush, George W. Speech to the NAACP 2000 Annual Convention. http://www.washington post.com/wpsrv/onpolitics/elections/bushtext071000.htm (accessed August 2008).

Butler, Judith. *Gender Trouble: Feminism and the Subversion of Identity*. New York: Routledge, 1990.

California Secretary of State. Official Voter Information Guide. http://vote2003.sos.ca.gov/propositions/2-3-4-text.html (accessed May 2009).

California Secretary of State. "Proposition 209." http://vote96.sos.ca.gov/BP209yesarg.htm (accessed August 2008).

Carby, Hazel. *Race Men*. Cambridge: Harvard University Press, 1998.

Carpio, Glenda R. *Laughing Fit to Kill: Black Humor in the Fictions of Slavery*. Oxford: Oxford University Press, 2008.

Chang, Jeff. *Can't Stop, Won't Stop: A History of the Hip-Hop Generation*. New York: Picador, 2005.

Chaudhuri, Una. "On Cultural Power: 13 Commentaries." *American Theatre*, May–June 1997, 61.

Chideya, Farai. *The Color of Our Future: Our Multiracial Future*. New York: William Morrow, 1999.

Chude-Sokei, Louis. *The Last "Darky": Bert Williams, Black on Black Minstrelsy, and the African Diaspora*. Durham: Duke University Press, 2006.

Claustro, Lisa. "Haysbert Says 24 Role Paved the Way for Presidential Hopeful Barack Obama." http://www.buddytv.com/articles/24/haysbert-says-24-role-paved-th-15880.aspx (accessed January 2009).

Clemetson, Lynette. "The Racial Politics of Speaking Well." *New York Times*, February 4, 2007. http://www.nytimes.com/2007/02/04/weekinreview/04clemetson.html?scp=1&sq=the%20racial%20politics%20of%20speaking%20well&st=cse (accessed January 2009).

Colleran, Jean, and Jenny Spencer, eds. *Staging Resistance: Essays on Political Theater*. Ann Arbor: University of Michigan Press, 1998.

Cotter, Holland. "Art Review; A Full Studio Museum Show Starts with 28 Young Artists and a Shoehorn." *New York Times*, May 11, 2001, E36.

Crouch, Stanley. "Race Is Over." *New York Times*, September 29, 1996, sec. 6, 170–71.

Crouch, Stanley. "Who's Zooming Who?" *Theater* 27.2–3 (1997): 20–23.

Daly, Sean. "The Warm and Fuzzy Side of Ice Cube." *Washington Post,* January 19, 2005, C01.

Darder, Antonia, and Rodolfo D. Torres. *After Race: Racism after Multiculturalism.* New York: New York University Press, 2004.

Davis, Clinton Turner. "To Whom It May Concern." *Theater* 27.2–3 (1997): 30–34.

Davis, Clinton Turner, and Harry Newman, eds. *Beyond Tradition: Transcripts from the First National Symposium on Non-Traditional Casting.* New York: Non-Traditional Casting Project, 1988.

Delgado, Richard, and Jean Stefancic, eds. *Critical Race Theory: The Cutting Edge.* 2nd ed. Philadelphia: Temple University Press, 2000.

Derecho (De Kosnik), Abigail. "Illegitimate Media: Race, Gender, and Censorship in Early Digital Remix Culture." Diss., Northwestern University, 2007.

Devil in a Blue Dress. Dir. Carl Franklin. DVD. Columbia TriStar Home Video, 1995.

Dickerson, Debra. *The End of Blackness: Returning the Souls of Black Folk to Their Rightful Owners.* New York: Anchor Books, 2005.

Du Bois, W. E. B. *The Souls of Black Folk: Authoritative Text, Contexts, Criticism,* ed. Henry Louis Gates, Jr., and Terri Hume Oliver. 1903. New York: W. W. Norton, 1999.

DuCille, Ann. "The Shirley Temple of My Familiar." *Transition* 73 (1997): 10–32.

Duke, Lynn. "South Africans Seek to Bring Home Bones of a Bitter Past; Tribes Say Colonial-Era 'Trophies' Don't Belong in European Museum Collections." *Washington Post,* February 7, 1996, A01.

Dyer, Richard. *White.* New York: Routledge, 1997.

Dyson, Michael Eric. *Race Rules: Navigating the Color Line.* Reading: Addison-Wesley, 1996.

E! Online. "One Hundred Years: Heartthrobs." http://www.eonline.com/Features/Specials/Century/Feb/05.b.html (accessed May 2003).

Elam, Harry J., Jr. *African American Performance and Theater History: A Critical Reader.* Oxford: Oxford University Press, 2001.

Elam, Harry J., Jr. *The Past as Present in the Drama of August Wilson.* Ann Arbor: University of Michigan Press, 2006.

Elam, Michele. "Obama's Mixology." http://www.theroot.com/views/obamas-mixology (accessed January 2009).

Entertainment Weekly online. "Washington Square?" http://www.ew.com/ew/article/0,,298675,00.html (accessed July 2008).

Epstein, Helen. *Joe Papp: An American Life.* New York: Little, Brown, 1996.

Fabre, Genevieve, and Robert O'Meally, eds. *History and Memory in African-American Culture.* New York: Oxford University Press, 1994.

Feldman, Allen. *Formations of Violence: The Narrative of the Body and Political Terror in Northern Ireland.* Chicago: University of Chicago Press, 1991.

Fichandler, Zelda. "On Cultural Power: 13 Commentaries." *American Theatre,* May–June 1997, 58.

Foster, Hal. *Recodings: Art, Spectacle, Cultural Politics.* Port Townsend: Bay Press, 1985.

Foucault, Michel. *Language, Counter-memory, Practice: Selected Essays and Interviews.*

Ed. Donald F. Bouchard. Trans. Donald F. Bouchard and Sherry Simon. Ithaca: Cornell University Press, 1977.

Gardner, James. "Lost in the Male—Whitney Museum of American Art, New York, New York; Various Artists." *National Review*, February 6, 1995, 76.

Gates, Henry Louis, Jr., ed. *"Race," Writing, and Difference*. Chicago: University of Chicago Press, 1985.

Gates, Henry Louis, Jr., ed. *Thirteen Ways of Looking at a Black Man*. New York: Random House, 1997.

Gilroy, Paul. *Against Race: Imagining Political Culture beyond the Color Line*. Cambridge: Harvard University Press, 2000.

Gilroy, Paul. *Postcolonial Melancholia*. New York: Columbia University Press, 2005.

Goldberg, David Theo. *Multiculturalism: A Critical Reader*. Cambridge: Harvard University Press, 1994.

Golden, Thelma. *Black Male: Representations of Masculinity in Contemporary American Art*. New York: Whitney Museum of American Art, 1994.

Golden, Thelma, ed. *Freestyle*. New York: Studio Museum in Harlem, 2001.

Gray, Herman. *Cultural Moves: African Americans and the Politics of Representation*. Berkeley: University of California Press, 2005.

Gray, Herman. *Watching Race: Television and the Struggle for Blackness*. 1995. Minneapolis: University of Minnesota Press, 2004.

Griffin, John Howard. *Black Like Me*. 1962. New York: Signet Group, 1996.

Griffith, D. W. *The Birth of a Nation*. Biograph Film, 1915.

Grindstaff, Laura. *The Money Shot: Trash, Class, and the Making of TV Talk Shows*. Chicago: University of Chicago Press, 2002.

Grisham, John. *The Pelican Brief*. New York: Island Books, 1992.

Guerrero, Ed. "Devil in a Blue Dress." *Cineaste* 22.1 (1996): 38, 40–41.

Guerrero, Ed. *Framing Blackness: The African American Image in Film*. Philadelphia: Temple University Press, 1993.

Guinier, Lani, and Gerald Torres. *The Miner's Canary: Enlisting Race, Resisting Power, Transforming Democracy*. Cambridge: Harvard University Press, 2002.

Hall, Kim. *Things of Darkness: Economies of Race and Gender in Early Modern England*. Ithaca: Cornell University Press, 1995.

Harlan, John. *Plessy v. Ferguson*, 163 U.S. 537 (1896). http://supreme.justia.com/us/163/537/case.html (accessed December 2008).

Harper, Philip Brian. *Are We Not Men? Masculine Anxiety and the Problem of African American Identity*. New York: Oxford University Press, 1996.

Hartman, Saidiya. *Scenes of Subjection: Terror, Slavery, and Self-Making in Nineteenth-Century America*. Oxford: Oxford University Press, 1997.

Hintzen, Percy, and Jean Mutaba Rahier, eds. *Problematizing Blackness: Self Ethnographies by Black Immigrants to the United States*. New York: Routledge, 2003.

Hobson, Janell. *Venus in the Dark: Blackness and Beauty in Popular Culture*. New York: Routledge, 2005.

Hollinger, David. *Postethnic America: Beyond Multiculturalism*. New York: Basic Books, 1995.

Holmes, Sarah. *African Queen: The Real Life of the Hottentot Venus*. New York: Random House, 2007.

Honegger, Gitta. "On Cultural Power: 13 Commentaries." *American Theatre*, May–June 1997, 16.

hooks, bell. *Black Looks: Race and Representation*. Boston: South End Press, 1992.

Horowitz, Jason. "Biden Unbound: Lays into Clinton, Obama, Edwards." *New York Observer*, February 4, 2007. http://www.observer.com/2007/politics/biden-unbound-lays-clinton-obama-edwards (accessed September 2009).

Internet Movie Database. http://www.imdb.com (accessed throughout 2008).

Jackson, John L., Jr. *Racial Paranoia: The Unintended Consequences of Political Correctness*. New York: Basic Civitas, 2008.

Jackson, John L., Jr. *Real Black: Adventures in Racial Sincerity*. Chicago: University of Chicago Press, 2005.

Jackson, Shannon. *Professing Performance: Theatre in the Academy from Philology to Performativity*. Cambridge: Cambridge University Press, 2004.

Jameson, Fredric. *Postmodernism, or, The Cultural Logic of Late Capitalism*. Durham: Duke University Press, 1991.

Jeter, Jon. "After 186 Years, Human Rites; S. Africa Buries Woman Caged and Humiliated by European Colonialists." *Washington Post*, August 10, 2002, A14.

Johnson, E. Patrick. *Appropriating Blackness: Performance and the Politics of Authenticity*. Durham: Duke University Press, 2003.

Johung, Jennifer. "Figuring the 'Spells'/Spelling the Figures: Suzan-Lori Parks's 'Scene of Love (?).'" *Theatre Journal* 58 (2006): 39–52.

Jones, James T., IV. "Yo, Hollywood: Rappers Are Here." *USA Today*, May 13, 1991, 6D.

Kaplan, E. Ann. *Women in Film Noir*. London: BFI Publishing, 1980.

Kelley, Robin D. G. "People in Me." *Colorlines: Race, Culture, Action* (Winter 1999): 6–8.

Kimmelman, Michael. "Constructing Images of the Black Male." *New York Times*, November 11, 1994, C1.

Kirkland, Bruce. "They're Hot about His Kiss: Denzel Washington's Passion in *He Got Game* Ignites Racial Anger." *Toronto Sun*, May 4, 1998, E42.

Klinghoffer, David. "No Bad Rap for Preachy 'Boyz'; Uneven Film Impossible to Dismiss." *Washington Times*, July 12, 1991, E3.

Kull, Andrew. *The Color-Blind Constitution*. Cambridge: Harvard University Press, 1992.

League of Resident Theatres. "LORT Member Theatres." http://lort.web.officelive.com/members.aspx (accessed December 2008).

League of Resident Theatres. "Objectives." http://www.lort.org/mission.htm (accessed July 2007).

Lee, James Kyung-Jin. *Urban Triage: Race and the Fictions of Multiculturalism*. Minneapolis: University of Minnesota Press, 2004.

Lee, Josephine. "Racial Actors, Liberal Myths." *Xcp: Cross Cultural Poetics* 13 (2003): 88–110.

Lorde, Audre. *Sister Outsider: Essays and Speeches*. Freedom, CA: Crossing Press, 1984.

Lormand, Richard. "Jennifer Beals Finds Success Courting Her." *Globe and Mail* (Canada), August 29, 1985. www.lexisnexis.com/us/lnacademic (accessed August 2008).

Loury, Glenn C. *The Anatomy of Racial Inequality*. Cambridge: Harvard University Press, 2002.

Lumenik, Lou. "Road Kill—Ice Cube Hits Dead End in 'Are We There Yet?'" *New York Post*, January 21, 2005, 39.

Magubane, Zine. "Which Bodies Matter? Feminism, Poststructuralism, Race, and the Curious Theoretical Odyssey of the 'Hottentot Venus.'" *Gender & Society* 15.6 (2001): 816–34.

Maslach, Christina. "Welcome from the Vice Provost for Teaching and Learning." http://americancultures.berkeley.edu/ (accessed August 2009).

Maslin, Janet. "Presenting Nancy Drew for the 90s." *New York Times*, December 17, 1993, C1.

McBride, Dwight. *Why I Hate Abercrombie & Fitch: Essays on Race and Sexuality*. New York: NYU Press, 2005.

McCauley, Robbie. "Working around Power." *Theater* 27.2–3 (1997): 34–38.

McKenzie, Jon. *Perform or Else: From Discipline to Performance*. New York: Routledge, 2001.

Mee, Charles. "A Note on Casting." http://www.charlesmee.com/html/cast.html (accessed August 2007).

Moran, Rachel F. *Interracial Intimacy: The Regulation of Race and Romance*. Chicago: University of Chicago Press, 2001.

Morrison, Toni, and Claudia Brodsky Lacour, eds. *Birth of a Nation'hood: Gaze, Script and Spectacle in the O.J. Simpson Case*. New York: Pantheon Books, 1997.

Mosley, Walter. *Devil in a Blue Dress*. New York: Pocket Books, 1990.

Motion Picture Association of America. *A Code to Govern the Making of Motion Pictures: The Reasons Supporting It and the Resolution for Uniform Interpretation*. New York, 1930–55.

Mullen, Harryette. "Optic White: Blackness and the Production of Whiteness." *Diacritics* 24.2–3 (1994): 71–89.

Munk, Erika. "Up Front." *Theater* 27.2–3 (1997): 5.

Murray, Rebecca. "Ice Cube Discusses His First Family Film, 'Are We There Yet?'" http://movies.about.com/od/arewethereyet/a/areweico11605_2.htm (accessed September 2008).

Nadel, Alan. "August Wilson and the (Color-Blind) Whiteness of Public Space." *Theater* 27.2–3 (1997): 38–41.

Newman, Harry. "Holding Back: The Theatre's Resistance to Non-Traditional Casting." *TDR* 33.3 (1989): 22–36.

Non-Traditional Casting Project. "Mission." http://www.ntcp.org/missionframe.htm (accessed January 2002).

Nunns, Stephen. "Wilson, Brustein & the Press." *American Theatre*, March 1997, 18.

Nyong'o, Tavia. *The Amalgamation Waltz: Race, Performance, and the Ruses of History*. Minneapolis: University of Minnesota Press, 2009.

Nyong'o, Tavia. "The Body in Question." *International Journal of Communication* 1 (2007): 27–31.

Omi, Michael, and Howard Winant. *Racial Formation in the United States: From the 1960s to the 1990s*. 2nd ed. New York: Routledge, 1994.

O'Sullivan, Michael. "Ice Cube's Rocky Road Trip." *Washington Post*, January 21, 2005, T43.

Oxford English Dictionary. www.oed.com (accessed June 2007).

Pakua, Alan, dir. *The Pelican Brief.* DVD. Warner Brothers, 1993.

Pao, Angela C. "Changing Faces: Recasting National Identity in All-Asian(-)American Dramas." *Theatre Journal* 53.3 (2001): 389–409.

Parker, Andrew, and Eve Kosofsky Sedgwick, eds. *Performativity and Performance.* New York: Routledge, 1995.

Parks, Suzan-Lori. *The America Play and Other Works.* New York: Theatre Communications Group, 1994.

Parks, Suzan-Lori. *Venus.* New York: Theatre Communications Group, 1997.

Pearce, Michelle. "Alien Nation: An Interview with the Playwright (Suzan-Lori Parks)." *American Theatre,* March 1994, 26.

Pellegrini, Ann. *Performance Anxieties: Staging Psychoanalysis, Staging Race.* New York: Routledge, 1997.

Race: The Floating Signifier. Dir. Sut Jhally. Videocassette. Media Education Foundation, 1996.

Reid, Mark A. *Redefining Black Film.* Berkeley: University of California Press, 1993.

Reinelt, Janelle G., and Joseph R. Roach, eds. *Critical Theory and Performance.* Ann Arbor: University of Michigan Press, 1992.

Rhoden, William C. *Forty Million Dollar Slaves: The Rise, Fall, and Redemption of the Black Athlete.* New York: Crown Publishers, 2006.

Richter, David H., ed. *The Critical Tradition: Classic Texts and Contemporary Trends.* 2nd ed. Boston: Bedford/St. Martin's, 1998.

Robertson, Campbell. "The World of Black Theater Becomes Ever Bigger." *New York Times,* February 12, 2007. http://www.nytimes.com/2007/02/21/theater/21urba .html?_r=1&pagewanted=all (accessed July 2009).

Robinson, Amy. "It Takes One to Know One: Passing and Communities of Common Interest." *Critical Inquiry* 20.4 (1994): 715–36.

Robinson, Cedric. *Forgeries of Memory & Meaning: Blacks and the Regimes of Race in American Theater and Film before World War II.* Chapel Hill: University of North Carolina Press, 2007.

Rokem, Freddie. *Performing History: Theatrical Representations of the Past in Contemporary Theatre.* Iowa City: University of Iowa Press, 2000.

Ryan, Suzanne C. "New FX Series Has Families Trading Races." *Boston Globe,* March 24, 2006. http://www.boston.com/news/globe/living/articles/2006/03/04/new_fx_series_ has_families_trading_races/ (accessed June 2009).

Samuels, Allison. "Will It Be Denzel's Day?" *Newsweek,* February 25, 2002, 60.

Sandoval, Chela. *Methodology of the Oppressed.* Minneapolis: University of Minnesota Press, 2000.

Schechner, Richard. "In Praise of Promiscuity." *American Theatre,* December 1996, 59.

Schechner, Richard. "Race Free, Gender Free, Body-Type Free, Age Free Casting." *TDR* 33.1 (1989): 4–12.

Schevitz, Tanya. "Prop. 54 Defeated Soundly: State Initiative on Racial Privacy Raised Issues about Health, Education." *San Francisco Chronicle,* October 8, 2003, A12.

Schneider, Rebecca. *The Explicit Body in Performance.* New York: Routledge, 1997.

Sharpley-Whiting, T. Denean. *Black Venus: Sexualized Savages, Primal Fears, and Primitive Narratives in French.* Durham: Duke University Press, 1999.

Shaviro, Steven. *The Cinematic Body.* Minneapolis: University of Minnesota Press, 1993.

Smith, Dinitia. "Novelists Get Back at Hollywood, Mostly Gently." *New York Times,* September 25, 1999. http://query.nytimes.com/gst/fullpage.html?res=9402E5D7133FF9 36A1575AC0A96F958260&sec=&spon=&pagewanted=all (accessed August 2008).

Sun, William H. "Power and Problems of Performance across Ethnic Lines: An Alternative Approach to Nontraditional Casting." *TDR* 44.4 (2000): 86–95.

Taylor, Diana. *The Archive and the Repertoire: Performing Cultural Memory in the Americas.* Durham: Duke University Press, 2003.

Torres, Rodolfo D., Louis F. Mirón, and Jonathan Xavier Inda, eds. *Race, Identity and Citizenship.* Malden, MA: Blackwell Publishers, 1999.

Wallace, Michele. "The Culture War within the Culture Wars: Race." In *Art Matters: How the Culture Wars Changed America,* ed. Brian Wallis, Marianne Weems, and Philip Yenawine. New York: New York University Press, 1999.

Warner, Sara L. "Suzan-Lori Parks's Drama of Disinterment: A Transnational Exploration of *Venus*." *Theatre Journal* 60.2 (2008): 181–99.

Weber, Bruce. "On Stage, and Off." *New York Times,* April 1, 1994, C2.

West, Cornel. *Race Matters.* Boston: Beacon Press, 1993.

Wiegman, Robyn. *American Anatomies: Theorizing Race and Gender.* Durham: Duke University Press, 1995.

Wiles, David. "Burdens of Representation: The Method and the Audience." In *Method Acting Reconsidered: Theory, Practice, Future,* ed. David Krasner. New York: St. Martin's Press, 2000.

Wiley, Ralph. "White Lies: HBO Gets It Half Right." November 14, 2002. http://espn.go.com/page2/s/wiley/021113.html (accessed February 2006).

Williams, Dana, and Sandra Shannon, eds. *August Wilson and Black Aesthetics.* New York: Palgrave Macmillan, 2004.

Williams, Linda. *Playing the Race Card: Melodramas of Black and White from Uncle Tom to O.J. Simpson.* Princeton: Princeton University Press, 2001.

Williams, Patricia J. "Racial Ventriloquism." *Nation,* June 17, 1999. http://www.the nation.com/doc/19990705/Williams (accessed January 2009).

Williams, Patricia J. *Seeing a Color-Blind Future: The Paradox of Race.* New York: Noonday Press, 1997.

Wilson, August. "August Wilson Responds." *American Theatre,* October 1996, 102–7.

Wilson, August. "The Ground on Which I Stand." *American Theatre,* September 1996, 14–16, 71–74.

Wiss, Rosemary. "Lipreading: Remembering Saartjie Baartman." *Australian Journal of Anthropology* 5.1–2 (1994): 11–41.

Worthen, W. B. "Citing History: Textuality and Performativity in the Plays of Suzan-Lori Parks." *Etudes Theatrales/Essays in Theatre* 18.1 (1999): 3–22.

Young, Harvey. "Touching History: Suzan-Lori Parks, Robbie McCauley and the Black Body." *Text and Performance Quarterly* 23.2 (2003): 133–52.

Young, Jean. "The Re-Objectification and Re-Commodification of Saartjie Baartman in Suzan-Lori Parks's *Venus*." *African American Review* 31.4 (1997): 699–708.

Zangwill, Israel. *The Melting Pot: Drama in Four Acts.* Norwood, MA: Norwood Press, 1909.

Index

McCarter Theater, 37
McCauley, Robbie, 63
McKenzie, Jon: *Perform or Else*, 1
Mee, Charles, 14
melodrama, 77, 110
    racial, 98, 99, 100, 103, 105, 109
melting pot, 8, 54
Mendes, Eva
    Out of Time, 191
    Training Day, 83, 190n86
Micheaux, Oscar: *The Homesteader*, 79
Miller, Arthur: *Death of a Salesman*, 16
Miller, Tim, 7
monoculturalism, 53, 181n71
Mosley, Walter: *Devil in a Blue Dress*, 97–98,
    101–10, 188n58, 190n79
Motion Picture Code, 79
MTV, 144, 148
    Making the Band, 143, 195n1
    Real World, The, 154, 157
multiculturalism, 3, 6, 7, 24, 32, 53, 57, 64, 67,
    112, 143, 145, 180n47
    principles of, 12
    shortcomings, 144
Mulvey, Laura, 138
Munk, Erika, 180n54
Murphy, Eddie, 169
Musée de l'Homme, 118, 119

NAACP
    Image Award, 103
    national convention, 181n77
Nadel, Alan: "August Wilson and the (Color-
    Blind) Whiteness of Public Space," 67
National Endowment for the Arts, 7
National Endowment for the Humanities, 52
NEA Four, 7
Neal, Larry, 64
Newkirk, Kori, 145, 196n7
Newman, Harry, 10–11, 12, 175n25
New Republic, The, 52, 182n89
New York City, 11, 60, 111, 187n41. *See also* Pub-
    lic Theater
New Yorker, 69
New York Shakespeare Festival, 14–15, 183n108
New York Times, 34, 106, 173–74n9, 187n40, 196n7
nontraditional casting, 9–18, 24, 63, 68, 85,
    175n29, 180n53, 184n126
    origin, 175n25

Non-Traditional Casting Project (NTCP), 10,
    12, 65, 68, 175n26
First National Symposium on Non-Tradi-
    tional Casting, 11
nonwhiteness, 17, 23, 45, 58, 67, 71. *See also*
    whiteness
Nora, Pierre: "Between Memory and History:
    Les Lieux des Mémoire," 115–18
Nyong'o, Tavia: *The Amalgamation Waltz*,
    177–78n70

Obama, Barack, 1, 180n34
    black performance in the age of, 25–31
    and feminists, 199n56
    "More Perfect Union," 30
    "Out of Many, One," 28
    post-election, 177n68
    racial signification, 177n70
Okudzeto, Senam, 145
Omi, Michael, 18
O'Neill, Eugene, 16
    Hairy Ape, The, 14
    Long Day's Journey Into Night, 17

Pakula, Alan: *The Pelican Brief*, 85, 87, 88, 89,
    90, 96, 101, 103, 104
Pao, Angela, 16–17
Papp, Joseph, 14–15, 183n108
Paramount, 49
Parker, Andrew, 19, 20
Parks, Suzan-Lori, 112–42, 183n117, 191n6
    "Equation for Black People Onstage, An,"
    113
    "Possession," 112
    Venus, 24, 66, 112, 113, 114
    as historical document, 115–25
    as literature, 125–35
    as show, 135–42, 194n89
Pasadena Playhouse, 183n125
Paterson, Eva, 4
People, 85
Perez v. Sharp, 98, 99
Pew Research Center, 27, 177n68
Phantom Menace, The, 173n9
Pierce, Wendell: *Waiting for Godot*, 10
playwrights, 7, 33, 44, 113, 175n29
    black, 39, 63
    See also individual names, e.g., Mee,
    Charles